T0041445

Too Much Information

Too Much Information

Understanding What You Don't Want to Know

Cass R. Sunstein

The MIT Press
Cambridge, Massachusetts
London, England

© 2020 Cass R. Sunstein

All rights reserved. No part of this book may be reproduced in any form by any electronic or mechanical means (including photocopying, recording, or information storage and retrieval) without permission in writing from the publisher.

This book was set in ITC Stone Serif Std and ITC Stone Sans Std by New Best-set Typesetters Ltd. Printed and bound in the United States of America.

Library of Congress Cataloging-in-Publication Data

Names: Sunstein, Cass R., author.
Title: Too much information : understanding what you don't want to
    know / Cass R. Sunstein.
Description: Cambridge, Massachusetts : The MIT Press, [2020] |
    Includes bibliographical references and index.
Identifiers: LCCN 2019047661 | ISBN 9780262044165 (hardcover)
Subjects: LCSH: Information behavior. | Disclosure of information. |
    Information policy.
Classification: LCC ZA3075 .S865 2020 | DDC 025.5/24—dc23
LC record available at https://lccn.loc.gov/2019047661

10   9   8   7   6   5   4   3   2   1

Yet ah! why should they know their fate?
Since sorrow never comes too late,
And happiness too swiftly flies.
Thought would destroy their paradise.
No more; where ignorance is bliss,
'Tis folly to be wise.

—Thomas Grey, *Ode on a Distant Prospect of Eton College*

I cannot bear not to know the end of a tale. I will read the most trivial things—once commenced—only out of a feverish greed to be able to swallow the ending—sweet or sour—and to be done with what I need never have embarked on. Are you in my case? Or are you a more discriminating reader? Do you lay aside the unprofitable?

—A. S. Byatt, *Possession*

Contents

Introduction   1

1   **Knowledge Is Power, but Ignorance Is Bliss**   11

2   **Measuring Welfare**   39

3   **Psychology**   79
with George Loewenstein and Russell Golman

4   **Learning the Wrong Thing**   109
with Oren Bar-Gill and David Schkade

5   **Moral Wrongs**   119
with Eric Posner

6   **Valuing Facebook**   135

7   **Sludge**   153

Epilogue   187

Acknowledgments   193
Notes   195
Index   227

Introduction

The primary question in this book is simple: When should government require companies, employers, hospitals, and others to disclose information? My proposed answer is simple, perhaps deceptively so: When information would significantly improve people's lives. Information can achieve that goal if it enables people to make better choices—for example, about their health, their time, or their finances. Information can also improve people's lives if it makes them happier. Unfortunately, some information does not improve people's lives in any way. It does not improve their decisions, and it does not make them happier. Sometimes it is useless. Sometimes it makes them miserable. Sometimes it makes their decisions worse.

It might seem obvious to emphasize the need to ask about the effects of information on human lives. But in public policy circles, many people think in very different terms. They emphasize the "right to know," urging that consumers and employers have a right to information, even if they will do little or nothing with it. Other people emphasize the relationship between information and personal autonomy, contending that people are freer with information than without it, even if it does not improve their lives. I will be rejecting the idea of a "right to know." I will also be urging that it is far less useful to focus on autonomy than on human well-being and on what information contributes to it. At least this is so when public officials are deciding when companies, employers, hospitals, and others must disclose information.

By specifying these claims, I hope to provide a framework to answer the wide range of questions that public officials all over the world are now confronting—about pandemics, cancer, smoking, climate change, poverty, loans, workers' rights, education, sex equality, genetically modified organisms (GMOs), and distracted driving. The proposed framework is meant to clarify not only when mandatory disclosure is a good idea, but also the form that mandatory disclosure should take. And to understand my primary question and my deceptively simple answer, we have to touch on even more fundamental questions about what human beings want to know and how much they want to know it—and whether in wanting to know, or not wanting to know, they might be making serious mistakes.

Ruining Popcorn

My interest in these questions was fueled during the Obama administration, when I was privileged to serve in the White House, helping to oversee federal regulation. A significant amount of my work involved regulations that required disclosure of information—about calories, nutrition, workplace risks, highway safety, fuel economy, greenhouse gas emissions, credit cards, mortgages, and a lot more. The Consumer Financial Protection Bureau had a relevant slogan: Know Before You Owe.

I was enthusiastic about disclosure as a regulatory strategy. I thought that it could make people's lives better.

One day I emailed a friend to let her know that the US Food and Drug Administration had finalized a regulation, on which I had spent a lot of time, requiring disclosure of calories at various restaurants, including movie theaters. I confess that I was enthusiastic, even excited, possibly a bit proud.

My friend's email response: "CASS RUINED POPCORN."

Those words were deflating, of course. But she had a point. At movie theaters, people want to have fun. They want to enjoy their popcorn. As the lights go down, they do not want to wonder whether they are getting fat. A calorie label might not exactly enhance their experience.

As we shall see, empirical work shows that my friend was right: Many people don't want to see calorie labels. In fact, they would be willing to pay real money *not* to see them.

Does this mean that calorie labels are a bad idea? Hardly. Their good effects might outweigh their bad effects. Some people might make better choices as a result of seeing them, and some of them might even learn to like healthier foods. This is a point about the shifting nature of tastes and values, which makes analysis especially complicated. For some people, salad tastes better, if you keep eating salad.

But the risk of ruining popcorn is important. It is a clue to something much larger and more interesting. It suggests that some information makes people feel worse or even terrible. That point might not be decisive. If you learn that you have strep throat, you will not be pleased, but you can probably find a way to get healthy. If you learn that you are performing poorly in your job, you might find a way to do better. But in some cases, ignorance really is bliss and people are better off if they are uninformed.

To the same effect, I received a much sadder lesson decades before. In 1976, my sixty-year-old, strong, very athletic father started to stumble on the tennis court. On several occasions, he nearly fell. My brother-in-law Roger, his frequent tennis partner, was deeply concerned. After a few weeks, my mother and I insisted on taking him to the hospital for a battery of tests. It was a difficult and exhausting day. My father had a flattened, glazed look in his eyes.

Several hours later, there was good news. After talking to the doctors, my mother came back into the hospital room with a bright smile on her face. She said to my Dad: "You have a reprieve! It's just normal headaches. You are going to be absolutely fine. They will do a few more tests, so you'll have to stay a little while. But they are sure that it's nothing." The three of us had a celebratory meal, there in the hospital.

An hour later, my mother brought me into the car, to drive home. She said, flatly and without much affect, "He's going to die of a fatal brain tumor. Probably in eighteen months. There's nothing they can do. Nothing. But we are *not* going to tell him."

We didn't. For a year, he was optimistic, even though the headaches got worse. At some point, it dawned on my father that his situation was grim. Not long before he died, he made that clear to me. His precise words are carved on my soul: "You're going to lose your father." That was over a year after my mother told me the same thing.

In hiding the truth, was my mother protecting herself? Yes, absolutely, no question about it. Was she protecting him? Yes, that too. Was she right? Decades later, I'm not sure, but I tend to think so. She knew a lot about my father, and she knew even more about herself. Whether it's right to disclose bad news depends on the people and the situation. One size does not fit all. I think that my mother knew what size best fit her, and her husband.

Here is a different tale. I purchase electric razors online. I know which brand I like, but when they arrive, they often come in a complicated package, with all sorts of wiring and plastic; it's not a lot of fun to extricate the razor itself. On Amazon, I recently noticed that you could buy a razor with "frustration-free packaging." I didn't know exactly what that meant, but I liked the sound, so that was the packaging I chose. Sure enough, the packaging was much easier to handle. It really was frustration-free.

A few weeks later, I looked up frustration-free packaging. Here is the brief summary:

Designed to reduce waste: Right sized and ships without Amazon packaging

Lab-tested protective design: Certified to minimize damage

Recyclable packaging materials: 100 percent curbside recyclable

Easy to open: No plastic clamshells, no wire ties

The point to note here is that frustration-free packaging is, in significant part, designed to minimize harm to the environment. It reduces waste, and all the materials are recyclable. But *it is not marketed that way*. Consumers are informed of something simple, which is that frustration will be taken away. Amazon must be making a judgment that the best way to inform consumers is to do the opposite, more or less, of ruining popcorn. The company is trying to induce positive emotions.

Often, it's right to ruin popcorn. Information can be essential; having it makes our lives incalculably better. That's true even if the news is terrible. But sometimes, it's best not to know. One of my primary goals here is to offer a plea for focusing intensely on the emotional effects of receiving information—on whether it makes people's days, weeks, months, and years better or worse. But one of my other claims is in some tension with that plea:

people often seek information not because it will make them happy, but because they believe that seeking it will lead to a fuller or richer life. That is a pedestrian observation, but we shall see that it helps unravel a paradox, and perhaps a few of them.

The Plan

Recall my primary question: When should government require people to disclose information? That question bears on what sellers should have to tell consumers, what employers should have to tell workers, what educational institutions should have to tell students, what companies should have to tell investors, and much more. To make progress on that question, it will be necessary to begin with more basic ones. Chapter 1 offers a general overview of why people might want information, why they might be indifferent, and why they might not want to know. It also explores why people might mistakenly want to know and mistakenly not want to know. To say the least, human nature is complicated on this count, and we know much less than we should (and much less than we should want to). My goal is to provide orienting principles.

Chapters 2 through 5 focus on warnings and mandatory labels. In asking whether disclosure of information increases human well-being, I focus on two questions. The first is what people can do with the information. Often they can do nothing at all. Perhaps the information has no connection to what matters to them. Perhaps it is too confusing and lengthy, so people say, "yeah, whatever." Many disclosures are essentially useless—all cost and no benefit.

The second question is how the information makes people feel. I place particular emphasis on the fact that *whether people seek or avoid information often depends whether they think that it will make them either happy or sad.* I also suggest that, in general, that is perfectly reasonable. People want to enjoy their lives. It is sensible to avoid things, including information, that will undermine that goal.

Importantly, enjoyment is not the only thing that matters. Life should be good, not merely fun. If bad news about a house you are thinking about buying makes you sad (perhaps it does not do well on an inspection), you are probably better off with that news in any case. Sometimes information makes life better and more meaningful even if it does not make it more enjoyable. But I will be placing weight on the emotional impact of receiving information, not because it is always the most important consideration, but because it is often neglected (by doctors, by marketers, by governments, by judges). Other things being equal, it is good not to ruin popcorn.

Because some people can use information that other people find useless, and because some people react very negatively to information that doesn't much bother other people, it should not be especially surprising to find a great deal of heterogeneity in information seeking and information avoidance. Some people enjoy information that pains others. As we shall also see, some forms of information disclosure are more likely to be useful than others, and some forms are especially likely to be impactful. (The term *frustration-free* is a clue. I love it; some people undoubtedly don't and would prefer something like *green packaging*.) But I do not aim to provide a how-to manual or a review of when labels and warnings work and when they do not. The broader goal is to provide a framework by which to organize and discipline findings about both success and failure.

Chapter 6 turns from mandatory disclosure to some related questions posed by social media platforms, which provide a lot of information. It asks whether they make people better off or worse off. The standard economic measures turn out to be inadequate. By itself, that is not exactly big news. But the reasons are intriguing, and the inadequacy of those measures has the advantage of shifting our attention to the right question, which is the actual effects of social media on people's lives. As we shall see, there is evidence that people are happier once they stop using Facebook, but even so, they are willing to demand a significant amount of money to get off the platform, apparently because it gives them information that they really want to have (even if it makes them unhappy). There is a large point here about how people seek information, broadly understood, in order to have a fuller or more meaningful life. Some things that we want to know do not make us happy; nonetheless, we want to know. But I shall also explore the possibility that those who want to continue to use social media are making a mistake. They may be in the grip of an addiction. They might not know that social media are having a harmful effect on their lives.

Chapter 7 shifts gears and explores the issue of too much information from another angle. In particular, it explores the problem of *sludge*: administrative burdens imposed by governments, generally asking people to provide information (and sometimes driving people crazy in the process). In short, I ask what government wants to know. Sometimes for good reasons, and sometimes for terrible ones, public officials ask people to hand over information. Sludge can impose high economic and psychological costs, including frustration and a sense of humiliation. It can hurt the most disadvantaged among us. The government needs to want to know less—and to reduce sludge.

In this short book, there are a lot of trees, but let us not lose sight of the forest. Information is a powerful tool—in some ways the most powerful of all. In countless contexts, government is entirely right to provide it or to require others to do so. We are better off with stop signs, with warnings on cigarette packages and prescription drugs, with GPS devices, with reminders that bills are due or that doctors' appointments are upcoming. But sometimes less is more. What is needed, for the future, is much more clarity about what information is actually doing or achieving. If we focus insistently on that question and on how to answer it, we will be able to make people's lives happier, freer, longer, and better.

1 Knowledge Is Power, but Ignorance Is Bliss

Suppose that you are moving to a new city. You probably want to know what it is like to live there. If you are buying a house, you probably want to know whether the roof needs to be fixed or whether the heating system is reliable. If you are buying a laptop, a car, or a cell phone, you are likely to want to know about the product's characteristics, including price, performance, and durability. If you are trying to decide for whom to vote, you probably want to know about the views of the candidates.

It is natural to assume that it is good to obtain information. But when exactly is information good? And exactly how good is it?

There is a great deal of information that people have no interest in receiving. It has no value for them. It clutters the mind. It is boring. In addition, there is a great deal of information that people want *not* to receive. It is unpleasant. It is painful. In some cases, people do not *want* to know, in the sense that they have no particular motivation to find out.[1] They will not take active steps to learn. In others, they want *not* to know, in the sense that they have a particular motivation not to find out. They will take active steps to avoid learning.

You might not much care to learn the number of hairs on the heads of people sitting at the next table at a restaurant, or the precise metals that were used to make your automobile, or whether the coffee beans at the local store came from Brazil, Colombia, Budapest, or somewhere else. You might not want to know whether you will get Alzheimer's disease, whether you have a genetic susceptibility to cancer and heart disease, what all of your colleagues really think about you, and the year of your likely death. You might not want to know about the health risks associated with consumption of beer, coffee, pizza, and ice cream—products that offer immediate pleasure but may create future harm. If your mind is full of those risks, consumption might produce fear, guilt, or shame. Ignorance might be bliss. (This very morning, I weighed myself. Doing that was not good for my mood.)

The general phenomenon of "information avoidance" suggests that people often prefer not to know and will actually take active steps to avoid information.[2] But what steps? And at what cost? I have said that the most fundamental question is whether receiving information increases people's well-being. That proposition argues in favor of a case-by-case approach, asking whether information would have that effect for the relevant population (even if it is a population of just one).[3] True, we have to say something about the meaning of *well-being*. Economists like to work with the idea of willingness to pay (WTP), insisting that it is the best measure we have of whether people will gain or lose from obtaining things—clothing, food, sporting goods, laptops, automobiles, or information.

I will have a fair bit to say about the willingness to pay criterion, much of it negative. What matters is human well-being, not willingness to pay. An obvious problem is that if people lack money, they will not be willing to pay much for that reason. But let's bracket that point and work with willingness to pay for now, seeing it as a way of testing whether people really do want something and how much. One of its advantages is that at least in principle, it should capture everything that human beings care about—everything that matters to them. In some cases, people are willing to pay a lot for information. In other cases, people are willing to pay exactly nothing for information. In other cases, they are willing to pay *not* to receive information.[4]

As we shall see, it is important to ask whether people's willingness to pay, or not, is informed and rational. Crucially, people might lack the information to decide how much they are willing to pay for information. If so, their willingness to pay might depend on an absence of information about the importance of that information. People's willingness to pay might also depend on deprivation and injustice, leading them to lack interest in information that could greatly improve their lives. People who do not know how much they might gain from learning about (say) how to save money might have no interest in obtaining that information. People's willingness to pay might also depend on some kind of cognitive bias, such as present bias (focusing on today and not tomorrow) or availability bias (making some risks, and not others, appear likely to come to fruition).

Willingness to pay might depend on a rational desire to avoid distress—or to preserve the capacity for surprise. We want information when we want it, not before and not after. A surprise party isn't much fun if it isn't a surprise, and a mystery novel needs to maintain its secrets. At the same time, people might underestimate their ability to adapt. They might avoid potentially distressing information about their health, even though the distress might turn out to be short-term (and medical help might be on the way).

Nonetheless, the fact that people are willing to pay a lot for some information but nothing for other information tells us something important. It is even more interesting that people are sometimes willing to pay real money to avoid information.

Two Reasons to Know

When people want to know, it is often for one of two reasons.[5] First, information may produce *positive feelings*. Information might provide joy, delight, amazement, or relief. Second, information may have *instrumental value*. It might enable us to do what we want to do, to go where we want to go, to choose what we want to choose, or to avoid what we want to avoid.

In behavioral science, it has become standard to distinguish between two families of cognitive operations in the human mind. System 1 is fast, automatic, intuitive, and sometimes emotional. System 2 is slow, calculative, and deliberative.[6] System 2 emphasizes the uses of information. It thinks: Can I do something with this? System 1 is attracted to or repelled by information. It thinks: Would knowing this make me happy or sad? Most people tend to think of information in the terms made relevant by System 2, and it is immensely important to do that. But in much of life, System 1 runs the show. When we are keen to know or repelled by the very prospect of knowing, it is usually because of the operations of System 1.

The idea of frustration-free packaging appeals mostly to System 1 (though System 2 also endorses it). For many people, the idea of green packaging appeals mostly to System 2 (though System 1 may well be enthusiastic too). Of course, there is heterogeneity on this count. In terms of System 1 or System 2, some people will care greatly about whether packaging is frustration-free and not at all about whether it is environmentally friendly. Other people might have the opposite preferences. The only point is that people's intuitive, emotional reaction to information, and to the prospect of receiving it, often determines whether they will seek or avoid it.

It follows that even if information is not useful, people might want it because they expect that it will make them feel great. If people learn that they will never get cancer or that they are unnaturally intelligent and good-looking, they are likely to be pleased, whether or not their behavior is altered. Information can create positive feelings of diverse kinds: joy, pride, satisfaction, contentment, relief, gratitude. In many cases, it is true and important to say that information has hedonic value—that is, it provides pleasure. Although I will use that term, it is inadequate to describe the relevant feelings as narrowly hedonic. They might have little or nothing to do with pleasure; they involve welfare in a much broader sense. They might produce a sense that life has meaning. We can use the term *affective value* to describe positive feelings of that kind.

The instrumental value of information is captured in the idea that knowledge is power. If people find out that their boss thinks that they are underperforming, they might be able to do better. If people learn that the stock market will go up in the next few months, they will have an opportunity to invest and to make money. If teachers learn that their students did not enjoy their course, they can try to teach better. If people learn that they are at risk of diabetes, they might take steps to reduce that risk. If people learn that their car is not fuel-efficient, they can buy a new and more fuel-efficient car. Often people act differently, and do better, once they know. Information saves money and lives.

Note here that the instrumental value might involve one's own well-being or instead the well-being of others. Consumers might want information about certain products so that they can increase social benefits or reduce social harms. Public officials might require disclosure of such information not because consumers are demanding it, but to trigger their attention, conscience, and concern and in that way affect social norms and promote social goals. Consider animal welfare and climate change.

For mandatory labels, instrumental value is usually primary, and hedonic value often matters. Because much of my focus is on such labels, I will be focusing largely on those two values. But they are certainly not exhaustive. People might believe that it is good to know about their country, their planet, and their universe, even if the information does not especially please them and even if they cannot do anything with it. They might want to know about life in other nations and about the history of the world's religions for reasons that have nothing to do with what they can do with that information or whether they will be pleased by what they learn. They might think that they have a moral obligation to know certain things. If people are suffering in their city or their country, or if there is a mass atrocity somewhere in the world, they might want to know about it.

More broadly still, people might think that certain kinds of knowledge make for a better or fuller or richer life, even if they lack instrumental or affective value. People might want to know something about their friends and family, even if that something does not make them happy and even if it cannot be used, because of their views about what makes a human life good or right. They might want to know about the life of William Shakespeare, the origins of Earth, the relationship between dogs and wolves, or the history of India, even if they are not rooting for a particular answer and regardless of whether or not they can use that information.

The Dark Side of Information

Much information does not enable people to do anything at all. If people learn the height of everyone born in Paris in 1920, the weather next week in a foreign city that they will not be visiting, or the words to twenty songs in a language that they do not understand, they are unlikely to live their lives differently. Finding out about those heights, that weather, or those words may not induce positive feelings. It might be useless as well as tedious.

Some information induces negative feelings. Do you want to know the year of your spouse's death? The year of your son's death? The results of a battery of medical tests? Whether the people who made your clothing were paid a decent wage? If the news could be bad or sad, people might want to avoid it for that very reason. And even if the news is likely to be relatively good, people might not want to take their chances on such questions. They might prefer a big question mark—or not to think about the matter. Information can produce distress, frustration, grief, rage, or despair.

Here is striking evidence. Sometimes people really do not want to know how much goods cost, and they will avoid information about price—*willfully*.[7] Price, too, can ruin popcorn, and people know that. More specifically, Linda Thunstrom and Chian Jones Ritten find that some people are "spendthrifts" by their own lights, in the sense that they agree that they spend too much for their own good. They find that spendthrifts tend to be inaccurate in their judgments about the costs of their own recent purchases. They also find that spendthrifts tend to agree with this statement: "When I engage in an enjoyable activity, I prefer not to think of the cost of that activity." Their evidence strongly suggests that spendthrifts take steps to reduce their attention to cost. To be sure, it may not be easy to ignore price entirely. But consumers can focus less on price, so that it is not so visibly on their viewscreen and so that they think and know less about it. Thunstrom and Ritten conclude that willful inattention to price is a justification for laws and policies that make prices transparent and salient.

Some information has *negative* instrumental value.[8] Suppose that you are a lawyer, representing a client accused of murder. Suppose that the evidence leaves significant doubt about whether your client is guilty or whether the police violated your client's constitutional rights. You might do a better job if you never know, for sure, whether your client is a murderer. Or suppose that you are fighting a serious illness. Your chances of success, and of a long life, might depend on not knowing the odds. (As Han Solo, the daredevil pilot in *Star Wars*, liked to say, "Never tell me the odds!") Or suppose that you are on a tennis team consisting of nine players, and the first team to win five matches wins the entire match. If you learn that four of your teammates are way ahead, you might not try so hard. You would be better off not knowing. Or suppose that you do not want to discriminate on certain grounds—sex, religion, age, race. You might fear that if you receive demographic information about a job applicant, you might discriminate. To avoid that risk, you might try not to know.

Some information has instrumental value but also induces negative feelings. If you learn that you are obese or that you suffer from high blood pressure, you are likely to be upset, but you can probably do something about it (which should reduce the negative affect). If you learn that your teacher thinks that you could do a much better job, you might be hurt and angry, but you might be able to take steps to improve your performance. If you find out that your spouse is upset with you, you will not be happy about it, but perhaps you can improve the relationship.

Some information has negative instrumental value but also induces positive feelings. If a high school student learns that she has gotten into the university of her choice, she might not work so hard during her last semester. If a football team learns that it has made the playoffs because its principal competitor has lost, it might not try so hard to win its next game. People might want to put off good news simply because it will adversely affect their performance.

For orientation, consider table 1.1. For different people, different information will occupy different cells. What is cell (1) for some people will be cell (7) for others, and what is cell (5) for some people will be cell (4) for others. A number of years ago, I had an endless series of medical tests for what was almost certainly a nonissue. It was a bit of a nightmare. In the tenth round,

Table 1.1
The value of information

		Instrumental value		
		Positive	Negative	None
Feelings	Positive	(1)	(2)	(3)
	Negative	(4)	(5)	(6)
	None	(7)	(8)	(9)

the kindly doctor said, "I think you are fine. But a lot of people can't sleep at night unless they have all relevant tests. I wouldn't get this if I were you, but it's up to you." He thought that for me, this might have been a case of cell (3) (no instrumental value, positive feelings from being tested), but he was wrong; I found it a case of (6) (no instrumental value, negative feelings from yet another test). The key point is that the value of information and the feelings that emerge as a result of that information can be positive, negative, or neutral, and that positive (or negative) value does not necessarily cause positive (or negative) feelings. Feelings and values can be mixed and matched in multiple ways.

A Bet

These are points about the effects of obtaining information, but when people say that they do or do not want to know, they will not know, in advance, what they will learn. They are making a kind of bet. The question is often to know *whether*, not to know *that*.

People might ask some question with a "yes" or "no" answer; a "yes" could induce positive affect and a "no" could produce misery ("Does she love me? Even a little bit?"). Or people might ask some question with ten, twenty, or a hundred possible answers ("What was my score on that test?" or "How much money will I be earning in ten years?"). Some of those answers will produce information that people could actually use, whereas others will not. It follows that when people are thinking about whether they want to know, they need to know both about expected outcomes and about the probability that they will occur. They will be interested above all in the probability that what they learn will induce positive feelings or will be useful. If the probability is very high (say, 90 percent), they might be more inclined to want to know than if the probability is very low (say, 10 percent). If people are confident that they will never get cancer—but are not quite sure—they might be interested in getting that information, simply because the odds seem to be in their favor. If a bad outcome is very bad, or if a good outcome is very good, their judgment will be affected, and this is true both for instrumental value and for hedonic value. Rational choosers, deciding whether to acquire or avoid information, would try to estimate some numbers.

Ideally, the decision of whether to know would turn on a rational assessment of everything that matters: people would figure out what they care about (peace of mind, longevity, money, cordial relations with others), and their decisions to acquire information would reflect that assessment.[9] But unjust background conditions or injustice can infect people's decisions about what information to acquire.[10] Under circumstances of poverty, deprivation, or discrimination, people might not have an interest in obtaining important information, and they might not have the capacity to get it even if they do have interest. In the worst cases, people's very preferences are adaptive to, or a product of, the injustice to which they are subject. If so, they might not seek information of immense importance.

Behavioral scientists have also shown that our decisions are not always entirely rational. People use heuristics, or mental shortcuts, which may lead them in unfortunate directions, and they are also biased in various ways. When people decide whether to obtain information, heuristics and biases matter as well. Of special importance is *present bias*, which means that people often focus on today and tomorrow, while neglecting the long-term.[11] Suppose that the question is whether to seek information from which you might suffer today, but which might be of great value over the long-term. You should seek that information. But you might not. The short-term distress might prove decisive. You might not want to know. (You might not weigh yourself. You might skip that annual appointment with your doctor, which might be especially foolish because the more you delay, the more fearful you might be.)

Some of the most illuminating work on information seeking emphasizes "strategic self-ignorance," understood as "the use of ignorance as an excuse to over-indulge in pleasurable activities that may be harmful to one's future self."[12] The idea here is that if people are present-biased, they might avoid information that would make current activities less attractive—perhaps because it would produce guilt or shame, perhaps because it would suggest an aggregate trade-off that would counsel against engaging in such activities. St. Augustine famously said, "God give me chastity—tomorrow." Present-biased agents think: "Please let me know the risks—tomorrow." Whenever people are thinking about engaging in an activity with short-term benefits but long-term costs, they might prefer to defer receipt of important information.[13] The same point might hold about information that could make people sad or mad: "Please tell me what I need to know—tomorrow."

Behavioral scientists have also emphasized *loss aversion*, which means that people particularly dislike losses; in fact, they dislike losses much more than they like equivalent gains.[14] If people are loss averse, they might be especially reluctant to get information if they think that the news might well be bad. If the news involves a potential cancer diagnosis, for example, they might think: "I feel fine now. I think that I will continue to be fine. If I get tested, I might get bad news. Why should I get tested?" It should be clear that present bias and loss aversion can be a potent combination, producing high levels of information avoidance. When people mistakenly avoid information, or do not seek information, it is often because of that potent combination.

An important finding here is that when people receive bad news—involving, say, a higher-than-expected risk of health problems—*their initial level of distress is high, but they recover quite quickly.*[15] If people anticipate the distress but not the recovery, they will avoid information that might save their lives and that might not have a terribly adverse effect on their feelings over time. An extensive review of fifteen studies about people's responses to predictive genetic testing shows something similar: if anything, it finds that people do not feel significant distress at all in response to predictive genetic testing.[16] The studies focused on such testing for a variety of conditions: hereditary breast and ovarian cancer, Huntington's disease, familial adenomatous polyposis, and spinocerebellar ataxia. Almost all involved adults (only one involved children). The general pattern was that during the twelve months after testing, neither carriers nor noncarriers were likely to show increased distress (understood as general and situational distress, anxiety, and depression). In only two of the studies did the outcome of the test predict distress more than a month after the test result. The authors conclude that that "those undergoing predictive genetic testing do not experience adverse psychological consequences," while also noting that the studies involve "self-selected populations who have agreed to participate in psychological studies."[17]

Even with that important qualification, I speculate that many people, in general and before undergoing genetic testing, would be surprised to learn of these findings—which supports the hypothesis that people overstate their likely reaction to unwelcome results from predictive testing. In addition to present bias and loss aversion, an inaccurate prediction might also be a product of the *focusing illusion*.[18] People often overestimate the effect of a particular event on their overall well-being, simply because they focus on it. As David Schkade and Daniel Kahneman have put it, "Nothing that you focus on will make as much difference as you think."[19] A cold rainy day, a shiny new car, an increase in salary, or even a serious illness might be anticipated to have a major impact, even though it quickly becomes part of the background, something like life's furniture. For that reason, people might exaggerate the welfare effect of bad news—and choose not to risk getting it.

At the same time, the desire to obtain information will also be affected by optimistic bias. If people think that they are likely to receive good news, they are more likely to want to know "whether." And indeed, most people do show unrealistic optimism, at least in the sense that they think that their personal prospects (with respect to health, safety, and other things) are better than average—and in fact better than statistical reality warrants.[20] Unrealistic optimism can counteract loss aversion and lead people to get information that might turn out to be exceedingly useful.

In assessing probability, people use the *availability heuristic*, which means that they ask whether relevant examples come to mind. How likely is a flood, an airplane crash, a traffic jam, a terrorist attack, or a disaster at a nuclear power plant? Lacking statistical knowledge, people try to think of illustrations. Thus, "a class whose instances are easily retrieved will appear more numerous than a class of equal frequency whose instances are less retrievable."[21] If people are aware of cases in which others received bad news, their probability judgments will be inflated accordingly. A set of cases of good news will have corresponding effects.

We should now be able to see that in any population, there is likely to be a great deal of heterogeneity. First, some people will be in a position to gain a great deal in instrumental terms from obtaining information about X, whereas other people will be in a position to gain only a little, and still others will gain nothing at all. Second, some people would be deeply alarmed at bad news, if it comes to that, whereas others would be mildly discomfited, and others would take it in stride. Many people are not resilient; many people are. Some people get hysterical; others get practical. A rational agent, deciding whether to seek information, would weigh both instrumental and affective values, and different rational agents, given their situations and sensibilities, would make different rational choices. Third, heterogeneity is greatly compounded in light of the fact that some people are more present-biased than others, more loss averse than others, and more optimistic than others. Fourth, the availability heuristic will lead some people to anticipate good news and others to anticipate bad news. For different people, different outcomes and events will be cognitively available.

Return to the problems of deprivation, inequality, and injustice. Some people are in a terrific position to benefit from information. Other people are not. Background information is often necessary to make sense of information, and some groups will lack that information. In thinking about mandatory disclosure of information, it is often important to confront issues of distributive justice and ask: Who is helped and who isn't?

In light of these considerations, it should be no wonder that some people want to get a lot of medical tests, and other people want to get exactly none. Nor should it be surprising that some consumers are keenly interested in energy efficiency and in learning about fuel economy, whereas others are indifferent or negative. Nor should it be surprising that some people care about and benefit from calorie labels, whereas other people (including people with little money or education) might neither care nor benefit, and might even think, "the more calories, the better." Of course, people have different moral convictions, and so some will want information relating to (say) animal welfare when others have no interest.

Clues

Using Amazon Mechanical Turk, I have conducted a series of studies of these issues, asking about four hundred Americans about whether they want information of diverse kinds and how much they would be willing to pay for that information. I hypothesized that I would find clear and clean evidence in favor of four simple propositions: (1) people want information if it would either be useful or produce positive affect; (2) people's willingness to pay for information would depend on (a) how useful it would be or (b) how happy it would make them; (3) when information would not be useful or would make people sad, they would be far less likely to want it; and (4) there would be a great deal of heterogeneity in people's answers.

I believe that all of these propositions are correct. I was hopeful of obtaining such evidence, because a growing body of research tends to support propositions 1, 2, and 3 in particular. For example:

1. People are more likely to check their investment portfolios and to learn whether they are gaining or losing money during

periods when the stock market is going up than during periods when it is going down—a clear demonstration of the "ostrich effect."[22] When the hedonic value of receiving information is likely to be negative, people are more likely not to seek information.

2. People want to see political views that align with their own, partly because they believe that seeing opposing views will make them sad or mad.[23] Here again, people anticipate that the information will create negative feelings, and so they are less likely to want to receive it. Interestingly, people make mistakes on this count; they overestimate the extent to which seeing opposing views will make them feel bad. On this count, people make an "affective forecasting error"; they do not accurately predict how information will make them feel. There is a large lesson here, bearing on health-related information in particular.

3. People are more likely to favor calorie labels, and to be willing to pay for them, if they do not suffer from self-control problems and hence are likely to be in a position to benefit from those labels.[24] Such people are not bothered by calorie labels; many of them even enjoy seeing them. They also believe that they can use them. By contrast, people who do suffer from self-control problems are more willing to pay *not* to see calorie labels. Apparently they believe that such labels will not help them and will just make them sad or upset.[25] (And indeed, they tend to have exactly that effect on people with self-control problems.) The conclusion is that making calories salient "positively affects consumer welfare, although heterogeneity over consumers is substantial—the consumer value ranges from positive to negative."[26] In addition, people with higher levels of self-control are more likely to benefit from

caloric information; those "with low self-control both experience a (higher) emotional cost from the nudge and no (or, at
best, few) benefits from consumption adjustments, compared
to higher level self-control consumers."[27]

4. Overwhelming majorities of people say that they do not
want to know when their partner will die or the cause of their
partner's death.[28] They also do not want to know when they
themselves will die or the cause of their own death.

5. With respect to their own performance on a task, people are
more likely to want information and to be willing to pay for
information if they think the news will be good—that is, if
they will learn that they performed well.[29] They are significantly less likely to want information and more likely to be
willing to pay not to receive it if they think that they performed poorly. The relevant research studied not only behavior but also brain regions. It found that those regions of the
brain that are associated with positive emotions are activated
by good news—strongly suggesting that affective reactions
help account for people's decision about whether to seek
information.

In these particular cases, hedonic value seems dominant in
determining whether people want to know. There is no more
reason to check your portfolio when its value is growing than
when its value is shrinking, though the latter is a lot less fun. But
instrumental value unquestionably matters as well. With respect
to calorie labels, it is reasonable to think that people's judgments
are mostly an answer to the question: Would I benefit from this
information? People with high levels of self-control would be
more likely to answer "yes" and so they would be more likely to
pay for the information. Similarly, people would undoubtedly be

more likely to want to know about the cause of a partner's death if they thought that they could do something about it—and eliminate that cause.

There are actually two separate questions here. The first is: Would I benefit? The second is: Can I change the outcome if I don't like it? The questions are closely related, but the second puts a spotlight on people's sense of agency. The capacity for control generates positive feelings in itself. It can produce a benefit, in terms of (say) health or economics, but it has independent value.

We could easily design cases for which instrumental value, understood in terms of both questions, would be dominant. For example, we might ask people whether they want to know what the weather will be for every day of the next year, what their bosses most like in their employees, or whether the stock market will go up or down next month.

My own evidence attests to the importance of both hedonic and instrumental value. A solid majority—about 60 percent—said that they want to know the annual cost of operating the appliances in their home. We could speculate that most people want that information so that they can save money. A solid majority—59 percent—also said that they would like to know how to fix their cell phones if they failed to connect to the internet. That would be handy information to have. About 58 percent wanted to know if a person for whom they have strong romantic feelings shares those feelings. In all of these cases, and perhaps especially the third, the relevant information is pretty useful.

It remains, of course, to explain why substantial minorities, in all three cases, are not interested in apparently useful information. The most plausible answers point to the word *apparently*—and also emphasize the importance of affect. In these cases, heterogeneity ought to be expected. Many people undoubtedly think that learning the annual cost of operating appliances is pretty dull stuff and that it would not do them a whole lot of good. Many others already have that information, or think they do, and so would not pay for it. Many others think, reasonably enough, that cell phones ordinarily connect to the internet, and if theirs do not, well, chances are that the problem will resolve itself. Many people fear that people toward whom they have romantic feelings probably don't share those feelings, which means that they would get bad news. Many others think that good news might be a bit dangerous. (By the way, I asked a group of about forty people in their twenties the same question—and all but one wanted to know!)

I asked several questions involving serious health conditions, and on those participants were almost evenly divided. For example, most people (53 percent) said that they did not want to know if they will get Alzheimer's disease. Half said that they want to know if they were at serious risk of getting diabetes. Slightly more (58 percent) said that they want to know whether they have a genetic disposition to cancer or heart disease.[30] The large percentages in favor of ignorance undoubtedly stemmed in large part from the negative emotions that bad news would induce. But while the answers to such questions could be alarming, many people evidently thought that forewarned is forearmed. Perhaps they could do something to reduce the risk of getting diabetes, cancer, or heart disease. Perhaps they could arrange their life a bit differently, or a lot differently, if they learn that they will get Alzheimer's disease.

I also asked questions about information of diverse kinds. About 57 percent would like to know whether their partner or spouse ever cheats on them. Only 42 percent would like to know what their friends and family members really think about them! About 42 percent want to know how much warmer the planet will be in 2100. Only 27 percent said that they want to know the year of their likely death. Amazingly, just 54 percent wanted to know how the stock market will be doing on a specified date in the future. (Apparently people did not think, as they should: If I receive that information, I can make essentially all the money I want.)

Strikingly, 71 percent want to know if there is life on other planets. Perhaps surprisingly, only a bare majority (53 percent) want to know if heaven really exists. Those who did not want to know probably fell within various categories: (1) those who are sure that heaven does exist, so the information would be worthless; (2) those who are sure that heaven does not exist, so the information would be worthless; (3) those who think that they will not get into heaven, so learning of its existence could only make them sad or upset; or (4) those who think that it is best to have a degree of uncertainty. A smaller number (44 percent) want to know if hell exists—which is probably testimony to the fact that if hell exists, a lot of people think that they will be in big trouble.

With respect to information that bears on consumption choices, only 43 percent said that they want to see calorie labels at restaurants. Their willingness to pay for that information was modest: the median was just $15 annually, and the mean was just $48.61. For information about the annual cost of operating appliances in the home, willingness to pay was comparable: a median of $15 and a mean of $43.71. These findings are of particular interest in light of evidence that an overwhelming majority of Americans favor a federal mandate requiring restaurants to disclose the calories associated with their offerings.[31] Many people who favor a federal mandate apparently believe that they themselves will not benefit from the information—and may even be harmed by it.[32] They want their government to require disclosure of information in which they have no interest (or which they would prefer not to get at all).

There is an evident paradox here. Why would people not want to see calorie labels—but nonetheless believe that the federal government should require restaurants to display them? It is reasonable to speculate that people believe that *other people* would benefit from that information. It is also possible that if people are asked whether companies should do something, they are willing to answer "yes," even if they would not benefit personally from that action.

Willingness to pay was somewhat higher for other kinds of information. For how the stock market will be doing on January 1, 2020, the median was $100 and the mean was $165.93. (Recall that that's wildly low, because you can make a ton of money with that information.) The median WTP of those who wanted to know whether they had a genetic predisposition to cancer was $79, with a mean of $115. For Alzheimer's, the corresponding numbers were $59 and $106.98; for the likely year of death, they were $93 and $154.44; for whether their partner or spouse ever cheats, they were $74.50 and $120.67. For the global temperature in 2100, the numbers were markedly lower: $19 and $59.37. Table 1.2 presents the key results.

Do Consumers Want to Be Informed?

I conducted a similar study, again using Amazon Mechanical Turk and four hundred Americans, exclusively involving information that might benefit consumers and of the kind on which

Table 1.2

Disclosure of potentially important information

Information offered	Annual willingness to pay		
	Want information	Median ($)	Mean ($)
Whether participant will get Alzheimer's disease	47%	59	107
Stock market performance on January 1, 2020	54%	100	166
The weather for every day of the remainder of the year	55%	70	121
Genetic predisposition to cancer or heart disease	58%	79	115
At serious risk of getting diabetes	50%	52	116
Whether participant's partner or spouse ever cheats	57%	75	130
Whether heaven exists	53%	200	221
Whether hell exists	44%	148	210
Whether ever get cancer	52%	26	101
Capitals of all the nations in Africa	20%	18	122
Winner of baseball's next World Series	42%	105	187
How to fix cell phone if it is not connecting to provider	59%	11	61
Whether there is life on other planets	71%	51	125
Whether person for whom you have strong romantic feelings shares those feelings	58%	67	114
The number of nations in the United Nations	30%	10	97

Table 1.2 (continued)

	Annual willingness to pay		
Information offered	Want information	Median ($)	Mean ($)
All of the terms and conditions, including possible late fees, associated with credit card	56%	1	60
The year of your spouse's death	26%	167	198
What your friends and family members really think about you	42%	88	130
Annual cost of operating the appliances in participant's home	60%	15	44
Global temperature in 2100	42%	19	59
Likely year of death	27%	93	154
Calorie labels at restaurants	43%	15	49

regulators have focused. All of that information would appear to be at least somewhat useful, though more so for some people than for others. Some of that information might not be a lot of fun to receive.

Here too, there was a great deal of heterogeneity, and many people showed no interest in receiving the relevant information. Only 62 percent of respondents wanted information about the standard fee for a late payment of their credit card bill. The remaining 38 percent might pay their bills on time or might not care about late fees. Only 60 percent wanted to know whether their food contains genetically modified organisms. Perhaps 40 percent already know or simply do not care.

Only 64 percent wanted to know about the amount of overuse charges for their cell phone. About 67 percent wanted information about the safety ratings for their tires. (This is relatively high; the word *safety* might be a trigger.) About 65 percent wanted information about the potential side-effects of pain relievers (such as Advil and Tylenol). About 55 percent wanted information about whether the products they buy contain conflict minerals (defined as minerals from the Democratic Republic of Congo [DRC] used to finance mass atrocities). It is reasonable to speculate that some people really care about the moral issue and would use the information in their consumption choices, and others just don't and wouldn't.

The median willingness to pay, in all of these cases, was pretty small: $8 for late payments ($103 mean); $24 for GMOs ($101 mean); $10 for overuse charges ($95 mean); $16 for safety ratings ($101 mean); $9 for side-effects of pain relievers ($85 mean); and $26.50 for conflict minerals ($109 mean). Table 1.3 presents the results.

It is safe to conclude that many people do not want to receive some information even if it seems relevant to their choices—and that when they do want that information, they do not place a high value on it. Many of them must think that the information would not affect their choices or that it would be unpleasant to receive it.

With respect to public policy, we should not take people's answers as authoritative. One more time: they might reflect an absence of information, unjust background conditions, or some kind of behavioral bias. But in light of these findings, we have some reason for personalized disclosure, giving information only to those who actually want it (assuming, perhaps inaccurately, that those who want it, and those who do not, do not

Table 1.3
Consumer disclosure

Information offered	Willingness to pay		
	Want information	Median ($)	Mean ($)
Standard fee for late payment of participant's credit card bill	62%	8	103
Food contains genetically modified organisms	60%	24	101
Amount of overuse charges for participant's cell phone	64%	10	95
Safety ratings for participant's tires	67%	16	101
Potential side-effects of pain relievers	65%	9	85
Products contain conflict minerals	55%	26.50	109

suffer from a relevant informational problem, background injustice, or some behavioral bias). Unfortunately, personalization is often infeasible. Information may be a public good, in the sense that if one person receives it, others do as well. Consider the case of calorie labels, which are provided to everyone, and cannot easily be personalized. But there is good news. In the future, new technologies will make personalized or targeted disclosure more feasible than it has ever been before.

I will explore this issue in due course. For the moment, let's step back from the details. When people want information, it is usually because it is useful to have, because it is pleasant to have, or both. In cases that are both common and hard, information is useful to have but unpleasant to have. (Welcome to the human condition.) In rare cases, information is pleasant to have but harmful to have. In many cases, the decision whether to seek information or instead to avoid it depends on a kind of bet. People are playing something like high-stakes poker. If they are optimistic, they might seek information even if it could make them feel terrible. If they are loss averse, they might avoid information even if it could save their lives. All this bears on major issues of public policy—issues that will rank among the most important of all in coming decades.

2 Measuring Welfare

Will disclosure of information promote human welfare? Are labels and warnings a good idea? When?

We have seen enough to know that these are impossibly abstract questions. Fortunately, the US government has a great deal of experience in trying to answer them in the process of investigating concrete proposals. Recall some defining examples: fuel economy labels, calorie labels, nutritional labels, energy efficiency labels, graphic health warnings for cigarettes. Informed by an understanding of why people may or may not want to know, I am going to focus here on whether and when it is a good idea to require information to be disclosed. Health and safety are particularly important, but it is also important to consider the risk of ruining popcorn.

To get hold of that issue, we should say something about why exactly a sensible government might mandate disclosure. My preferred answer is simple: because it promotes human welfare. If a disclosure mandate does not do that, it should not be imposed. But as we have seen, some people who champion disclosure mandates do not see things that way. They insist that their goal is to ensure that people's decisions are informed—period. If that is the goal, then we might approve of disclosure mandates even if they do not really improve human welfare at all. True, we will want to ensure that any such mandate is *effective*. If the result is to overwhelm people with thirty dense pages that they cannot understand, they will not be informed. But so long as disclosure does inform people, some policymakers would declare victory. But why? If a mandate does not make people better off, or if it makes them worse off, what is the point?

A possible answer points to a different master concept: autonomy. On one view, the whole purpose of disclosure mandates is to ensure that people can make autonomous choices. We might add that if they are consumers, workers, or patients, people should be treated with respect, and ensuring that choosers are informed is a way to do that. Philosophers and others vigorously argue over the choice between welfarism, applied here and growing out of the utilitarian tradition inaugurated by Jeremy Bentham and John Stuart Mill, and deontological approaches, focused on the idea of autonomy and respect for persons, championed and defended by Immanuel Kant.[1]

In 2019, the US Food and Drug Administration (FDA) ventured in the direction of autonomy in justifying its proposed regulations, calling for new warnings and graphic images on cigarette packages.[2] Instead of claiming that the warnings and images would reduce smoking and save lives, the agency said that they would promote "a greater public understanding of the negative health consequences of cigarette smoking." That greater understanding was, in the agency's view, the principal benefit of its regulation—apart from its consequences for public health. It is not clear whether the agency thought that the greater understanding was valuable in itself, was valuable instrumentally for multiple reasons (having to do with human welfare), or was valuable instrumentally because it would eventually lead to less smoking. But the agency emphasized that a better understanding was intrinsically valuable.

This is not the space to venture a full argument on behalf of welfarism. For the most part, I shall simply assume that it is the most helpful way to approach the question whether government should mandate disclosure of information. I shall also attempt to make the argument plausible by reference to a host of examples. The good news is that for the most part, welfarist and deontological approaches do not lead in dramatically different directions, at least for my purposes here. Even if one rejects welfarism and embraces a commitment to autonomy, it hardly follows that mandatory disclosure of information is generally a good idea. A central question is what kinds of information people need to have to be autonomous. An equally central question is what and whether autonomous agents would want to know. If information would not improve their decisions, and if it would make them miserable, they might want not to know. If we want to respect their autonomy, we should respect that preference, at least as a presumption.

Consider an analogy. Reasonable choosers often choose not to choose. That is one way that they exercise their autonomy. They delegate choices to others (doctors, lawyers, engineers, investment advisers). They might do so because they think that others will chose better. They might do so because they do not like choosing. They might do so because they are busy and want to focus on other matters. They might think that if they delegate choice, they will have more freedom. In these circumstances, to force them to choose is disrespectful of their autonomy. So too with information: if people do not want it, forcing them to get it, or throwing it in their faces, is not exactly respectful. It is true, of course, that a lack of information, background injustice, or a behavioral bias might be distorting people's decisions about whether to seek or avoid information. The only point is that if we are concerned about people's autonomy, it is not clear that we should provide them with information in situations in which they do not want it.

If we start with the idea of welfare, we should note that the idea needs to be specified. In the abstract, it could mean any number of things.[3] For now, let us emphasize just one point: Distributional concerns greatly matter. We need to know who is helped and who is hurt. If information disclosure helps people who are educated and wealthy but does not help people who are uneducated and poor, there is a serious problem. If wealthy people use information but poor people do not, policymakers need to take that point into account. They might want to do something different. Philosophers have defended the idea of *prioritarianism*, a form of welfarism that puts special weight on the well-being of those who are worst-off.[4] In a sensible regulatory system, prioritarianism plays a large role in the design of disclosure policies.

Four Questions

In most nations, the law does not take an explicit stand on the largest theoretical questions. But when they issue significant regulations, federal agencies in the United States have been asked, for decades, to answer four questions with an unmistakably welfarist orientation, focusing on the human consequences of their policy choices:[5]

1. When exactly should government require disclosure—or, in other words, in what circumstances is there some kind of market failure?

2. What would be the costs and benefits of disclosure?

3. How can those costs and benefits be measured?

4. Would disclosure of information do more good than harm, by reference to cost-benefit analysis or some other metric?

Starting with President Ronald Reagan in 1981, both Republican and Democratic presidents have issued Executive Orders that require agencies, such as the US Environmental Protection Agency (EPA) and the US Department of Transportation, to answer all of those questions whenever they are issuing important regulations, including those that mandate disclosure. To many people, such requirements are mysterious. They need not be. They are best understood as a way of testing whether disclosure of information will promote human welfare.[6] Analysis of costs and benefits is a highly imperfect but administrable way of answering that question. Suppose, for example, that a disclosure requirement would impose $500 million in costs but produce $10 in benefits. If so, we have good reason to think that the requirement will not promote human welfare.

I am aware that this claim raises many questions and doubts. The fact that a requirement imposes monetary costs in excess of monetary benefits does not *necessarily* mean that it will fail to promote human welfare. The fact that a requirement confers monetary benefits in excess of monetary costs does not *necessarily* mean that it will promote human welfare. Again: distributional effects should be considered. I will have a great deal to say about the relationship between cost-benefit analysis and human welfare. For now, let's simply underline the goal of the four questions: to focus on the actual consequences of disclosure for human beings. (I will have something to say about nonhuman animals as well.)

These questions arise in many contexts, involving calorie labels, mortgage disclosures, energy efficiency labels, conflict of interest disclosures, health disclosures, fuel economy labels, credit card disclosures, labels for genetically modified food, nutrition facts panels, country of origin labels, dolphin-free tuna labels, sunscreen labels, conflict minerals disclosures, graphic warnings for cigarettes, and much more. Some of these labels are designed to enable consumers, workers, patients, and others to protect themselves from risks involving money or health. Some of them attempt to protect third parties or respond to moral concerns—as, for example, when labels offer information that bears on animal welfare. Some of them respond to some kind of consumer (or interest group) demand for government action, whether or not risks are actually involved. Figure 2.1 shows three prominent examples of mandatory labels.

Chasing Numbers

Assessment of the effects of mandatory disclosure can be daunting. The first problem is that sometimes government agencies *do not know how people will respond*. If people are informed that certain refrigerators or microwave ovens are energy efficient, or are given clear information about the costs of operating household appliances, how will their behavior change? If they are given a great deal of information about the costs associated with taking out a mortgage, what will they do, compared to what they would do if they did not receive that information?

The second problem is that even if agencies can predict how people will respond, they may find it hard to translate people's responses into monetary equivalents. If agencies learn that disclosure of caloric information leads people to consume

(a)

(b)

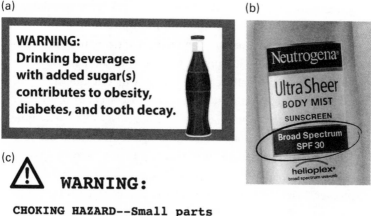

(c)

WARNING:

CHOKING HAZARD--Small parts
Not for children under 3 yrs.

Figure 2.1
Three disclosure labels: (a) a warning about the effect of drinking sugary beverages, (b) an indicator of a sunscreen's type and extent of sun protection; and (c) a choking hazard warning.

fewer calories or that disclosure of the use of genetically modified organisms leads to different consumption choices, what exactly is the benefit? To be sure, many people will be skeptical of the whole idea of monetary equivalents. What matters is welfare, so the real question is how responses to labels actually affect people's lives. Recall that we are using monetary equivalents not because they tell us everything that we need to know, but because they are an available proxy for what we need to know—a way of getting important information about the welfare effects.

We have seen that if the goal is to obtain monetary equivalents, economists tend to think that private willingness to pay is the best approach in theory.[7] To many people, that claim is not exactly intuitive; it might even seem preposterous. But we have also seen that on identifiable assumptions, it should capture everything that people stand to gain and lose from information. It should take account of the fact that some information has no benefits at all because people will not care about it, use it, or understand it. It should also take account of the fact that some information produces welfare gains, while other information produces welfare losses—and that some information will do both at the same time. The challenge is that to come up with willingness to pay figures, people have to solve a prediction problem. They have to figure out the effects of information on their welfare. However, there are two reasons why solving that problem may be exceedingly difficult.

I have already pointed to the first reason: people often lack the information that would enable them to decide how much to pay for (more) information. As Kenneth Arrow put it long ago, "There is a fundamental paradox in the determination of demand for information; its value to the purchaser is not known until he has the information, but then he has in effect acquired it without cost."[8] If people do not have information, they may not know enough to know whether and how much to pay to receive information! The point bears on questions of distributional fairness: some people might have enough information to want information, and other people might not. At the very least, these points raise serious problems for before-the-fact estimates of willingness to pay. After-the-fact estimates may be better. After people have obtained information, they might have a much better sense of its value.

The second reason is that even apart from this problem, willingness to pay, stated in advance, may fail to capture the actual welfare effects of information. In some contexts, people's preferences shift over time. Once informed about the health risks associated with certain foods, people might (begin to) develop different tastes. They might start to like brownies much less and salad much more. On plausible assumptions, for example, salt and sugar labels can lead to transformations in tastes. One reason is that our tastes are a product of our beliefs, which is to say information itself. Another reason is that even if we hold beliefs constant, people may start to like different things as they develop different desires. What once tasted good might start to taste horrible and vice versa. If so, before-the-fact willingness-to-pay figures will be insufficiently informative about the welfare effects of disclosure requirements. (I used to hate egg sushi, known as Tamago Sushi. Because everyone else hated it and because it seemed to come with most sushi combinations, I decided to try to like it. I succeeded. It's pretty good.)

There is a more general point here. Disclosure of information is a kind of nudge, understood as a choice-preserving intervention that steers people in certain directions.[9] Nudges include reminders, warnings, the layout of a cafeteria or a grocery store, statements about existing social norms, and default rules. In some cases, nudges succeed in moving human behavior in the desired directions, producing significant benefits.[10] In some cases, they fail.[11] They might have no effect at all. They might even be counterproductive. Some of the welfare effects of informational nudges, both positive and negative, should not be so difficult to catalogue. If people stop smoking, we might be able to project a reduction in premature deaths. If people buy more expensive, energy-efficient refrigerators, we know that those people will spend more up front but save money over time, and that there will be environmental benefits. Ideally, we want to identify the magnitude of all of these effects.

However, suppose that people experience a welfare loss *as a result of the nudge itself*, or *as a result of the very behavior that the nudge induces*. For example, people might not enjoy a reminder or a warning; neither of these may be a lot of fun to receive. Recall that many people experience a welfare loss when they are informed about risks that they are running, even if on balance they are better off as a result of obtaining that information. The welfare effects of learning about a risk of heart disease or cancer must include consideration of the potential hedonic loss associated with that very information. In addition, the behavior change induced by nudges may include a loss of welfare; consider exercising, when exercising is not pleasant.

An illustrative example is the debate over prostate-specific antigen (PSA) testing, designed to help reduce prostate cancer deaths. Some experts believe that early detection can save lives by increasing early treatment of aggressive cancers. Others believe that it can cause serious harm by subjecting men to the various adverse effects of radiation, surgery, and other treatments. Suppose that as a matter of fact, PSA testing does result in early detection and treatment but that it does not improve survival, or that it improves survival only modestly. For many men, not knowing might well be best.

Within the medical profession, that much is common ground. What I mean to add here is simple: the argument for not knowing is strengthened if a bad result on a test produces real anxiety and distress (which are not pleasant and which may induce health problems). It is true that if patients fear that they will react strongly to bad news, and prefer ignorance for that reason, they might be suffering from present bias. But perhaps they are making a reasonable all-things-considered calculation, leading them to want not to know.[12] There is an important point here for medical practice, which is that we should want a degree of personalization. If doctors are dealing with patients who have a lot of anxiety if they get even mildly bad news, ignorance might be best. If patients are intensely curious and can easily handle bad news, the argument for testing is stronger. Good doctors take individual differences into account.

Of course it is also true that information, or nudges, might produce benefits rather than costs—again, not because of how they change behavior, but because they confer hedonic benefits. Those who emphasize the costs might have the sign wrong. For example, people might enjoy learning for its own sake; exercising might be pleasant, fun, or rewarding. Recall from chapter 1 that most people actually enjoy seeing calorie labels. But my principal emphasis here is on losses rather than gains.

A note about the scope of the discussion: The focus of this chapter is on the welfare effects of information, not on the appropriate design of particular forms of disclosure. It is well-known that labels might be framed in such a way as to be highly effective, or not.[13] Framing matters. A complex and confusing disclosure policy might overload consumers and thus have little or no effect—costs with no benefits. A simple disclosure might misinform consumers and potentially have negative welfare effects for that reason. The question here is not how to design or frame disclosures, but more broadly how to assess their benefits and costs. The design question is taken up in chapter 3.

Does Information Actually Help?

No one should doubt that information can improve people's decisions. A GPS device helps people to get to their preferred destination. Traffic lights enable people to know when to stop and when to go. On a beach, a sign that says No Swimming reduces danger. If an over-the-counter medicine is labeled Allergy Relief, Pain Relief, or Cough Suppressant, people will know what the medicine is for. If food contains allergy warnings—peanuts, seafood—disclosure of that fact will likely have significant benefits. When cities and airports have clear signs, people can find their way. Information helps people to navigate life, and in that sense it increases freedom, and is even indispensable to it.

Essential information is all around us, and in that light, it seems preposterous, a form of pointless contrarianism, to question the proposition that it can be beneficial. Nonetheless, a number of researchers have been making powerful arguments against disclosure mandates. They note that the government is requiring a large assortment of disclosures. In their view, people are not paying the slightest attention to many of them, which means that they are essentially a waste—a way of making policymakers think that they are improving health or safety when they are doing nothing of the kind.

In one form, the central objection is to complexity, length, or unintelligibility.[14] Disclosure might have no benefits if it consists of seventy-five pages of technical jargon. When people take out a mortgage, they are assaulted with a ridiculous amount of information, most of it useless. When people go to a doctor, they might well find themselves confronting privacy disclosures that are barely intelligible and that will not affect their behavior in any case. It is pointless, a form of meaningless expressivism (or a way of protecting against lawsuits).

It is true that complex, lengthy, or unintelligible disclosures may do no good at all. This is a crucial point, and it casts grave doubt on the wide assortment of disclosures that are all around us. If disclosure would have no benefits, it should not be mandated. That simple point suggests the importance of actually evaluating disclosure requirements to see if they are accomplishing anything, with an eye toward improving or perhaps eliminating them.

Consider a little tale. For many years, the United States relied on the Food Pyramid as its central icon to promote healthy eating. Created by the Department of Agriculture, the website with the Food Pyramid was one of the most visited in the entire US government. Generations of children used it. Figure 2.2 shows what one version looked like.

The pyramid was supposed to convey information, but it was long criticized as hopelessly uninformative. The reason is that it does not provide people with any kind of clear path. A shoeless

Figure 2.2
Food pyramid

person appears to be climbing to the top of a pyramid. But why? What's that white triangle at the top? The pyramid is organized by five stripes. (Or is it seven?) What do they connote? At the bottom, you can see a lot of different foods. But it's a mess. Some of the foods appear to fall in several categories. Are some grains vegetables? Is milk a fruit? Is meat a milk?

People are unlikely to change their behavior if they have no idea what to do. A lot of people are interested in healthy eating, but they are unaware of the concrete steps that they should take. The Food Pyramid did not much help.

In 2011, the Department of Agriculture consulted with a wide range of experts, with backgrounds in both nutrition and communication, to explore what kind of icon might be better. In the end, the department replaced the pyramid with a new, simpler icon, consisting of a plate with clear markings for fruit, vegetable, grains, and protein (figure 2.3).

The plate is designed to give clear, simple guidance—to be a kind of map. At the same time, the plate is accompanied by straightforward verbal tips, available on choosemyplate.gov, giving people information about how ant to make good nutritional choices. The tips include these:

- Make half your plate fruits and vegetables.
- Drink water instead of sugary drinks.
- Switch to fat-free or low-fat (1 percent) milk.
- Choose unsalted nuts and seeds to keep sodium intake low.

If the goal is to ensure that information is actually helpful, then "plate, not pyramid" is a good orienting slogan. But it must be confessed that even now, we do not have much data about whether the food plate is proving to be beneficial—which signals the possibility of a more fundamental objection to disclosure

Figure 2.3
Food plate

policies. According to that objection, such policies are *typically* unhelpful, because people ignore them even if they are clear and simple. For those who embrace this objection, mandatory labels are a distraction and a waste. If we want to shift people's behavior, more aggressive interventions are necessary.

Is the objection correct? To know, it would be best to have randomized controlled trials, in which some people receive information and others do not, allowing us to identify the difference that information actually makes. Importantly, such trials have been used to study the effects of some labels on consumers, such as calorie labels.[15] We also have information about the effects of such labels on retailers[16] and the effects of pictorial warnings on smokers.[17] The challenge is that with respect to information, randomized controlled trials are difficult to undertake, and they are not yet common.[18] Often we have "before and after" studies, which cannot offer firm conclusions. Such studies give us helpful clues, but they do not isolate the effect of information or warnings. If a lot of people quit smoking after the introduction of graphic health warnings, we may not know that they quit smoking *because* of the introduction of graphic health warnings.

Obtaining a clear sense of the actual effects of warnings, or mandatory labels, is a work in progress. Randomized controlled trials have the advantage of allowing us to specify the relevant effects. Over the past few years, some such trials have provided important information about when warnings or disclosure actually help.[19] But there is much more to learn, and such trials will and should be undertaken far more in the future.

Even now, we know enough to know that an across-the-board objection to mandatory disclosure is far too categorical, a kind of polemic.[20] There are far too many success stories. Consider a few examples:

1. Requiring home sellers to provide buyers with certified audits of residential energy efficiency has succeeded in significantly encouraging investments in energy efficiency technologies, by both sellers and buyers.[21]

2. A multistore field experiment in the United States found that when coffees were labeled Fair Trade, sales increased by nearly 10 percent.[22]

3. Dolphin-safe labeling for tuna played a role in reducing dolphin deaths in the United States—according to one estimate,

from one hundred thousand per year in the 1970s to under five thousand per year in 1992.[23]

4. Nutrition labels have been found to have beneficial effects on the diets of college students, leading to significantly healthier choices.[24]

5. In 2006, the US Food and Drug Administration required the reporting of trans fat content on its nutrition facts labels. The Centers for Disease Control and Prevention found a significant reduction in trans-fatty acid blood levels by 2009, in part as a result of the labeling mandate.[25]

6. A traffic lights program—labeling food as red, yellow, and green, corresponding to health effects—has been found to have a beneficial impact on consumer choices, leading to significantly healthier selections.[26]

7. Energy-efficiency labels are favored by most customers, who have been found to be willing to pay more for energy-efficient appliances.[27]

8. The effects of mandatory calorie labels are disputed,[28] and in some places they seem to be harmful. There is evidence that in low-income communities, many consumers think that their limited dollars are best spent on high-calorie items, which means that labels can increase obesity.[29] At the same time, there is evidence that in aggregate, such labels reduce calorie intake, at least among people who are obese.[30] Intriguingly, some evidence suggests that if calories are presented on the left rather than the right, they have a larger impact,[31] apparently because when people see calories first, their decisions are more likely to be affected than if they see the food item first.

These examples should be taken as merely illustrative. Some of them are controversial; the conclusions can be contested. The only point is that with respect to mandatory labels, generalized pessimism is unwarranted by what we know. Information can save money and lives. When it does not do that or does not produce benefits on net, disclosure should not be mandated.

Four Approaches

I have said that US agencies have often faced considerable difficulty in quantifying the costs and benefits of disclosure requirements. A general problem, to which I mean to draw attention here, is that they often do far less quantifying than they might. In fact, they have adopted four distinctive approaches, imposing increasingly severe information-gathering demands on those producing regulatory impact analysis. It is not always easy to explain why agencies choose one or another approach in particular cases.

The first approach, and sometimes the most candid, is to confess a lack of knowledge by acknowledging that, in light of existing information, some costs and (especially) benefits simply cannot be quantified.[32] The problem with this approach is that it suggests that the decision to proceed is essentially a stab in the dark. When the stakes are large, that seems unacceptable, certainly for policymakers. It is also a disservice to the public. Should regulators impose significant costs on the private sector without making every effort to be transparent about the benefits that disclosure might confer? To be sure, quantification may turn out not to be feasible.

The second approach involves *breakeven analysis*, by which agencies describe what the benefits would have to be in order to justify the costs—and suggest that the benefits are indeed likely or not likely to be of the requisite magnitude. Suppose, for example, that a disclosure requirement would impose annual costs of $10 million and that the product is purchased by fifty million consumers annually. Agencies might ask: Is the label worth twenty cents annually to the average consumer? A question of this kind might have an obvious answer.

In principle, this approach is better than a simple confession of ignorance, at least if the agency can show that the benefits have a lower or upper bound. In the case of a lower or upper bound, the decision whether to go forward might become clear. Breakeven analysis is sometimes the only possible path forward. But in hard cases, it involves a high degree of guesswork, and without a lower or upper bound, it seems to be a mere conclusion, a kind of ipse dixit, masquerading as an analytic device. Without reasonable identification of lower or upper bounds, it is not so different from a confession of ignorance.

The third approach is to attempt to specify outcomes in terms of end points, such as economic savings or health gains. The advantage of this approach is that it actually points to concrete benefits, and it tries to measure and to monetize them. But it too runs into serious difficulties. The first is epistemic: agencies may lack the information that would enable them to specify what the benefits are. They might have little idea, for example, how much consumers would save as a result of fuel economy labels or how much they would benefit from a warning that, below a specified SPF, sunscreen does not reduce the risk of skin cancer.

The second problem is that even an accurate specification of end points will not give a full picture of the actual benefits; in crucial respects, it will almost certainly overstate them. (It may also understate them, as we will see.) We already have a preliminary sense of why: people might experience significant losses as a result of receiving information. Suppose that they dislike receiving it because it saddens or frightens them or that they switch to a product that is inferior along certain dimensions. An account of end points will ignore those losses.

The fourth approach is to identify consumers' willingness to pay. We have seen that one of the advantages of this approach is that it should capture both positive and negative welfare effects and allow regulators to take account of people's willingness to pay *not* to receive information. If people do not care about calorie labels, their willingness to pay nothing will be part of the calculation. If they gain and lose from calorie labels, the net number will capture both gains and losses. If they prefer not to receive the information, a negative willingness to pay will register as well.

At the same time, willingness to pay runs into serious and perhaps insuperable objections, some of which are distinctive to the problem of information disclosure, some of which involve the limits of the willingness-to-pay criterion in general. Recall that when people offer their willingness to pay, they are attempting to solve a prediction problem. That problem may be difficult to solve, perhaps especially (but not only) when people are asked about whether they want to receive information. For one thing, people tend to underestimate their own resilience, which may mean that they will avoid information when it really would help them or that they will seek information when it really will not do them much good. "Even in ordinary circumstances people tend, for example, to overestimate how unhappy a bad outcome will make them and to underestimate their ability to cheer themselves up."[33]

In short, we may be dealing here with a possible gap between *decision utility* (the utility expected at the time of decision) and *experienced utility* (the utility actually experienced).[34] The most obvious solution would be to try to convey experienced utility to people in advance so as to reduce the gap. In principle, informed people will know what their experience actually was, and they can describe it to people who are choosing. In practice, however, it may not be feasible to give people a concrete, vivid sense of actual experience, especially if their preferences and tastes might change.

For that reason, willingness-to-pay measures are often an unacceptably crude proxy for the actual welfare effects of obtaining information. I mean this point to raise a concern about willingness to pay for information, but it applies more broadly—for example, to the valuation of morbidity risks. If we see willingness to pay as an effort to solve a prediction problem, we might wonder whether it is likely to be a sufficiently accurate measure of the actual welfare effects of (say) a severe concussion, chronic bronchitis, ringing in the ears, or a nonfatal heart attack. Of course, it is true that more accurate measures may be unavailable.

Costs

On the cost side, some of the questions are relatively straightforward. Regulators may well be able to learn the total cost of (for example) producing fuel economy labels and placing them on new vehicles. Production of labels might itself be relatively cheap, but it might turn out to be costly to obtain the information that would end up on the labels, especially if acquiring that information entails a great deal of work and monitoring. In the context of genetically modified food, the US Department of Agriculture concluded that the first-year cost of labeling may be as high as $3.9 billion, with annual costs thereafter in the general vicinity of $100 million—not massive, in the scheme of things, but not exactly small.[35]

A separate difficulty, which US agencies have often ignored, arises *when the information itself imposes costs on consumers*. It is a mistake to ignore those costs, even if they prove difficult to quantify, and even if consumers benefit on net. Those costs come in several different forms. Some of them will usually be low, but not always.

A Small Cognitive Tax

A cost is involved in reading and processing information. For each consumer, that cost is usually likely to be low. But if customers are asked to read dozens of pages of paper before they engage in some transaction, we are not speaking of a quick glance or a few minutes. Across a large number of purchasers, the cognitive cost might turn out to be significant. Information disclosure is, in a sense, akin to a paperwork burden. True, consumers are usually not compelled to read and process what is disclosed. But even for those who seek to ignore it, its very presence may operate as a kind of cognitive tax. Because people have limited mental bandwidth, that tax may not be safely ignored. (If there is a hell, it is filled with warnings.)

The problem will turn out to be especially serious if labels are complex or if people are deluged with multiple labels. Information overload might result in significant aggregate costs on individuals—and might also ensure that the benefits of labels are low.

Ruining Popcorn, 1: A Hedonic Tax on Those Who Do Not Change

Much more importantly, the cost may be hedonic, not cognitive. Suppose that smokers are given information about the harmful effects of smoking or that visitors to chain restaurants are given information about the caloric contents of food. Many members of both groups will suffer a hedonic loss. Consider smokers who cannot or will not quit and customers who decide to choose high-calorie foods notwithstanding the labels. In hedonic terms, such people will lose, rather than gain, if they are miserable or at least sadder at the time of purchase.

To be sure, there is a normative question whether regulators should count, as costs, the adverse hedonic impact of truthful information. Is it a cost or a benefit if people learn, truthfully, that they have diabetes or cancer? In welfare terms, that might well be a benefit on net, at least if they can do something about the problem. (If they cannot or do not, it might be a cost, on net, at least in terms of subjective welfare.) But there is a cost as well, and potentially a large one, even if the net effect is positive. So long as we are operating within a welfarist framework, the hedonic loss must be treated as a cost. It might turn out to be low, but regulators should not ignore it, as they typically do.

It is true that we might find ourselves in deep philosophical waters here. Welfarism might seem objectionable if it treats the receipt of truthful, personally relevant information as a cost. Maybe people are in an important sense more free, or living a more authentic life, if they get that information. But if they suffer, that should probably count.

Many people do not want to get blood tests, even if doctors advise them to do so, because they do not like the risk of getting less than good results. We have seen that the failure to get the tests might be a product of a behavioral bias, such as present bias or loss aversion. But it might also be a product, in whole or in part, of a rational aversion to receiving negative information. Recall that large numbers of people do not want to know if they have a genetic disposition to cancer or heart disease; one reason must be the hedonic loss of receiving that information. Some labels belong in the same category, in the sense that they give people information that they are unhappy to hear (again, this is so even if on balance, they are better off with it than without it).

Personalization to the Rescue?

I have said that ideally, disclosure would be personalized, and indeed, markets and life allow for a lot of personalized disclosure. You can check your bank balance a lot or a little. You can weigh yourself every day or never. You can get a Fitbit and see how much exercise and sleep you are getting; maybe you would enjoy that and maybe it would help you to improve your health. Or maybe you would find a Fitbit to be a bit of a nightmare. If you want a Fitbit, or despise the idea, you might suffer from a lack of information or a behavioral bias. But you might not.

Personalized disclosure has large advantages, precisely because it ensures that people who would benefit from information—in instrumental terms, in hedonic terms, or both—will actually get it. In markets, disclosure is generally personalized in that way. You can learn things if you want to, but if you don't, you needn't. In the same vein, government might try targeted disclosures, on the theory that it would have far higher net benefits. It might, for example, give information about high-calorie foods to people who want or need that information, and decline to give it to people who have neither interest nor need. In principle, personalized disclosure has significant advantages.[36]

For some policies, of course, information cannot easily be provided to one person without being provided to many or all. A fast-food restaurant might be asked to post nutritional information, and if it does, everyone who goes there will get that information. But apps can easily be used to increase the level of personalization by allowing people to get information if and only if they want it. Even without apps or something like them, officials might provide some brief, simple information (about, e.g., fuel economy) to all, while also making detailed information available to those who want it. That approach can also promote personalization.

For defenders of personalized disclosure, the considerations marshaled in chapter 1 provide strong support and also some cautionary notes. With respect to the latter: People who do not want information may suffer from an informational deficit, deprivation, or behavioral biases, leading them not to want information from which they might benefit. To be sure, the very factors that lead them not to want information might lead them not to use it in any way—in which case there is no gain from providing it to them. But we can certainly imagine cases in which people might not particularly want information, but act very differently after receiving it, helping themselves or perhaps others. If people learn about potential economic savings from energy conservation or harms to others associated with a particular product, they might choose differently.

Ruining Popcorn, 2: A Hedonic Tax on Those Who Do Change

Even if people might be able to quit smoking or end up choosing lower-calorie items, and will hence benefit greatly on net, they will incur a cost by seeing something that inflicts pain. That cost should also count, even if it is greatly outweighed by benefits. The point is not that the hedonic cost is necessarily a trump card: if people make different choices once they are informed, the presumption should be that they are better off. But by how much?

To answer that question, the hedonic cost must be taken into account. For many people, a calorie label imposes a cost, simply because it informs them that the delicious cheeseburger they are about to eat is also going to make their belly bulge. It is true that there is a difference between theory and practice and that in practice, reasonable regulators might not know how to calculate this hedonic cost (other than perhaps to recognize it without quantifying it). The only point is that the cost is real.

A Consumer Welfare Loss

There is a fourth loss, in the form of a consumer welfare loss. Suppose that people decide that on balance, they should have a salad rather than a cheeseburger, on the ground that the latter has many more calories. If they choose the salad because of a calorie label, they are probably better off on balance—and in a sense, they are sadder but wiser (and healthier). They are sadder to the extent that they enjoy their meal less.

Assessment of the magnitude of the loss poses serious conceptual and empirical challenges (to be addressed in due course). Here as well, there will be heterogeneity within the population. Some people will be much sadder, and some people will be only a little bit sadder. But there is no question that a consumer welfare loss will occur and that it might turn out to be a nontrivial fraction of the benefits. In principle, if the hedonic loss is almost as high as the health gain, a decision to forgo the hamburger might make people only modestly better off. Whenever a mandatory label leads people to substitute product A for product B, there is a welfare loss to the extent that aside from the characteristic on which the label gets people to focus, product B is better than product A.

Suppose, for example, that consumers are choosing between two essentially equivalent cars. The more fuel-efficient one would cost $2,000 less annually to operate because of its greater fuel efficiency. The less fuel-efficient one would cost $500 more up front. Imagine that because of the fuel economy label, they select the fuel-efficient car. For each such consumer, we might be tempted to say that the label has produced $1,500 in gains. But in actual practice, the effects of a fuel economy label will be much more complicated to assess. Some consumers will end up purchasing cars that are more fuel efficient but inferior along some dimension, so that they will gain $1,500 minus X, where X refers to the desirable features of the unchosen car that they otherwise prefer. It is hard for public officials to know whether X is, on average, $100 or $1,000 or $1,450.

The (Critical) Problem of Endogenous Preferences

All this assumes that preferences are fixed, consistent, and exogenous. In some contexts, however, that assumption is not correct.[37] People's preferences are labile; they change over time, sometimes as a result of information, sometimes as a result of experience. Whether and when preferences will change can be unpredictable. On the one hand, familiarity breeds contempt. On the other hand, there's no place like home. These points complicate the forgoing analysis and create a risk that analysis of costs will ignore shifts in tastes that are induced by information itself.

Suppose that at time 1, people enjoy hamburgers a lot and enjoy salads only a little. Now suppose that having seen calorie labels, people switch to eating salads at time 2 because they want to make healthier choices. At time 2, they suffer costs as a result of the switch; they miss hamburgers (delicious!) and they do not much like salad (boring!). But at time 3, people might come to dislike hamburgers (disgusting!) and to love salad (fresh!). Changes in people's preferences over time must be taken into account by the considered cost-benefit analyst, even though doing so presents serious empirical challenges. What was once a high cost might turn into a low cost. It might be difficult to know the magnitude of the change and even the sign. Perhaps those who switch to salad will learn to love it, or perhaps they will crave hamburgers and grow to despise salad.

Benefits

On the benefits side, the assessment can be even more challenging.[38] If the government mandates a fuel economy label, agencies might want to project the economic and environmental benefits from the mandate. At the outset, it should be clear that any projection would be challenging to produce. To project benefits, regulators should identify the effect of labels on behavior, at least if they are concerned with economic or other end points. We have seen that in principle, a randomized controlled trial would be valuable for that purpose. If one group sees a particular label and a similar group sees a different label (or no label), regulators should be able to specify the effect of the label on purchasing decisions. Armed with that information, they could estimate economic and environmental consequences (at least if they could generalize from the trial).

As we have also seen, it can be difficult to run randomized controlled trials. In these circumstances, making any kind of projection of how consumers will react to a label is exceedingly difficult. Agencies might rely on surveys or on focus groups, which can provide relevant information. Carefully designed surveys might tell us a great deal about how consumers and workers will respond to information.[39] Even so, it might be hazardous to project, from survey research, specific numbers with respect to behavior change.

Agencies sometimes attempt to identify likely end points in terms of money or health. If they do not have randomized controlled trials, they might use surveys to test whether people will spend less, save more, or avoid risks. The results might be surprising; people might overreact or underreact to information. If agencies were able to make accurate projections, they would know something important. Suppose, for example, that with graphic warnings on cigarette packages, there would be twenty-five thousand fewer annual deaths from smoking-related causes, or that consumers would save $120 million from a well-designed fuel economy label, with environmental benefits in the same vicinity. Some agencies make estimates of exactly that kind. Perhaps technological innovations will make accurate projections increasingly feasible.

Agencies sometimes know a lot, and with such innovations, they will know much more. That is great. The problem is that for the reasons given thus far, such projections would not give a complete estimate of the (net) benefits. Even if we have a randomized controlled trial showing that a fuel economy label saves specified amounts of money, we do not know the net welfare benefits. Because end points do not include a series of cognitive and hedonic costs, they might well be an upper bound. They might also fail to include some hedonic benefits, in which case they might turn out to be a lower bound.

Willingness to Pay

We have seen that regulators might explore the issue from another direction. Rather than asking about the economic savings from the fuel-efficient car, they might ask an entirely different question: How much would consumers be willing to pay for a fuel economy label? As we saw in chapter 1, that is easy to do.

It is true that if people are asked about their willingness to pay for information in the abstract, they will have to answer some tough questions. How will they use that information? How much will they gain from it? They might have little or no idea. It is also true that in surveys, answers to questions about risk reduction raise serious puzzles. Surveys find, for example, that there is a large disparity between willingness to pay and willingness to accept, and also that some consumers would be unwilling to accept *any* finite payment to purchase and use risky products.[40] Findings of this sort raise questions about whether willingness-to-pay figures for information (potentially leading to economic savings or risk reduction) adequately capture welfare effects (see chapter 6). But at least in principle, those figures should be both informative and useful. They should capture everything that people care about—not simply end points, but the full range of costs and benefits of information.

In the context of reports about home energy use, Allcott and Kessler offer an important study of willingness to pay.[41] Those reports provide information, but of a distinctive kind. They tell people how their energy use compares to that of their neighbors, and they also give people some tips about how people can save energy (figure 2.4).

On average, people end up saving about $6 per year as a result of such reports. Allcott and Kessler find that on average,

(a)

Last Month Neighbor Comparison | You used **42% more** natural gas than your efficient neighbors.

Efficient Neighbors	19 Therms*
YOU	27
All Neighbors	28

How you're doing:

Great ☺ ☺

▶ **GOOD** ☺

More than average

* Therms: Standard unit of measuring heat energy

Who are your Neighbors? | ■ **All Neighbors:** Approximately 100 occupied, nearby homes that are similar in size to yours (avg 1,517 sq ft) | ■ **Efficient Neighbors:** The most efficient 20 percent from the "All Neighbors" group

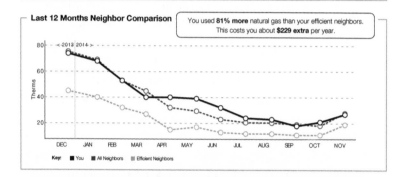

Last 12 Months Neighbor Comparison | You used **81% more** natural gas than your efficient neighbors. This costs you about **$229 extra** per year.

Therms

80
60
40
20

DEC JAN FEB MAR APR MAY JUN JUL AUG SEP OCT NOV

Key: ■ You ■ All Neighbors ■ Efficient Neighbors

(b)

Personalized tips | For a complete list of energy saving investments and smart purchases, visit **utilityco.com/rebates**.

Quick Fix
Something you can do right now

☐ **Open your shades on winter days**
Taking advantage of winter's direct sunlight can make a dent in your heating costs. Open blinds and other window treatments during the day to capture free heat and light.

South-facing windows have the most potential for heat gain, and the sun is most intense from 9 a.m. to 3 p.m.

When you let the sun in, remember to lower the thermostat by a few degrees. These two steps combined are what save money and energy.

SAVE UP TO
$**10** PER YEAR

Smart Purchase
An affordable way to save more

☐ **Program your thermostat**
A programmable thermostat can automatically adjust your heat or air conditioning when you're away, then return to your preferred temperature when you're home to enjoy it.

If you don't already have a programmable thermostat, look for one at your local home improvement store. For comfort and convenience, be sure to program your thermostat with energy-efficient settings.

If you need help installing or programming your thermostat, consult your manual or call the manufacturer for assistance.

SAVE UP TO
$**65** PER YEAR

Smart Purchase
An affordable way to save more

☐ **Weatherstrip windows and doors**
Windows and doors can be responsible for up to 25% of heat loss in winter for a typical home.

If you're comfortable doing the task yourself, you can weatherize your home in just a few hours. Seal windows for about $1 each with rope caulk, or install more permanent weatherstripping for $8-$10 per window. Also, install sweeps at the bottom of exterior doors.

A professional can help you with this work if you prefer.

SAVE UP TO
$**10** PER YEAR

Figure 2.4
Home energy report: (a) social comparison, and (b) tips.

people are willing to pay *something* for those reports, but the average amount that they are willing to pay is far less than the average economic savings that people enjoy as a result of the reports—only about $2.80. One implication is that the standard evaluation, focusing on average economic savings, greatly overstates the net welfare gain from the reports. It is not clear why the willingness-to-pay figures are so much lower than the economic gain: Why would people pay (say) $2.80 for a report that would enable them to save (say) as much as $7?

But on reflection, the answer is not so mysterious. The relatively lower WTP probably reflects an assortment of welfare losses from receiving the report: the time spent reading it, the emotional tax of receiving less than good news, the time spent taking steps to reduce energy use. Whatever we think of the precise numbers given by Allcott and Kessler, willingness to pay should capture factors of this kind. In some cases, it should capture the fact that some or many people would be willing to pay nothing for information or might even pay something not to receive it. In fact, that is exactly what Allcott and Kessler find. The clear conclusion is that many people really do not want the information contained in the reports. It ruins popcorn!

Of course, some people undoubtedly *enjoy* reports of the kind that Allcott and Kessler studied, which suggests that a full accounting would also have to identify the hedonic *benefits* of receiving information. (Recall that many people enjoy calorie labels as well.) Consistent with this point, Allcott and Kessler find a high degree of heterogeneity. A number of people are willing to pay more than $7 for the reports. An important lesson, properly stressed by Allcott and Kessler, involves the potential welfare gains of targeted policy, ensuring that the reports go only to people who want them.

Under ideal conditions, and bracketing the fact that people's preferences and values might shift, the right question for regulators to ask involves willingness to pay. They should not focus solely on the economic benefits that consumers might receive if (for example) they purchase more fuel-efficient cars. One more time: On optimistic assumptions, the willingness-to-pay question ought to include everything that matters to consumers. Of course it is true that the question will not fully capture third-party effects, and it will not capture welfare effects if preferences and values shift over time.

Information and Biases

As an empirical matter, it may not be easy to obtain a reliable answer to the willingness-to-pay question, or anything close to it. We might simply ask people, as Allcott and Kessler did, and as I also have done (see chapter 1). But for their answers to be relevant, it is important to provide pertinent information—for example, about the potential benefits (purely economic and otherwise) of labels. We want *informed* willingness to pay, rather than willingness to pay in an informational vacuum. If people say that they are willing to pay $2.80 for a home energy report, or $1.00, or $15.00, aren't they just making a stab in the dark? Maybe. What standing do such figures have? Maybe none.

Unfortunately, providing the key information might "anchor" consumers and hence bias their answers. Suppose that consumers were told that the average family saves $7 per year as a result of receiving home energy reports or that fuel economy labels lead people to save $100 annually, on average, as a result of purchasing more fuel-efficient vehicles. Respondents would likely anchor on such numbers. If so, it is not clear what their answers would tell us. Anchored answers would not be especially informative about welfare effects.

Imagine that the problem of anchoring could be overcome and that informed consumers would be willing to pay (say) $10, on average, for home energy reports. If so, we might have some sense of the benefits, at least if behavioral biases are not distorting people's answers. In actual practice, however, such biases might well produce distortions; recall present bias and optimistic bias, which may lead to willingness-to-pay figures that are unduly low or unduly high in light of the welfare benefits. If we are dealing with survey evidence, people's answers are imperfectly reliable, in part because real money is not being exchanged. Even if it is, there remains the difficulty of informing consumers in a sufficiently neutral way.

For health-related disclosures, the problem is even harder. Consumers might not know enough to give good answers to the questions how much they are willing to pay for information. One goal of calorie labels is to reduce obesity, which causes an assortment of health problems, including premature mortality. If consumers are asked how much they would pay for such labels, they would have to try to answer some questions about their likely effects—about whether calorie labels will enable them to improve their health, and if so to what degree. Those are not easy questions to answer. (How much would you be willing to pay to have calorie labels on your food for the next year? Why exactly did you produce that figure?)

It is true that if *regulators* are focusing on end points rather than willingness to pay for labels, they have established ways to turn health effects into monetary equivalents. In the United States, a statistical death is now valued at about $9 million.[42]

But how many premature deaths would be prevented by calorie labels? And what would be the effect of such labels on adverse health outcomes short of death? To answer such questions, regulators have to undertake two tasks. First, they must begin by making some prediction about the effect of calorie labels on what people choose to eat. Second, they have to follow that prediction by specifying the health consequences of lower levels of caloric intake. At least it can be said that if they can accomplish those tasks, they will have some sense of the benefits of the labels, once—and this is a third task—they turn the various consequences into monetary equivalents. After undertaking all three tasks, regulators will have specified end points, which is good—but for the reasons given, a specification of end points will overstate benefits because it will not include various cognitive and hedonic losses. (As noted, there may also be hedonic benefits.)

But we are focusing now on willingness to pay, not on end points. We could ask how much people would be willing to pay for calorie labels.[43] As before, asking that question is, in principle, preferable to an effort to assess health states, because willingness to pay will capture all variables that matter to consumers.[44] Also as before, there are formidable challenges in using surveys to elicit reliable numbers, informed and free from biases of various kinds. And if preferences are shifting and labile, willingness-to-pay numbers might greatly understate the welfare gain from labels. Recall that people might develop tastes for the products to which they shift. I am also bracketing the questions raised by addictive goods, such as cigarettes, for which labels might be beneficial on welfare grounds precisely because they help break the hold of the addiction. Note the claim that cigarette taxes might well make smokers happier.[45]

Predicting Welfare

Recall that when consumers state their willingness to pay, they are solving a prediction problem. To take a mundane case: When a consumer decides to spend $30,000 for a new car rather than $25,000 or $35,000, she must be making a prediction about the welfare effects of the expenditure. In choosing among three cars, the solution to a prediction problem, for individual consumers, is not all that easy. Can consumers reliably foresee the welfare effects, for them, of each of the cars? Maybe so, but actually, the prediction problem is much harder than that. Consumers should be asking about the range of alternative uses for the money. That may be difficult. For goods that are relatively familiar, most consumers may have enough experience or sensible rules of thumb and so do not go far wrong—but still.

Turn now to health risks: a broken back, a severe concussion, heart disease, diabetes. Not long ago, I was hit by a car and had a severe concussion. Before the fact, I had no idea what a severe concussion was like. (It's bad.) Deciding how much to pay to eliminate a $1/n$ risk of some health problem requires a judgment about what it would be like to suffer from that problem. Are consumers in a good position to make that judgment? Often not. Are they in a good position to make judgments about how worthwhile it is to obtain information that would permit them to reduce the risk of suffering from those conditions? Often not.

In light of these challenges, regulators have two highly imperfect options. First, they can work on two tracks to try to produce answers: identifying end points (economic savings, health benefits) and enlisting surveys to learn what people want to know, preferably accompanied by relevant information to assist respondents. On prominent occasions, US agencies have emphasized end points in particular.[46] Second, regulators can acknowledge the difficulties, confess that they cannot surmount them, and use breakeven analysis to decide whether to proceed.

Suppose that an energy-efficiency label for refrigerators would cost $10 million annually and that eight million refrigerators are sold in the United States every year. Even if the average consumer saves only fifty cents annually as a result of the label, the cost will be made up in just three years. Perhaps regulators can specify a lower or upper bound on benefits, thus allowing breakeven analysis to have some discipline. Breakeven analysis can be crude, but in some cases, it will suggest that the argument for disclosure of information is either very strong or very weak.

A vivid example comes from 2019, when the US Food and Drug Administration proposed to require new warnings, including graphic images, on cigarette packages and in cigarette advertisements.[47] As we have seen, the agency offered a distinctive justification for the graphic warnings. Instead of speaking in terms of public health, the agency said that it would promote "a greater public understanding of the negative health consequences of cigarette smoking." To show that the warnings would achieve that goal, the agency began by emphasizing that the current text-only warnings, issued in 1984, are inadequate. Many people (including adolescents) "do not see or read, and do not remember," those warnings. Nor do they then think about them even if they do remember them. By contrast, pictorial warnings heighten both attention and awareness. For that reason, they increase knowledge about smoking-related health outcomes (including stroke and cancer).

The FDA itself undertook a research program to test which textual warnings and which graphic images would increase public understanding. A proposed new warning reads: "Smoking can harm your children." On the basis of its research, the FDA found that that this warning, and a dozen others, would attract people's attention—and would be remembered. It also used individual interviews, focus groups, and online research panels to determine which images would improve people's understanding of health risks.

What about the costs and benefits? The agency said that the annual expense of adopting, designing, rotating, and advertising the various labels will be in the vicinity of $110 million. With respect to benefits, the agency acknowledges that they "are difficult to quantify." The reason is simple: if we are speaking of increasing public understanding rather than reducing illness and death, it is hard to speak in terms of monetary savings. To defend the rule, the FDA briefly undertook breakeven analysis. It noted that if the benefits of the graphic warnings were as low as one cent per pack, they would be sufficiently justified. Surely—it implied— a greater public understanding of the health risks of smoking is worth at least a penny a pack.

It is not obvious that a greater understanding, taken only as such, is actually enough to justify the regulation. But it is plausible to think that that understanding would ultimately produce less in the way of smoking. If a life is valued at $9 million, and if we focus only on premature deaths, the graphic warning rule would be justified if it would prevent as few as thirteen premature deaths each year! It is an excellent bet that it would do much more than that.

Taking Stock

The central purpose of disclosure requirements is to increase human welfare—to make people's lives better. In numerous contexts, Congress has required or authorized federal agencies to impose such requirements. In all those contexts, executive agencies are required, by executive order, to try to catalogue the benefits and costs of disclosure requirements and to demonstrate that the benefits justify the costs (a proxy for welfare). Such agencies face persistent challenges in projecting benefits, and they use four different approaches: a refusal to do so on the ground that quantification is not feasible; breakeven analysis; projection of end states, such as economic savings or health outcomes; and estimates of willingness to pay for the relevant information.

Each of these approaches raises serious questions and runs into reasonable objections. On highly optimistic assumptions, the right question generally involves willingness to pay, which should capture everything that matters, including health benefits and the hedonic losses associated with receiving information (and thus the possibility that on balance, people would be willing to pay nothing, or would even be willing to pay something not to receive information). One of the advantages of asking about willingness to pay is that it puts a spotlight on the potential of personalized disclosure, ensuring that information goes only to the people who want it. In countless settings, markets allow for personalized disclosure; in the future, regulators might inquire into that possibility, at least where information is not a public good.

But there are major problems with willingness to pay. Sometimes people do not have much money, which means that their willingness to pay is low, even if information would greatly improve their lives. In practice, people often lack enough information to give a sensible answer to the question of how much they would be willing to pay for (more) information. How much would you be willing to pay for information about the presence of chemical XYZ in your favorite food, when you know little or nothing about chemical XYZ or its effects? People do not only lack information; they might also suffer from behavioral biases (including present bias and unrealistic optimism).

We have also seen that when preferences are shifting and labile, even a sensible answer to the willingness-to-pay question may fail to capture the welfare consequences, because *people may develop new tastes and values as a result of information.* Willingness-to-pay figures require people to try to solve a prediction problem, and in some cases people are not in a good position to do so. In these circumstances, breakeven analysis is the very least that should be required, and it is sometimes the most that agencies can do. If agencies can identify lower or upper bounds, a breakeven analysis will sometimes show that mandatory disclosure is justified on welfare grounds—and sometimes that it is not. For that reason, that form of analysis is often a terrific idea.

The challenge is that breakeven analysis is a confession of ignorance, and without lower or upper bounds, it will leave us at sea. In the future, it would be far better for agencies to make progress in answering difficult questions about the actual effects of information on people's lives. Those effects might be strongly positive or strongly negative. The next generation of work on disclosure requirements—and regulatory benefits in general—should make it a priority to produce those answers.

3   Psychology

with George Loewenstein and Russell Golman

An important advantage of disclosure, as opposed to more aggressive forms of regulation, is its flexibility and respect for the operation of free markets. Regulatory mandates are blunt swords; they tend to neglect heterogeneity and may have serious unintended adverse effects. For example, energy efficiency requirements for appliances may produce goods that work less well or that have characteristics that consumers do not want. Information provision, by contrast, respects freedom of choice. If automobile manufacturers are required to measure and publicize the safety characteristics of cars, potential car purchasers can trade safety concerns against other attributes, such as price and styling. If restaurant patrons are informed of the calories in their meals, those who want to lose weight can make use of the information, leaving those who are unconcerned about calories unaffected. Disclosure does not interfere with, and should even promote, the autonomy (and quality) of individual decision-making. If properly designed, it should also increase efficiency.

How should we think about proper design? The question is put in sharp relief by Omri Ben-Shahar and Carl Schneider in an essay provocatively titled, "The Failure of Mandated Disclosure."[1]

The authors devote twelve pages to listing some of the numerous and sometimes absurd disclosure requirements embedded in federal and state statutes, administrative regulations, and court rulings. These requirements apply to virtually all types of loans, bank accounts, mutual funds, credit cards, securities brokers, credit reporting agencies, investment advisors, ATMs, pawnshops, payday loans, rent-to-own contracts, installment sales, all types of insurance contracts, vehicle rentals, self-storage facilities, car-towing companies, car repair shops, and much more. Perhaps the most amusing (if somewhat macabre) example is the requirement that funeral operators in California disclose to casket purchasers that "THERE IS NO SCIENTIFIC OR OTHER EVIDENCE THAT ANY CASKET WITH A SEALING DEVICE WILL PRESERVE HUMAN REMAINS."

Ben-Shahar and Schneider are deeply skeptical of disclosure requirements—in part because disclosure is often poorly designed, in part because they think that it is usually doomed to fail. Whether or not they are right, perusal of their list suggests a common pattern in situations in which mandatory disclosure requirements are imposed. In general, such requirements are applied when less informed consumers interact with better-informed sellers and when the incentives of the consumers and sellers are at least arguably misaligned. (Note that in many important cases the sellers and consumers are providers and recipients of advice.) These features characterize situations such as the following:

- Interactions between an automobile seller and potential customer. The seller has better information about the safety of the cars it sells, but the customer may have a greater interest in driving a safe car.

- Interactions between a chain restaurant and its patrons. The restaurant has better information about the nutritional properties of the food it sells, but the customer may have a greater interest in eating nutritious food.

- Interactions between a physician and a patient. The physician has better information about the appropriateness of different tests and treatments, but may also have incentives to recommend specific tests, drugs, or services (such as surgery) that may not be in the patient's best interest.

- Interactions between (a) manufacturers that outsource production to establishments that mistreat workers or engage in environmentally destructive patterns of behavior and (b) consumers who, while appreciating low prices, have a desire to consume "green" or socially conscientious products.

In addition to situations in which disclosure addresses standard economic market failures created by asymmetric information and misaligned incentives, there are situations in which disclosure serves the purpose of helping to protect consumers against themselves. Psychology and behavioral economics provide a new rationale for regulation that supplements traditional economic accounts. The new rationale involves what might be called "behavioral market failures." Analogous to the concept of externalities in standard economics, behavioral economics enlarges the potential scope of justifiable regulation by introducing the concept of *internalities*—costs that individuals impose on themselves but fail to internalize at the time of decision. For example, smokers may enjoy smoking, but not so much lung cancer. Those who eat a lot of food, and gain weight, may love their meals, but not the health problems that come from them. Those who spend a lot of money today may not be so happy to find that they have nothing to spend tomorrow.

Note that internalities alone do not provide an adequate rationale for mandatory disclosure regulations; at least some kind of misalignment of incentives is important in this case as well. Suppose that at time 1, a consumer is making a decision that will harm herself at time 2, with the long-run cost exceeding the short-term benefit. If the seller's incentives are aligned with the consumer's long-term interests, the seller will provide information or products intended to reduce or eliminate the internality.

For obvious reasons, this may not be the case. If fast-food customers fail to take account of the health consequences of calories, for example, then fast-food restaurants can exploit this failure by offering enticing but unhealthy menu options that are cheap to produce. Likewise, if car purchasers pay insufficient attention to fuel costs, then car manufacturers can offer gas guzzlers that are cheaper to produce and more attractive with respect to the attributes to which consumers attend.

Information disclosure can take a variety of forms. The most appropriate form of disclosure depends on the situation in which a market failure arises. It is important to distinguish between situations in which information is verifiable (and misinformation can be punished) and those in which information is unverifiable. The calorie claims of a fast-food restaurant and the fuel economy claims of an automobile manufacturer, for example, can be scientifically validated. However, if a doctor expresses the view that a patient is ideally suited for a clinical trial, there is no way to verify whether he really believes that or is conveying it because he will benefit by receiving a referral fee.

When information is verifiable, disclosure can focus on rectifying an information asymmetry—on providing information to the less informed buyer or advice recipient in order to level the informational playing field. When a drug company is required to include a warning label with a prescription drug, for example, the warning is designed to mitigate the asymmetry in information that exists between the manufacturer of the drug, who has access to data on potential side effects, and the patient, who, in the absence of the disclosure, does not. The same is true when an automobile company is required to include a label with the fuel economy of cars.

When information is unverifiable, however, mandatory disclosures attacking the information asymmetry would be useless because there would be no way to know if the disclosed information is accurate.[2] In this case (as well as in the case of verifiable information), the informed party could still be required to disclose the misalignment of incentives. In New York State, for example, prospective home buyers and sellers have been required to sign (to verify that they have been shown) a disclosure form designed to inform "potential buyers or sellers with whom [real estate licensees work] of their agency relationship and the rights and obligations it creates. This disclosure will help you to make informed choices about your relationship with the real estate broker and its sales agents."

One might think it should be obvious to disclosees when interests are misaligned, so that no disclosure is necessary, but existing research suggests that many recipients of advice are not aware of misalignments, or at least behave as if they are not, taking advice from conflicted sources at face value.[3] Beyond suggesting to information recipients that they should perhaps mistrust information coming from advisors with misaligned incentives, awareness of the misalignment could also encourage advisees to seek out advisors with competing interests in order to hear both sides of an argument.[4] However, disclosure of the misaligned incentives could actually be harmful. People might overreact to disclosure, which might prevent an individual from getting good advice—as would be the case if, for example, a sick patient avoided the doctor altogether upon learning of her conflict of interest. In addition, when advisors are ethically motivated to provide unbiased advice, disclosure of misaligned incentives can potentially undermine this motivation (a phenomenon of moral licensing, which is discussed in more detail below).

Disclosures can also be *delivered* in various ways. In the case of a physician, for example, disclosure of a potential conflict of interest could come directly from the physician during the doctor-patient interaction or could be provided in a less personal fashion (e.g., via printed information given to the patient by the receptionist in the waiting room). Disclosures can also be accompanied by greater or lesser efforts to ensure that consumers actually pay attention to them. For example, chain restaurants might be required merely to make nutritional information available to those who request it, or, as the Affordable Care Act mandates, to post the information on menu boards. From an economic perspective, some of these details might appear inconsequential, but in reality they matter profoundly.

Psychological Mechanisms

When presented with information, people react based on several psychological mechanisms.

1: Limited Attention and Awareness
A growing body of research in economics confirms what psychologists have known and studied for decades: there are serious

limitations on the amount of information to which people can attend at any point in time. The standard economic account would emphasize that attention is a scarce resource and suggest that people make rational (even if fairly rapid) decisions about how to allocate it. Research in psychology, by contrast, suggests that people do not *decide* how to allocate attention; certain items capture attention, while others disappear into the background, even if they are exceedingly important and even if it would be rational to focus on them. The distinction between the two accounts matters for some purposes but not for others. The most general point is that limits on attention may well be the most important factor affecting the efficacy of disclosure.

Bounded attention renders many disclosures useless because consumers ignore them. They respond, "yeah, whatever," and move on. For example, fewer than 3 percent of consumers read the privacy disclosures that are so ubiquitous on websites,[5] and 75 percent of consumers think that the existence of a privacy policy implies privacy protection,[6] even though the actual thrust of such policies is often the opposite—to secure the consumer's acquiescence in relinquishing privacy.[7] Disclosures are so ubiquitous that we tend to be unaware of them, and when the implicit is made explicit, one cannot help but be struck by the impossibility that anyone could attend to even a fraction of the disclosures to which we are exposed.

One of the most common, and obviously important, forms of disclosure involves product warning labels. Summarizing results from approximately four hundred articles dealing with on-product warning labels, McCarthy et al. conclude that "on-product warnings have no measurable impact on user behavior and product safety."[8] The conclusion seems far too pessimistic, but it is telling. And when disclosure requirements turn out to be ineffective, it might be worthwhile to consider improved approaches that nonetheless involve information or other regulatory approaches, including default rules.

2: Inattention to Missing Information

A key assumption of the economic analysis (leading to the conclusion that disclosure is unnecessary when disclosed information is verifiable) is that people are aware not only of information that they are presented but also of currently undisclosed information that could be presented. More specifically, the standard economic analysis assumes that when companies provide individuals with selected information, people fill in the blanks with the worst possible values, assuming that if the information was favorable it would be disclosed. Research in psychology suggests that this key assumption is unlikely to be true. We have seen that people have only limited capacity to attend to information that they are presented with; other research shows that people typically pay even less attention to the absence of information than to its presence, even when both are equally informative.[9]

Powerful evidence of inattention to missing information in a real-world market context comes from research examining the *cold release* of movies—that is, the release to consumers without first giving access to reviewers. Studios cold-release movies when they are confident that the reviews will be unfavorable, and consumers should ideally draw the logical inference from the release of movies with no prior reviewer coverage. But in fact, cold-released movies initially do better than movies that are prereleased to critics only to receive predominantly negative reviews.[10]

The consequence of people's inattention to missing information is that voluntary disclosure policies will often turn out to be quite ineffective. If, for example, physicians could sign up for a clean conflict of interest certification, patients might infer from the lack of such a certification that a doctor must be conflicted. But if patients systematically fail to notice the absence of the certification, then doctors would be commensurately less motivated to eschew conflicts.[11] Similarly, prior to the Nutritional Labeling and Education Act, makers of salad dressings with higher fat content chose not to label these products voluntarily. But with mandatory disclosure, their sales declined.[12]

3: Motivated Attention

Even when people have the cognitive capacity to attend to the information provided by a disclosure, they do not always do so. As we have seen, information is not only an input into decision-making; it is a source of utility in its own right.[13] Recall the importance of hedonic effects. When information is unpleasant to deal with, people often fail to attend to it. We have seen that investors tend to log in and look up the value of their portfolios after a rise in the market, but put their heads in the sand after the market declines.[14] Research on medical testing for conditions such as HIV finds that the people who are most at risk often do not get tested because the prospect of the disease is too scary to think about or because they are afraid to expose themselves to the risk of getting bad news.[15]

One such study examined the decisions of individuals at risk for Huntington's disease about whether to get tested.[16] Even though knowing whether one has the disease should be an enormously valuable input into decisions (such as whether to have children), many people chose not to get tested until they started experiencing symptoms. Even more interestingly, those who did not get tested made life decisions, such as whether to have children, that did not differ from those who were tested and discovered they did not have the disease. For purposes of decision-making, people appeared to treat the absence of testing results as tantamount to the absence of the disease.

With respect to medical disclosures, the psychological story is of course complex. Different patients react differently to the same disclosures. There is a correlation between a person's baseline anxiety and psychological distress levels and the effect of a medical disclosure on that person.[17] For example, people with high levels of anxiety will react more strongly to a diagnosis of cancer. In addition, it may matter whether a medical disclosure concerns someone's own health or instead someone for whom they care, such as a child. For many parents of children with Down syndrome, the more information the better, even if the information may include bad news, presumably because parents think that more information helps them be better caregivers.[18] The impact of bad news will also be affected by patients' preexisting beliefs about their health. Patients who think that they have a significant risk of developing a serious disease will be more likely to interpret test results in that way, and those who do not think that they face such a risk will think their test results support their view as well.[19] This is a clear case of motivated attention.

The most obvious implication of motivated attention for mandatory disclosure policies is that disturbing messages might well be ignored or downplayed. Research on the impact of emotional health warnings—so-called fear appeals—does in fact show that scary warnings unaccompanied by immediate options for remediating action can backfire, apparently because people are deterred by fear from thinking about, and hence become less likely to respond to, the risks.[20] In a similar phenomenon, people have been shown to suffer from unrealistic optimism, especially with respect to personal risks,[21] and unrealistic optimism could well weaken the effects of disclosure.

A subtler implication is that disclosure policies intended to mitigate selective provision of information by firms may not work as well as might be expected. Even if *companies* do not engage in selective withholding of information (whether voluntarily or due to disclosure regulations), consumers may, in effect, take up the slack by paying attention to information that supports decisions that they may have already decided to make and ignoring or downplaying that which does not. If ice cream parlors would prefer not to post calorie information, but are forced to do so by regulations, consumers who like ice cream may take over the "editing" role that regulations prevent the parlors from implementing, by ignoring information that, if attended to, would reduce their pleasure.

4: Biased Probability Judgments

Although standard economics allows for the idea that probability judgments might incorporate random error, the conventional assumption is that people do not display systematic biases—that, on average, people estimate things correctly. For a variety of reasons, this is not the case.[22] Research has found that people have systematically biased beliefs about, for example, food calorie content,[23] returns to schooling,[24] and the impact on energy consumption of driving cars differing in fuel economy.[25]

Misestimates of probabilities can have important implications for disclosure. For example, providing information about the health consequences of smoking is intended to deter people from smoking, and calorie information is intended to help people cut down on their calorie intake. But these effects are likely to occur only if, prior to disclosure, people are systematically biased in a direction that promotes the undesirable behavior, which may not be the case. Some research finds that both smokers and nonsmokers tend to *overestimate* the health risks of smoking[26]—though it is important to add that most smokers have been found to underestimate their *personal* risk even in the face of accurate estimates or overestimates of statistical risks.[27] To the extent that some or many smokers overestimate the risks of smoking, it is possible that disclosure of the true risks of smoking could end up promoting smoking.

There is a larger point here. Some medical tests and procedures do very little to reduce absolute risks. For purposes of illustration, some forms of cancer screening might prevent one death in a population of a thousand. People might believe, in advance, that cancer screening has a much larger impact in preventing deaths. If they are informed of the actual numbers, there is a good chance that cancer screening will go down. In my view, that is a good thing, but reasonable people might differ about that conclusion.

5: Moral Licensing

There is by now a large literature in behavioral and experimental economics demonstrating what many people might find obvious—that people are powerfully driven by other-regarding motivations such as altruism, fairness, and a desire to perceive themselves as good people, and that, all else held equal, people prefer to tell the truth[28] and also expect others to do so.[29] These motivations can be important for disclosures for moral reasons (as in the case of animal welfare) and also in the types of misaligned relationships that are the common focus of disclosure policies, They can motivate sellers to behave in the interests of buyers even when they have material incentives not to do so.[30]

The fact that people are intrinsically motivated to provide unbiased advice and high-quality products (even when they could pass off inferior ones to naïve consumers) is highly relevant to the effects of disclosures of conflicts of interest. In some situations, such disclosures can undermine that salutary motivation through a complex phenomenon known as *moral licensing*.[31] Moral licensing occurs when people feel that they have been licensed to do something that they would otherwise consider wrong. In conflict of interest cases, the perception that an advisee has been warned, via disclosure, of an advisor's potential bias makes the advisor feel less responsible for giving unbiased advice. The empirical literature on moral licensing is very much in a state of development; the brief discussion here is meant as an effort to identify a potential risk of disclosure.

In a study demonstrating the phenomenon, Cain et al. asked respondents to a survey to imagine that they were participating in an experiment in which they played the role of advisor and gave advice to another person (the estimator), who would make money by accurately estimating how many jellybeans were in a jar that was depicted in a photo.[32] Participants were all given a (hypothetical) conflict of interest: "Suppose that you are paid a $50 bonus if the estimator overestimates the number of jellybeans in the jar." Participants were also told that the jar actually contained between 1,900 and 2,900 jellybeans. All participants were asked to rate how ethical it was to suggest a number above 2,900 (in hopes that the estimator overestimates the number of jellybeans). In one condition, estimators were told that "the estimator is unaware of your $50 incentive," and in the other they were told that "the estimator is aware of your $50 incentive." Consistent with moral licensing, respondents reported that it would be more ethical to overstate the number when the estimator was aware of the conflict.

In a series of stylized experiments, the same authors showed that when a conflict was disclosed, moral licensing was sufficiently strong that conflicted advisors were better off and advice recipients were worse off, as compared to the same situation but without disclosure.[33] These findings were later replicated and extended in an experiment modeling a real-life situation of a homebuyer and a conflicted real estate agent.[34] These studies show that disclosure of misaligned incentives can backfire, hurting those it is intended to help. The conclusion is not that such disclosure is a bad idea, all things considered. In some cases, disclosure of conflicts might improve the quality of advice. But there is a risk that those who receive information about conflicts will not be better off as a result—and they might be worse off.

Panhandler and Insinuation Anxiety Effects

Two additional psychological phenomena raise further concerns about the potential for disclosure of misaligned incentives to backfire. Disclosing that an advisor has a conflict of interest does have the intended consequence of decreasing advisee trust. But perversely, due to two psychological mechanisms, it can also increase pressure to comply with the distrusted advice.

The first mechanism, the *panhandler effect*, results from the fact that once a conflict has been disclosed, the advisor's interests become common knowledge, and, in some situations, advisees may feel pressured to help advisors obtain their personal interests. For example, once a doctor discloses that he or she earns a large referral fee if their patient enrolls in a clinical trial, the patient may implicitly feel that he or she is being asked to "help" the doctor get the fee.

Insinuation anxiety arises from the advisees' fear that rejecting advice (after learning about a conflict of interest) sends a negative signal that in their view, the advice is biased and the advisor is corrupt. Without disclosure, investors might not want to invest in a new mutual fund recommended by their financial advisor due to risk aversion or satisfaction with current investments. However, after the investment advisor has disclosed that he/she will receive a financial benefit if investors buys into the new fund, they may fear that their failure to follow the advisor's recommendation to do so is likely to be interpreted as a signal of distrust—an indication that they doubt the advisor's ability to transcend the conflict.

In a pair of papers, Sah et al. report on the results of lab studies involving hypothetical and real outcomes, as well as field studies, in which conflicted advisors interacted with advisees who either were or were not informed of the conflict.[35] In all experiments, disclosure increased distrust in advice but, due to either the panhandler effect or insinuation anxiety, also increased advisees' feelings of pressure to comply with it. In several of the experiments, the latter influence was stronger than the former, so that advisees ended up being more likely to comply with the advice, even though they trusted it less.

The Spotlight and the Telltale Heart Effect

Psychology does not always work against the effectiveness of disclosure. On the contrary, the *telltale heart effect* suggests that psychological factors may *increase* the effectiveness of disclosure when, from an economic standpoint, it might be expected to be superfluous. Mandatory disclosure can lead disclosers to "clean up their act."[36] For example, hygiene ratings of restaurants in LA affected patronage patterns, which then motivated restaurants to improve their sanitation practices.[37] In more intriguing situations (to some extent including the case of restaurant hygiene ratings), *an industry response can be found amid little evidence of a consumer response.*

This pattern raises an obvious question: Why are providers changing their products in response to disclosures that their customers are largely ignoring? On the basis of profit considerations alone, consumer inattention should lead producers to do exactly what they were doing before. Evidently some disclosers either have an exaggerated expectation of the likely consumer response or feel guilty or ashamed about the information disclosed. We suspect that sellers may well have an inflated sense of the public salience of disclosures, in a phenomenon related to the spotlight effect,[38] by which people exaggerate how much other people are looking at them, and also analogous to the confession of the protagonist in Edgar Allen Poe's famous short story, "The Tell-Tale Heart," who imagines that the police can hear the heartbeat of the man he has killed and buried beneath the floorboards of his apartment.[39]

Some current evidence seems to suggest either a modest effect or no effect, on consumers, from calorie labeling.[40] But in a study that provides evidence suggestive of a telltale heart effect, researchers combed an archive of publicly accessible web pages for changes in posted menu offerings at fast food restaurants between 2005 and 2011, a period during which several municipalities introduced calorie posting.[41] Menus from five fast-food chains with outlets in areas subject to menu-labeling laws were compared with menus from four chains operating in areas not requiring labeling. Although the overall prevalence of healthier food options remained low over the period, restaurants located in areas that implemented calorie labeling increased healthier entrée options.[42]

Increasing the number of healthy options does not, however, mean that consumers will necessarily choose them. In a study showing that a greater prevalence of healthy options can end up backfiring by creating a "halo effect," Chandon and Wansink find that consumers significantly underestimate the calories in an ostensibly "healthier" meal from Subway than for a comparable meal from McDonald's.[43] The same study also finds that health claims can lead consumers to order sides and beverages that contain more calories, a kind of substitution effect also observed in a field experiment conducted at Subway, in which consumers were nudged toward lower calorie entrees via a "convenience menu" that included only low-calorie sandwiches.[44]

Further evidence suggestive of a telltale heart effect comes from the literature on appliance purchases, which to date provides relatively weak evidence of consumer responsiveness to energy-efficiency labeling, but much stronger evidence of manufacturer responsiveness. Newell et al., for example, find just that for energy-efficiency labeling.[45] After such labeling was mandated in the United States, responsiveness of energy-efficient innovation in appliances to energy price changes increased substantially. Waide documents a trend toward more efficient products in the European Union that began right after the onset of labeling and that was so strong that market saturation of certain appliances with an A rating led regulators in the EU to create A+ and A++ ratings to encourage greater efficiency through product differentiation.[46]

One situation in which a telltale heart effect may be especially effective is corporate ethics and socially responsible behavior.

Writing not only about corporations' concern for their public image, but also about consequent potential benefits of information disclosure regulations, Estlund contends that

> the lengths to which leading firms go to advertise their virtuous performance on matters of sustainability, diversity, ethics, and overall social responsibility suggest that more is at work than ordinary labor market or product market competition. . . . Mandatory disclosure of accurate information about socially salient conditions of employment (as well as other objects of CSR [corporate social responsibility] claims), would help ensure that there is a factual basis for firms' claims of social responsibility, and that firms cannot easily buff up their reputation for good citizenship without improving their actual practices.[47]

The telltale heart effect is likely to be playing a role here.

Making Disclosure Work

How can disclosure policies be improved? An understanding of behavioral science provides an assortment of answers.

Simplification and Salience

Given the limits of human attention, the most obvious way to improve the effectiveness of disclosures is to simplify them and thus to increase their salience. As Ripken writes, "In order for a disclosure system to be effective, not only must the information that is supplied be disclosed completely, clearly, and accurately, but it must also be read and comprehended by the consumer. Here is where disclosure today fails in its purpose."[48] Ripkin's focus is on financial disclosure, where the problem is especially acute. Corporate disclosure documents tend to be packed with abstruse text written to protect companies from liability rather than to provide investors with comprehensible information. But the point is broadly applicable. It certainly applies to efforts to help consumers, workers, and others.

Simplification accomplishes a number of goals at the same time. It increases the likelihood of understanding. It focuses people's attention. It increases the salience of whatever it said. There are ways to increase salience while maintaining complexity—as, for example, with large fonts or bold type—but because simplification and salience often march hand in hand, I treat them together here.

Barghava and Manoli provide evidence for the benefits of simplification.[49] In a field experiment testing different interventions to increase take-up of the Earned Income Tax Credit (EITC) using mailed communications, they found that decreasing the complexity relative to a baseline notice (which itself produced take-up of 14 percent) increased take-up by six percentage points. Also consistent with an important role for simplicity, increasing complexity decreased take-up by four percentage points.

If simplification is, in principle, a good thing, exactly *how* to simplify information is anything but a simple problem, and again some obvious approaches may have unexpected pitfalls. Studies conducted both in the United States and abroad have shown that using categorical labels, such as stars or letter grades, rather than a continuous scale, leads to better comprehension, a faster grasp of label information, and greater ease of use.[50] Newell and Siikamäki, for example, found that consumers who were exposed to different energy-efficiency disclosures and made hypothetical choices between water heaters (in a within-subjects experiment) were more responsive to, and more likely to make cost-efficient decisions after receiving, simple as compared with complex energy efficiency labels.[51] Consumers were most influenced by simple information about the monetary value of saving energy; additional information about placing this cost within a range of comparable models did not have significant additional value. Perhaps most importantly, a categorical label leads to increased self-stated motivation on the part of the consumer to consider energy efficiency as part of the purchase decision.[52]

We have seen that the evidence with respect to calorie labels is mixed, and briefly referred to research finding that a small and simple fix might make a big difference: put the calorie labels on the left side of menu items, rather than the right.[53] That is an intriguing finding because it has implications for design choices by the private and public sectors in countless domains. The research was conducted via three different experiments. The first was undertaken at a chain restaurant on a college campus. About 150 participants were randomly assigned to one of three paper menus: no calorie information, calorie information on the right, and calorie information on the left. Putting the information on the right had no effect. But when calories were put on the left, participants reduced the number of calories ordered by 24.4 percent.

The second study was an online survey involving about three hundred people asked to choose among food items on a menu. About half saw calorie labels on the left and half on the right. Participants were also asked to say what factors influenced their choice (such as taste, size, price, value, and calories). When calorie information was placed on the left, people said that they would order significantly lower-calorie meals. In addition, they were much more likely to say that calories influenced their choices.

The third study was the most ingenious. The researchers recruited about 250 Hebrew-speaking Israelis. Unlike English,

Hebrew is read right to left. Dallas and his colleagues hypothesized that for speakers of Hebrew, their central finding would be reversed: calorie information would have a greater impact if it was placed on the right. As in the first experiment, participants were divided into three groups: calories to the left, calories to the right, and no calorie information. As in the second experiment, participants were surveyed about their choices. When calories were placed to the left, Hebrew speakers were unaffected; the number of calories ordered was the same as in the no-calories condition. But when calories were placed to the right, participants ordered significantly fewer calories.

Here is a simple explanation for these findings: Salience greatly matters, and people are greatly influenced by what they see first. If they see "cheeseburger" first, they might well think, "That's exactly what I want!" If they see "300 calories" right after, they might think, "OK, but that's exactly what I want!" If they see "300 calories" first, they might well think, "That's a lot of calories." If they see "cheeseburger" right after, they might think, "OK, but that's a lot of calories!" In other words, what we see first, on a menu or anywhere else, might orient us and prove decisive when we assess what we see second, third, and fourth.

If simplification and salience are the general goals, perhaps the most obvious change in policy with respect to mandatory disclosure regulations is one that would be most difficult to implement: *reduce the number of less important disclosures so as to increase the salience of the most important ones*. In today's regulatory environment, the obstacle to such a change is that disclosure regulations arise from a wide range of legislative and regulatory sources at the federal, state, and local levels. Warnings and labels can be seen as forms of sludge (see chapter 7), and sludge reduction can make the most important ones more effective.

Standardized and Comparative Information

People are generally able to make more coherent and rational decisions when they have comparative information that allows them to assess relevant trade-offs.[54] This point suggests that disclosures that provide comparisons, or information in standardized formats that facilitate comparisons, may have the greatest impact and benefit. If information is presented in a way that does not allow comparisons, it may not be meaningful, especially because people might not do the cognitive and other work that would enable them to make such comparisons on their own.

Energy-efficiency labels for automobiles and appliances in the United States are only two examples of many disclosures that do provide comparative information—in such cases, about how the operating costs of the car or appliance in question compare to those of others. Another example is the College Scorecard from the US Department of Education, which is intended to promote better postsecondary education choices. The scorecard provides standardized information that allows prospective college students to compare costs, graduation rates, loan default rates, amounts borrowed, and employment for every degree-granting institution in the country.

Although (and perhaps *because*) the benefits of providing standardized information about alternative products appear manifest, there is not a great deal of research that examines whether such information makes a difference. Some evidence does, however, suggest that comparative information along with other interventions can be effective. It does so because it overcomes "comparison friction," understood as the friction that people face when they try, all on their own, to make comparisons among offerings and options. In a randomized field experiment, senior citizens choosing between Medicare drug plans were randomly selected to receive a letter with personalized, standardized, comparative cost information.[55] Plan switching occurred with 28 percent of the intervention group, but only 17 percent of the comparison group, and the intervention caused an average decline in predicted consumer costs of about $100 a year among letter recipients. Note, however, that this intervention combined a number of different aspects (comparative and personalized information), so we cannot isolate a single mechanism that explains its effectiveness.

In a revealing study, prospective payday borrowers, already routinely provided with the APR of payday loans (typically around 450 percent), were also provided comparative information about the cost of other types of loans.[56] In one treatment, the typical APR of a payday loan was contrasted with that of other loans that consumers were likely to be familiar with, such as car loans (typical APR of 18 percent), credit cards (16 percent), and subprime mortgages (10 percent). In another treatment, the dollar costs of payday loans of durations ranging from two weeks to three months were contrasted against the much lower dollar costs of credit card debt. A third treatment provided information about the (high) fraction of people taking out payday loans who end up renewing the loans. The dollar cost information condition had the largest, although somewhat modest and only marginally significant, impact, both on loan initiation and loan amount. Note that this was not the only comparative condition; it was also the only condition involving dollar as opposed to percentage information. For that reason, dollar information may have been the key aspect of the intervention that increased its

impact. Indeed, an experiment examining the choice of investment funds differing in fees by workers without much financial literacy also found a greater impact on choice of presenting
information in dollar, rather than percentage point, terms.[57]

Other research suggests that merely providing comparative
information is insufficient to enhance choice; it is important
how information is sorted. In a study of the impact of the US
News & World Report college rankings, Luca and Smith exploited
a natural experiment that resulted from a change in how universities were listed.[58] From 1989 to 1994, the top twenty-five
universities were listed in order of rank, but the next twenty-five
were listed alphabetically (though reporting rank). In 1995, US
News began listing all of the top fifty universities in order of
rank. The authors found that a change in rank for universities
in the bottom half of the one to fifty range had a significant
impact when all fifty were ordered by rank (high salience), but
no impact when the focal universities were ordered alphabetically (even though rank was reported).[59] The evident reason is
that with the alphabetical listing, some cognitive work had to be
done to ascertain ranking. Even though that work was modest,
people declined to do it.

A different study examined the impact of simplified school-
level academic performance information on the school choices
of parents in the Charlotte-Mecklenburg Schools district.[60]
The study produced less encouraging results both for simplification and ordering. In a randomized field experiment (one
of two studies that the authors report), parents of children in
randomly selected schools who were provided with statistics on,
and sorted by, different schools' academic achievements did not
make better school choices than those who did not receive the
information.[61]

Social Comparison Information

Media mogul Ted Turner once complained that *Forbes* published a list of the wealthiest Americans but not the most generous, an omission that was later corrected by *Slate*. Research suggests that social competition can encourage generosity.[62] Social comparison information can operate through a variety of channels. Beyond playing on the natural human desire to be above average on almost anything that can be measured, social comparison information can potentially establish descriptive norms (stating what most people do, as in, "95 percent of people pay their taxes on time") and also injunctive norms (stating what people think ought to be done, as in, "95 percent of people think that citizens should pay their taxes on time").[63] Perhaps surprisingly, descriptive norms are often more powerful than injunctive norms; people usually want to do what others actually do, not what others merely think should be done. Social comparison information provides descriptive norms, and it may carry an injunctive norm along with it.

Perhaps the most carefully studied intervention, discussed in chapter 2 in connection with work by Hunt Allcott and Judd Kessler, provides homeowners with information about how their energy use compares with that of their neighbors. As we have seen, Opower, a company based in Virginia, works with utilities to send people a personalized Home Energy Report, which includes a comparison to their neighbors (e.g., "great," "good," and "more than average") and is accompanied by "energy-saving tips," such as "move your thermometer up two degrees" and "when you're away, set it higher." Evaluations of the Opower intervention have found that when people learn that they are using more energy than similarly situated others and are provided with tips on how to reduce energy use, their energy use declines significantly.[64] Although the effects are not large (approximately a 2 percent reduction), the cost-effectiveness of the intervention compares favorably to that of other, more standard programs designed to promote energy conservation.

It is important to emphasize, however, that the causal mechanisms are not yet well identified because the program combines comparative information with tips (sometimes described as *channel factors* in the psychological literature), and existing designs cannot exclude the possibility that the effects result from an increase in mere energy awareness on the part of the consumer as a consequence of receiving the report, regardless of its specific content. It should also be noted that several studies have found little or no impact of social comparison information, and at least one study (the previously discussed study by Barghava and Manoli[65]) actually found that social comparison information had a perverse effect, decreasing take-up of the Earned Income Tax Credit by 4.4 percent.

Public ratings of corporations and other institutions have also been found to influence their behavior. One study focused on the release of toxic chemicals, as reported to the US Environmental Protection Agency's Toxics Release Inventory. It examined the impact on firm behavior of being suddenly included among the ranks of firms whose relative performance was publicly graded.[66] The researchers found that firms that initially rated poorly subsequently improved their performance, as compared to firms that were never rated or rated more favorably. Other studies of the same program also find significant effects, which the authors attribute to a fear of "environmental blacklisting."[67]

Social comparison information also seems to have played a role in positive progress made in reducing certain types of conflicts of interests in academic medical centers (those associated with gifts to physicians from pharmaceutical companies and device manufacturers). The American Medical Student Association PharmFree Scorecards grade conflict of interest (COI) policies at US academic medical centers, and these appear to have encouraged the implementation of stronger COI policies in many academic medical centers.[68] In Washington, DC, mandatory disclosure of marketing costs for prescription drugs lowered marketing expenditures by pharmaceutical companies, including gifts to physicians, from 2007 to 2010. In addition, the announcement of the names and amounts received from industry by the top eight physician speakers in 2009 resulted in a significant drop in the amounts received by this group in the subsequent year compared to a comparison group (the next eight speakers whose names and industry amounts were not disclosed).[69]

These and many other examples suggest that "regulation by shaming" can be an effective strategy for improving the performance of firms and other organizations.[70] At the same time, it is important to note that such regulation can produce perverse effects. Rankings of schools by the media can produce a kind of self-reinforcing dynamic by which low ratings lead to a drying up of resources and decline in the quality of students, making it difficult if not impossible for schools to rectify problems identified by their rankings.[71] Moreover, social comparison information does not even always lead to a desire to improve, at least on the intended dimension. In the case of Opower, providing the social comparison information does seem to lead to an average net decrease in electricity usage, but some studies have documented so-called boomerang effects, whereby those discovering that they are consuming less than average actually increase their usage.[72]

Vividness

It is well-understood that vivid displays often have a larger impact than dry, statistical information.[73] This point has significant lessons for disclosure policies. In the context of smoking, for example, many studies indicate that warnings that combine pictures and text are more effective than text alone in decreasing demand for cigarettes—perhaps by triggering strong emotions, perhaps by increasing awareness of risks, and perhaps by promoting thoughts about quitting.[74] The relevant pictures can be gruesome or shocking, such as images of diseased organs, and these images have been found to have a greater impact on smokers than words suggesting more abstract injury.[75] As discussed earlier in the context of motivated attention, however, there is some danger that the use of pictorial warnings could backfire; consumers might direct their attention away from the gruesome pictures and thus insulate themselves from the warning information.[76]

Smart Disclosure and the Role of Intermediaries

In some situations, exemplified by the abstruse legalistic disclosures accompanying securities transactions, the language or underlying information is far too complex for a layperson to digest. In other situations, exemplified by the privacy notifications that almost no one reads on internet sites, the volume of information is overwhelming and not worth the investment one must make to read it. In still other situations, exemplified by conflict of interest disclosures, the disclosures are neither complicated nor long, but their implications for behavior are difficult to assess. If a doctor informs a patient that she will receive a referral fee if the patient enters a clinical trial she recommends, should the patient decline to enroll? Making this determination requires a difficult judgment about whether the doctor's recommendation has been colored by the disclosed conflicts.

In all of these situations, unsophisticated recipients of advice could likely benefit from the intervention of more savvy intermediaries to help them make sense of the information. Many nonprofit organizations, such as Consumers' Checkbook (http://www.checkbook.org/), already perform this function. Instead of attempting to provide information directly to consumers, disclosure requirements could make information available in standardized formats so that intermediaries can arise to process it, make sense of it, and (perhaps for a fee) provide it in a form that is usable to its end users. Such an approach might well yield benefits beyond those contemplated by its implementers.

Consider GPS information, which is used in creative and useful ways that early proponents of its release could never have anticipated. Consistent with this goal, the Smart Disclosure initiative, undertaken by the Obama administration,[77] was designed to encourage providers to disclose downloadable, machine-readable information, in part so that intermediaries can help consumers of (for example) energy and health care to learn about their own behavior and, as a result, make more informed choices.

Complicating Life

Psychological factors severely complicate the standard arguments for disclosure requirements. Because attention is both limited and motivated, disclosures may be ignored, especially if they are complex. New disclosures, even of significant information, may distract attention from older and possibly more important ones. As a result of limited attention and other psychological factors discussed in this chapter, disclosure requirements appear to have been less effective in changing recipient behavior than their most ardent proponents assume.

At the same time, disclosure may have large effects on producers, which presents an independent puzzle: If consumers are unaffected by disclosure requirements, why would producers change their behavior? Providers of information may well overestimate the likely effect of disclosure on consumers, partly because that disclosure seems so salient to providers. But producers may also feel guilt and shame, and they care about their reputations. As a result of the telltale heart effect, information disclosure can have beneficial effects even when it fails to change consumer behavior.

Unfortunately, disclosure of misaligned incentives can have perverse effects on the producer side of the equation. Advisors who would have otherwise been intrinsically motivated to provide unbiased advice can feel morally licensed to provide biased advice after a conflict of interest has been disclosed. Because of panhandler and insinuation anxiety effects, advice recipients may feel greater pressure, following disclosure, to follow the now less trusted advice.

Psychologically informed strategies would make disclosure far more effective. Promising examples include simplification, standardization, and the use of social comparisons. Further research is needed to gain a better understanding of when, why, and how disclosure policies have intended or unintended consequences, as well as how such policies can be improved. But one thing is clear: psychology changes everything.

4 Learning the Wrong Thing

with Oren Bar-Gill and David Schkade

Red Auerbach, the late, great coach of the Boston Celtics, liked to say, "It's not what you say; it's what they hear." What do consumers "hear" when the government mandates the disclosure of a certain ingredient or a characteristic of a product? They may hear something altogether different from what the government intends to convey. The result can be a serious welfare loss to producers and consumers alike.

Imagine, for example, that the government mandates a warning that cigarettes cause cancer. Consumers will hear, "DANGER! DON'T BUY!!" That is precisely what the government wants consumers to hear. In cases of this kind, the government concluded, on the basis of scientific evidence, that the relevant product or ingredient is harmful to consumers. It is trying to use a disclosure mandate to convey that information and reduce demand for the harmful product.

In other cases, however, the government does not want to send a "DANGER!" signal. Imagine, for example, that government mandates disclosure of whether food is genetically modified, or bioengineered. In such cases, there may be no scientific basis for concluding that the ingredient or characteristic is harmful. The disclosure mandate may be motivated by a belief that consumers have a right to know what they are buying, whether or not the ingredient or characteristic is harmful. Or it may be motivated by interest group pressures. Or the government may be recognizing some kind of social value (say, on behalf of products bought in the country in which they are sold) or moral commitment (say, on behalf of animal welfare) that has nothing to do with health risks.

Or, perhaps, there is some preliminary evidence of possible harm, but far from enough to merit a "DANGER! DON'T BUY!" warning; only, maybe, a much weaker message: "Some preliminary, inconclusive cause for concern. Not sure if you should buy or not." In recent years, the Environmental Protection Agency has seriously considered listing certain chemicals as "chemicals of concern"—not because there is anything close to authoritative evidence of health risks, but because the preliminary evidence is suggestive and because some officials think that it would be a good idea to inform the public of that fact. The US government has thus far refused to produce such a list, in part because of a fear that people will draw a false inference: "DANGER! DON'T BUY!" The problem is general. In many cases, consumers may hear "DANGER!" even though the government does not mean to issue that kind of warning at all.

Consumers face an *inference problem* whenever the government decides to mandate disclosure of an ingredient or a characteristic of a product. The consumer's postdisclosure beliefs about the product will be influenced by (1) the consumer's predisclosure beliefs, (2) the consumer's estimate of the accuracy of the government's information, and (3) the consumer's beliefs about the government's motives.[1] Suppose that before learning of the government's decision to mandate disclosure, the consumer is fairly certain that the ingredient or characteristic is harmful. A consumer might believe, for example, that nicotine is addictive. If so, the disclosure mandate will have a minimal effect on the consumer's postdisclosure beliefs (and perhaps none at all). Or suppose that prior to disclosure, the consumer is essentially certain that an ingredient or characteristic is harmless, thinking (say) that genetically modified food poses no health risks. Here as well, the disclosure mandate will have a minimal effect on the consumer's postdisclosure beliefs (and perhaps none at all). When consumers are already well-informed, or think that they are well-informed, the additional signal derived from the government's decision to mandate disclosure carries little or no weight. Consumers who are fairly certain about the truth will be unaffected by mandatory disclosure.

Now turn to cases in which consumers are uncertain about whether an ingredient or characteristic is harmful or not. We might be dealing with genetically modified food; with trans fats; or with bisphenol A (BPA) and bisphenol S (BPS), two chemicals believed by some to impose significant risks. In such cases, the government's decision to mandate disclosure will carry more weight. That may be a good opportunity, to be sure. But it also means that we should be most worried about potentially misleading decisions to mandate disclosure when many consumers are uncertain about whether the ingredient or characteristic is harmful. In many areas, consumers, or a large number of them, are indeed uncertain because the underlying questions are technical, complex, or subject to competing (but apparently plausible) interpretations.

The perceived quality or accuracy of the government's evidence about whether the ingredient or characteristic is harmful also affects the consumer's postdisclosure beliefs. When the government is thought to have superior information, the decision to mandate disclosure will naturally carry more weight. It follows that the perceived professional expertise of the government agency that decides to mandate the disclosure will affect the inferences that consumers draw from any such mandate. And this is all as it should be: consumers should give more weight to the government's decision to mandate disclosure when they believe that the government has better information and greater expertise. The concern that a disclosure mandate will mislead consumers arises when consumers over- (or under-) estimate the quality of the government's information or its level of professional expertise.

Finally, and perhaps most interestingly, the government's perceived motivation for mandating disclosure will critically influence the inferences that consumers draw from a decision to mandate disclosure. If consumers think that the government requires disclosure because it found that the product is harmful, they will naturally be more likely to revise their beliefs about the product's harmfulness. If, by contrast, consumers think that the government requires disclosure because it believes in a right to know or because it succumbed to interest group pressure, then they will be less likely to revise their beliefs about the product's harmfulness. Again, this is all as it should be.

The risk is that a decision to mandate disclosure will mislead consumers. This concern arises *when consumers misperceive the government's motives*—for example, if they think that the government decided to mandate disclosure because it concluded that the product is harmful, when in fact the disclosure mandate was motivated by a belief in a right to know. With respect to genetically modified food, several studies find that the concern is quite real. One study finds that GMO disclosure significantly worsens consumers' perception of GMO safety, even if the government does not intend to produce that effect.[2] A related study finds a serious risk of false inferences from disclosure.[3] The US government has itself been concerned with the risk that consumers might be misled in this context. In 2015, the US Food and Drug Administration noted:

> A statement may be false or misleading if, when considered in the context of the entire label or labeling . . . it suggests or implies that a food product or ingredient is safer, more nutritious, or otherwise has different attributes than other comparable foods because the food was not genetically engineered. For example, the labeling of a bag of specific type of frozen vegetables that states that they were "not produced through modern biotechnology" could be misleading if, in addition to this statement, the labeling contains statements or vignettes that suggest or imply that, as a result of not being produced through modern biotechnology, such vegetables are safer, more nutritious, or have different attributes than other foods solely because the food was not produced using modern biotechnology.[4]

Welfare Costs

What are the welfare costs of false inferences? Putting quantitative assessments to one side, the qualitative answer is obvious. False inference leads to misperception of risk. Consumers will either over- or underestimate the risk associated with an ingredient or characteristic of the product. Consumers who overestimate the risk might decline to purchase the product. Instead they will purchase an otherwise less attractive alternative (or decide not to purchase any product in this category), which will reduce their welfare. Consumers who underestimate the risk might purchase the product when in fact they should be purchasing a less risky alternative. Again, the result will be a reduction in their welfare.

Table 4.1
Predisclosure vs. postdisclosure misperceptions

Case	Predisclosure misperception	Postdisclosure misperception
1	Underestimation of risk	Less underestimation of risk
2	Underestimation of risk	Overestimation of risk
3	Overestimation of risk	More overestimation of risk

When deciding whether to mandate disclosure, the government agency must compare the welfare cost from false inferences to the welfare cost in the absence of the disclosure mandate. In the absence of a disclosure mandate, consumers may be imperfectly informed—namely, they will suffer from under- or overestimation of risk. The question is whether the predisclosure misperception is better or worse than the postdisclosure misperception. To answer this question, it is helpful to distinguish among three cases, described in table 4.1.

In case 1, predisclosure consumers suffer from underestimation of risk, and the disclosure mandate reduces the degree of underestimation. Consumers' risk estimate is now closer to the objectively correct estimate, and so their purchase decisions are more efficient and their welfare is higher. In case 2, predisclosure consumers suffer from underestimation of risk, and postdisclosure they suffer from overestimation of risk. The purchase decisions are distorted in both cases: excessive purchase predisclosure and insufficient purchase postdisclosure. The effect on consumers' welfare is indeterminate in the abstract; empirical work would be needed to tell. In case 3, predisclosure consumers suffer from overestimation of risk. and the disclosure exacerbates this bias. Consumers' risk estimate is now farther from the objectively correct estimate, and so their purchase decisions are less efficient and their welfare is lower.

Quantification is of course challenging. But at least in principle, the preceding analysis lends itself to direct implementation by regulators. Survey studies can provide information about the direction and even the magnitude of the misperception pre- and postdisclosure. On the basis of this information, the policy prescriptions in case 1 and case 3 are straightforward: mandate disclosure in the former, but not in the latter. Case 2 poses a more difficult problem. In the absence of disclosure, underestimation of risk leads to overconsumption of the product, whereas disclosure results in overestimation of risk and thus underconsumption of the product.

It is important but insufficient to compare the magnitudes of the two misperceptions. Even if the underestimation is smaller than the overestimation, it may have a larger effect on consumption. Ideally, the regulator should assess the elasticity of demand with respect to risk perceptions (emphasizing that this elasticity can be quite different for under- versus overestimation of risk). As noted, surveys might provide relevant information. If sufficient information cannot be obtained, regulators should, consistent with standard practice, candidly acknowledge uncertainties. When quantification is not possible and significant uncertainties remain, regulators have some helpful strategies, including the use of lower and upper bounds.[5] In some cases, it is imaginable that existing knowledge will make it difficult to decide whether the benefits of disclosure justify the costs.

Counteracting False Inferences

From the point of view of regulators, it is also important to ask whether false inferences might be combated with more disclosure or with improved framing. If so, the welfare costs would be reduced or eliminated. One question is whether voluntary disclosure can be expected to provide a corrective. Another question is whether supplemental disclosure might be mandated.

Consider a mandate that requires all sellers who use BPH (an imaginary chemical) in their products to include a BPH label on their packaging, and assume that this disclosure mandate is not based on evidence that BPH is harmful to consumers. Sellers of BPH products would have a clear incentive to educate consumers and convince them that BPH is harmless (or, at least, that there is no evidence to the contrary). The question may not be hypothetical. In the United States, sellers of genetically modified (GM) food might want to engage in an advertising campaign or add a disclosure: "There is no evidence that GM food is hazardous to human health."

For two reasons, however, such voluntary disclosure might not always occur. First, it might be futile or even counterproductive. A statement that GM food has not been found to be hazardous to human health places *GM food* and *hazardous* in the same sentence. Many consumers might not be assured by that kind of proximity; their concern might even grow. Rational sellers would take that possibility into account. Second, the necessary information triggers a collective action problem: a single seller will be reluctant to invest millions of dollars in an advertising campaign to educate consumers about the safety of GM food if all sellers of GM food would reap the benefits of such a campaign. Perhaps an industry group could solve this collective action problem, or perhaps a simple label, including a corrective statement, would have benefits in excess of costs (assuming the proximity problem could be solved).

Should a federal agency mandate some kind of corrective disclosure, to combat the risk of false inferences? For instance, if there is concern that a GMO disclosure would lead to over-estimation of risk, the government can mandate a supplemental disclosure: "The best scientific evidence suggests that GMOs carry no health risks." On plausible assumptions, such a mandate would make sense. It would reduce the welfare costs of false inferences without imposing costs on those who do not draw such inferences (assuming the costs of the disclosure are themselves modest). One question is whether the proximity problem just identified would mean that the mandate would be futile or counterproductive. Another question is the magnitude of the welfare loss from false inferences and whether it can be reduced or eliminated through voluntary action. If the loss is large, if voluntary action is insufficient, and if the loss can be successfully combated through a corrective mandate, such a mandate would deserve consideration.

5　Moral Wrongs

with Eric Posner

Thus far I have been focusing mostly on situations in which people seek information because it will affect their own lives. But in many contexts, people want information, or the government requires disclosure of information, in order to improve the lives of others. The main point of disclosure is *moral*. It is to help those who are deprived, hurt, vulnerable, or at risk. Disclosure is a way to confer benefits or to reduce harm—and also to allow or to encourage people to register their moral convictions. In addition, disclosure might be an effort to trigger or heighten moral concern and in that way change social norms.

When disclosure is animated by such concerns, popcorn might well be ruined. It might not be a lot of fun to buy a cell phone that has some label saying, "Workers were abused in the making of this cell phone," or a meat product with the words, "The cows that you are about to eat were treated horrendously," or clothing with the label, "The women who made this product were sexually harassed." Perhaps for that reason, a standard approach to adverse effects on third parties is to *accentuate the positive*. Products might be labeled Cruelty-Free, Animal Welfare Approved, Certified Humane, or Organic. Whether negative or positive, the questions remain: What are the actual effects of morally motivated information? Should disclosure be mandated? When?

Righting Wrongs

To concretize these questions, consider the following cases:

1. Congress has directed the US Securities and Exchange Commission (SEC) to issue a regulation to ensure disclosure of "conflict minerals"—minerals used to finance mass atrocities.[1] Should the SEC try to identify the benefits of disclosure? Should it attempt to specify the beneficial effects of disclosure on people who would otherwise be subject to atrocities? The SEC is also aware that many consumers are interested in the relevant information. How, if at all, should the SEC quantify and monetize that interest?

2. The Dolphin Protection Consumer Information Act provides labeling standards for tuna products.[2] It includes standards by which companies may label their products dolphin safe.[3] How should the public officials try to identify the benefits of the labels for dolphins? Should it offer some numbers?

3. A federal law requires the Department of Transportation and the Environmental Protection Agency to produce fuel economy labels, which must contain information about greenhouse gas emissions. Should the agencies quantify the effects of the labels in reducing emissions? Many consumers care a great deal about greenhouse gas emissions from their vehicles; they want to reduce climate change. How should the agencies deal with that fact?

4. Many consumers are concerned about genetically modified food.[4] While some of them are concerned about health and

the environment, others believe that genetic modification of food is "just wrong." Congress has required the Department of Agriculture to label GM food as such.[5] How, if at all, should the department take account of consumer sentiment in cataloging the rule's benefits?

In some important contexts, governments require disclosure of information in order to protect children, people in other nations, victims of some kind of wrongdoing, animals, or even nature.[6] In most cases, the goal is to reduce concrete harms, such as lives lost, which are what trigger the moral concern. In some cases, it is difficult or perhaps impossible to identify concrete harms, but people nonetheless favor disclosure as a way of expressing and realizing their moral commitments. The principal question here is how regulators should take account of those commitments. Figure 5.1 shows a few examples of the kinds of disclosure that fall into the category I have in mind.

Assessing Welfare Effects

When third parties are at risk, the central question is simple: What are the welfare effects of disclosure? The principal benefit, of course, is to the relevant third parties. That is what most matters. Are they really being helped? By how much? For example: What is the effect of fuel economy labels containing information about greenhouse gas emissions?

From chapter 2, the central features of the analysis should be familiar. The first question is the magnitude of the consumer response. Will people buy more fuel-efficient cars? How many people, and how much more fuel-efficient? The second question is the effect of the response on emissions. Are greenhouse gas

Figure 5.1
Morally motivated labels: (a) dolphin-safe label, (b) conflict-free minerals label, (c) fuel economy label, and (d) non-GMO label.

emissions reduced by 1 percent? By 2 percent? By 5 percent? The third question is the effect of that reduction on anticipated warming. The fourth question is the ultimate effect on what matters, such as human health, economic growth, animal welfare, and endangered species. In the United States, policymakers have tried to monetize those effects through the "social cost of carbon," which was about $40 under the Obama administration and is in the vicinity of $6 in the Trump administration.

Whatever one thinks of those numbers, answering the four questions is daunting, but necessary if the goal is to understand what disclosure requirements actually achieve. To be sure, assessing the effects of fuel economy labels on greenhouse gas emissions is especially challenging. But in some cases, agencies have enough information to make real progress in identifying the effects of disclosure requirements on third parties. They can make projections about the likely consumer response, and with that response, they can make some projections about the real-world impact. If they cannot, breakeven analysis may be the best that they can do.

On the cost side, the analysis is nearly identical to what we saw in chapter 2, with just a few twists. As usual, we need to know the purely economic costs of disclosure, which may include production of labels and verification of the underlying information. In some cases, those costs can be quite high, at least if numerous products are involved. Recall that in the context of genetically modified food, for example, the Department of Agriculture projected first-year costs of up to $3.9 billion and recurring annual costs in the general vicinity of $100 million. In principle, we should also consider the cognitive burden on consumers, though perhaps the economic equivalent is low enough to be safely ignored.

Again, there is also the hedonic burden on consumers. If consumers suffer when they learn negative information about a product they love or enjoy, they incur a cost, and it may be high. Should that be included? The answer is intriguingly unclear. On the one hand, it is a genuine welfare loss. People are sadder; they might also be upset. A welfare calculation determined to count everything that actually happens would have to take that into account. But on ethical grounds, it is not at all clear that government should count, as a loss, the suffering that people experience when they learn truthful information that troubles them from a moral point of view. It is one thing if people learn that popcorn might make them fat. It is another thing if people learn that popcorn was produced through processes in which workers were mistreated. There is a good argument that regulators should not attend to the hedonic loss that comes from suffering induced by learning the truth.

But what about the loss that consumers incur if they do not buy a product that they would otherwise want or if they shift from one product to another? Suppose, for example, that consumers do not purchase a car that they really like because it emits high levels of greenhouse gases, and so they shift to a car that they like a bit less. Or suppose that people restrict themselves to chocolate that has a Fair Trade label, even though they prefer chocolate without that label. In such cases, consumers are suffering a loss. It must be included.

Vindicating Moral Commitments

There is a more exotic question.[7] Many consumers want their moral commitments to be vindicated. Their main commitment is to those they hope to benefit; it is not selfish. But if their moral commitments are vindicated, they themselves gain, for that very reason. To capture that gain, regulators might well ask: How much are people willing to pay to honor their moral commitments? Evidence might be available to answer that question. For example, people might be willing to pay $200 for a specified diminution in greenhouse gas emissions.

To be sure, asking about willingness to pay might seem jarring, because the question of what morality requires usually is not answered by asking how much people are willing to pay to promote their moral commitments. But from a welfarist perspective, it is both relevant and important to answer that question. Suppose that a consumer, John, cares about an assortment of things, including his longevity, his health, his comfort, and dolphins. Suppose that a substantial component of his welfare is the welfare of dolphins. If they suffer, he suffers. But how much does he suffer? Here as elsewhere, and despite its limitations, his willingness to pay might turn out to be the best available measure.

As it happens, this kind of issue has been studied empirically in the context of dogs. In the United States, households spend about $70 million annually on their pets. But how much are they worth? Careful research surveyed dog owners to ask how much they would be willing to pay to reduce mortality risks faced by their dogs.[8] Specifically, dog owners were asked about their WTP to reduce the risk of death from canine influenza. The value of a dog's life, or more precisely "the value of a statistical dog life," turns out to be $10,000. That is strikingly lower than the corresponding number for human beings; as noted, it is around $9 million. Still, it suggests that people would pay a great deal to prevent mortality risks to (their own) dogs. The finding strongly suggests that human beings are willing to pay real money to save nonhuman life.

It is true that for life-saving policies, what most matters is the lives saved, not the feelings of those who seek to save them. If the goal is to prevent mass atrocities in a foreign country, Americans' willingness to pay to prevent mass atrocities hardly exhausts the welfare effects of preventing mass atrocities. But people's welfare may well be affected and even profoundly affected by the realization or frustration of their moral commitments, as demonstrated by willingness to pay. If people lose welfare because of the suffering or death of others—people in other countries, their own children, rape victims, dolphins, members of future generations—their loss ought to be counted.

To be sure, the welfare loss might be hard to measure, and in many cases it might turn out to be relatively or even trivially small, not least because people's budget constraints might mean that they are unwilling to spend a great deal to vindicate any particular moral commitment. But in principle, there is no justification for refusing to include, in a cost-benefit analysis, people's willingness to pay to protect such commitments.

The question of how to address people's moral commitments in cost-benefit analysis is of great importance, and not only because many regulations advance moral goals. The problem for agencies is that when Congress commands them to advance such goals, it rarely provides guidance about the level of costs that should be imposed on the private sector in the course of achieving those goals. The SEC calculated that its conflict minerals regulation would cost industry about $5 billion, and in its view, the relevant statute required it to pay that price to enhance disclosure of conflict mineral use.[9]

But what if a slightly more effective regulation, also in compliance with the underlying statute, would have cost $50 billion or $500 billion? What if a slightly less effective regulation, again in compliance with the underlying statute, would have cost $1 billion or $2 billion? Should the SEC have imposed huge costs on the private sector in order to improve disclosure by only a tiny amount? If agencies try to quantify the moral benefits of regulations, they will be in a better position to decide on the stringency of regulations in a nonarbitrary way. In some cases, monetization of moral benefits will justify stronger regulations.

To understand the problem, compare Jane and Sam. Jane suffers from seafood intolerances, as a result of which she greatly benefits when food products include labels that disclose whether trace amounts of seafood are present in a product. Before the Food Allergen Labeling and Consumer Protection Act was passed, she bought organic foods from specialty stores that cost about $1,000 per year more than comparable food products sold in supermarkets.[10] As a result of the law, Jane can now shop at supermarkets; she is at least $1,000 better off per year and can use this money to buy goods and services that she could not afford in the past. So long as she uses this money for saving and consumption, the $1,000 amount is a reasonable approximation of the impact of the law on her well-being; it might well be a lower bound.

Sam does not suffer from food intolerances, but he cares deeply about the well-being of dolphins. He donates $1,000 per year to a charity that lobbies for laws that protect dolphin populations from harm by drift nets used to catch tuna. When Congress enacts the Dolphin Protection Consumer Information Act, Sam is very happy. But he is not sure whether the law should affect his charitable giving. He still cares about dolphins and thinks that the $1,000 he donates might be used to lobby for a stricter law that bans drift nets or for some other law that will help dolphins. But he also needs to pay his mortgage.

The Allergen Labeling Act improves Jane's well-being in a straightforward way. But does the Dolphin Act improve Sam's well-being? A tempting position is that while the law helps advance one of Sam's moral commitments, it does not affect his well-being. It does not improve his health or safety, give him goods or services to consume, or (directly) enhance his wealth. Another way to make this point is to imagine a world in which people like Sam disappear. No one cares about dolphins anymore. Nonetheless, it remains wrong to kill dolphins unnecessarily with drift nets. A utilitarian will probably believe that the well-being of animals has independent moral importance.[11] In fact, that was Bentham's view,[12] and I agree. But even philosophers who do not embrace utilitarianism often believe that an objective moral reality exists and does not depend on what people's moral beliefs are at any given moment. They believe, for example, that slavery is morally wrong even if no one in society, not even the slaves themselves, believe it is morally wrong. On this view, the moral worth of dolphins does not depend on whether Sam exists or whether many or few people agree with Sam.

This view seems to have a surprising implication: regulators must take into account Jane's self-regarding preferences and disregard Sam's moral beliefs. To understand this argument, consider the Benthamite view. If one hundred thousand dolphins exist, then their continued existence has moral value reflecting the well-being of those dolphins. If we take Sam's $1,000 charitable donation as an approximation of his willingness to pay to keep the dolphins alive, this would imply that the moral value of the existence of the dolphins is $1,000. If one thousand people agree with Sam, their moral value equals $1 million. And if the Sams disappeared, the moral value of dolphins in a cost-benefit analysis would fall to zero.

But as we have seen, the moral value of the dolphins is not a function of the number of people who care about dolphins. This means that the cost-benefit analysis should not treat Sam's willingness to pay as a reflection of their moral value. On this view, a regulatory agency charged with implementing the Dolphin Act should conduct cost-benefit analyses, but insofar as it is doing so, it should ignore moral valuations. To be sure, moral arguments, captured in the commitment to the well-being of dolphins, matter and deserve independent consideration. But Sam's moral views are irrelevant.

This conclusion is not correct. The first and more minor point is that when Sam donates $1,000 to the dolphin charity, he has $1,000 less to spend on his own well-being. If we want to be precise, we need to analyze Sam's motivations. If the regulation causes Sam to spend that entire amount on himself, then the regulation does make him better off by $1,000. If a regulation that helps dolphins causes Sam to reconsider his moral priorities and donate the money elsewhere, then it is harder to know whether and to what extent it improves Sam's well-being.

But there is a far more fundamental point, which bears directly on that question. Suppose that Sam's subjective welfare is affected by what happens to dolphins. When he hears about them being caught in drift nets, he experiences a loss of welfare, probably captured in some kind of distress or unhappiness. This sense of empathy is a psychological reaction, akin to disgust, anger, and fear, and it is highly relevant to Sam's welfare. Certainly in principle, the cost-benefit analysis should take account of the positive psychological effect on people of protecting those about whom they care. People are willing to pay to improve their welfare, and affective states are an important component of welfare. (Recall the data on dogs, suggesting that people are willing to pay a lot to reduce risks to them.)

It follows that if the entire dolphin population were eliminated, or if a significant number of dolphins were killed, then there would be two separate effects: a *moral effect* and a *welfare effect*. (To be sure, the moral effect is a kind of welfare effect, but it does not involve consumers or even human beings.) Both effects should count. If dolphins are eliminated, a moral wrong has taken place, and it is independent of the welfare effects on humans. The elimination of dolphins also harms human welfare by causing unhappiness or other welfare loss among people who care about dolphins. This harm can be measured, at least in principle, and is of course a function of the size of the human population that cares about dolphins.

Here, in short, is the central claim: when regulators analyze the welfare effects of disclosure requirements, they should include valuations that reflect how much benefit people receive from seeing their moral beliefs vindicated. Those valuations will hardly capture everything that matters, but they are an important point of a full accounting.

Mass Atrocities and Consumer Choices

In the Dodd-Frank Act, Congress required the Securities and Exchange Commission to issue regulations requiring firms to disclose their use of conflict minerals, which are minerals mined in the DRC and other countries where armed groups fund themselves by managing and extorting mining operations.[13] The SEC issued those regulations, which were challenged in court by the National Association of Manufacturers (NAM). Among other things, NAM argued that the regulations were arbitrary and capricious under the Administrative Procedure Act because the SEC did not conduct an adequate cost-benefit analysis. Although the SEC calculated the cost of the regulations to industry, it did not estimate the benefits of the regulations, on the ground that it was not feasible to do so. The court rejected NAM's argument that the agency's analysis was legally insufficient.[14]

The SEC concluded that the disclosure regime would impose a one-time cost of $3 to $4 billion on industry and another $207 to $609 million per year.[15] At the same time, the SEC explained that it was "unable to readily quantify" the benefits.[16] The principal reason did not involve translating the relevant benefits into monetary equivalents; it involved the difficulty of knowing what the benefits might be even before monetization was ventured.

The SEC thought that it was impossible to know whether disclosure would reduce violence in the DRC, and if so, by how much. The chain of causation was long and complex: (1) consumers would need to read or learn about the disclosures; (2) this information would need to cause them to reduce their purchases from firms that use conflict minerals; (3) the reduction in demand would need to be sufficient to cause firms to switch to suppliers of nonconflict minerals; and (4) the loss in revenue to armed groups in the DRC would need to cause them to lay down their arms and negotiate peacefully. If (4) happened, or something close to it, we would need to know what would happen on the ground. With all that in mind, the SEC concluded that any effort at quantification would be doomed to failure. As a matter of law, it emphasized that Congress had mandated its action and thus, in effect, determined that the benefits were sufficient by enacting the law.

The court upheld the agency's decision.[17] In the court's view, the regulation was not required to pass a cost-benefit analysis because Congress required the agency to act whatever the outcome of that analysis. In any case, the agency did not act arbitrarily in concluding that the moral value of the regulation could not be quantified and put in monetary terms. The court added: "Even if one could estimate how many lives are saved or rapes prevented as a direct result of the final rule, doing so would be pointless because the costs of the rule—measured in dollars—would create an apples-to-bricks comparison."[18]

The court was surely on solid ground when it held that the SEC did not act arbitrarily in concluding that it could not estimate the benefits for people living in the DRC. It is possible, on admittedly speculative assumptions, that the benefits were zero—that the disclosure regime would have no effect on fighting in the DRC, or even a perverse effect by depriving honest mining operations of revenue and thus very poor workers of their wages. It is also possible, also on admittedly speculative assumptions, that the benefits were very high. In the abstract, and even after careful exploration of the evidence, it would be difficult to be confident about the level of benefits.

But there is a separate point. Suppose that many Americans believe that American companies have a moral obligation not to use conflict minerals in their operations. Or suppose that many Americans believe that they have a moral obligation not to use products that contain conflict minerals, and therefore that American companies should disclose to them whether their products contain conflict minerals so that Americans can avoid using those products if they choose to. How should such moral considerations be valued?

The SEC might have made some effort to determine how much Americans are willing to pay in relation to these moral concerns. In the context of this regulation, the question is how much Americans benefit from learning that corporations use conflict minerals or do not use conflict minerals. How much would Americans be willing to pay to receive that information? Survey information could provide a rough answer to this question. The firms themselves may have information as well. There are many ways to gain indirect insights. First, do Americans read or seek access to disclosures of this kind as a general matter? Second, if Americans learn that a company uses conflict minerals, will they stop using its products?

It is reasonable to suspect that firms' opposition to the regulation is based not so much on the compliance costs as the fear that they will lose sales if Americans learn about their use of conflict minerals. If so, the SEC could ask the firms for estimates, grounded in market data, on the likely effect of the regulation on sales.

It is possible, of course, that the monetized moral benefit of the regulation is small. Consider an American, named Joan, who pays $420 for a cell phone because it was not manufactured with conflict minerals rather than $400 for an otherwise identical cell phone that was manufactured without conflict minerals. We infer that Joan is willing to pay at least $20 to avoid using conflict minerals, but it is also the case that Joan is made worse off to the tune of $20 as a result of the price increase. Yet in the case given, the benefit is not zero; Joan is better off on net. She prefers the more expensive cell phone. Other people, like Joan, might believe themselves to be better off if, as a result of the regulation, products with conflict materials are used less often. In principle, surveys can be used to estimate the aggregate welfare benefits of the regulation. People do receive hedonic benefits—a kind of warm glow—from helping others. Those benefits should be counted.

The most important point lies elsewhere. When disclosure is motivated by moral concerns, agencies should do the best they can to determine whether disclosure will, in fact, counteract a moral wrong or produce a moral right—and by how much. There is a risk that morally motivated disclosure requirements will be merely expressive, producing a sense that something has been accomplished without actually helping anyone. It is essential to do whatever can be done to understand the likely consequences.

6 Valuing Facebook

If you want information, you will probably go online to get it. Some of it has instrumental value. If you want to know how to get from one place to another, you might use Google Maps. If you want to know to handle a sprained ankle, you can find a great deal of useful information. Or you might go online to learn what it pleases you to learn, even if you cannot use it. If you enjoy learning about the history of popular music, you can do exactly that.

Much of the available information is abstract, but it is possible to obtain personalized information as well. You can find out your life expectancy, given certain basic facts. You can find out a great deal about your health risks, your economic prospects, even your personality. What is available now is unfathomably more detailed than what was available ten years ago. What will be available ten years from now will be unfathomably more detailed than what is available now.

In this chapter, I am going to cover a lot of territory, and it will be useful to put the main point on the table at the outset. There is evidence that use of Facebook makes people, on average, a bit less happy—more likely to be depressed, more likely to be anxious, less satisfied with their lives. The effect should not be overstated. It isn't large. But it is real. At the same time, people who have ceased using Facebook, and experienced evident increases in well-being, *very much want to continue to use Facebook*. In fact, they would demand a lot of money to give it up. Why is that? We do not know for sure, but a plausible explanation is that the experience of using Facebook, including the information its use provides, is valuable even if it does not make people happier. Ignorance isn't bliss. People know that. They want the relevant information because they like or even cherish a sense of connection with relevant others.

It is important to emphasize that social media do not simply provide information, at least not in the sense that I have been emphasizing here. You might use Facebook to connect with family or friends. You may or may not think that you will learn something that matters to your economic situation or to your health. But social media are, in one or another respect, about the transmission of information, even if the category is understood more broadly than I have been doing thus far. A central question is this: How valuable are they, really?

On social media, much of the relevant information is free, at least in the sense that you can get it without turning over money. You might be paying by providing your attention or your data. Companies such as Facebook and Twitter obtain revenue from advertising. But in light of continuing controversies, there have been serious discussions about changing the business model to one in which users are asked to pay for use of the relevant platforms and the services that they provide.[1] These discussions have been accompanied by more theoretical discussions about the appropriate economic valuation of their platforms. What if people were required to pay to use Facebook? How much would they be willing to spend?

The answers would tell us something important about the value of social media and information in general. Answering those questions might also help answer more fundamental questions about economic valuation; about the potentially expressive quality of some consumption decisions; and about the disparity between traditional economic measures and actual human welfare, emphasized in chapter 2. An answer would bear on policy and regulation as well.

A general issue, of special interest in behavioral economics, is the potential disparity between willingness to pay (WTP) and willingness to accept (WTA). If we are interested in welfare, is the best question how much people would be willing to pay to use (say) Facebook, or instead how much they would demand to stop using it? A great deal of work has explored the *endowment effect*,[2] which suggests that people demand far more to give up certain goods than they would pay to obtain those goods in the first instance. The endowment effect is controversial, at least in the sense that there is a debate about its domain, its sources, and its magnitude.[3] We might wonder whether WTP to use social media is greater than WTA not to use social media and, if so, whether the standard explanations account for any such disparity.

An equally general and even more basic question involves the relationship between WTP or WTA measures and human welfare. We have seen that within economics, it is common to say that people's WTP for goods is the best available measure of the welfare effects of having those goods. Of course, WTP is the standard measure in actual markets. Recall, however, that to produce a WTP figure, people have to solve a prediction problem—that is, they have to predict the effects of the good on their welfare. Solving that problem may seem easy, especially for familiar commodities with which people have experience (shoes, shirts, soap). But for some goods, finding a solution may be especially difficult, as in the case of unfamiliar commodities for which people lack experience. How is it possible for people to generate a monetary measure to capture the likely welfare effects of a good that they have never had?

For many people, Facebook, Twitter, Instagram, and other social media platforms are anything but unfamiliar; people have a great deal of experience with them. But for reasons that we will explore, it is not easy for users of social media to value such platforms in monetary terms. An understanding of WTP in the context of social media tells us something general about the uncertain link between WTP and welfare in the context of information seeking—and should motivate a more direct inquiry into welfare effects. WTP is a mere proxy for those effects, and in some cases, it is not a good one. The task is to figure out exactly why and to design substitutes. My goal here is to make some progress on that task.

A Superendowment Effect

In April 2018, I conducted a pilot experiment to obtain some preliminary answers to valuation questions. Using Amazon Mechanical Turk, I asked 439 demographically diverse Facebook users to say how much use of the platform is worth.[4] More specifically, I asked 215 Facebook users a simple question: "Suppose that you had to pay for the use of Facebook. How much would you be willing to pay, at most, per month?" At the same time, I asked 234 other Facebook users a different question: "Suppose that you are being offered money to stop using Facebook. How much would you have to be paid per month, at a minimum, to make it worth your while to stop using Facebook?"

The first question asks about WTP, whereas the second focuses on WTA. According to standard economic theory, the two questions should produce identical answers. But behavioral economists have shown that in important contexts, they do not.[5] In many experiments, WTA is about twice as much as WTP. This is evidence of the endowment effect, which means that people want to hold onto what they already have, and value what they have far more than what they do not have, even if the two commodities are identical.[6] For example, people would pay less to buy a coffee mug or lottery ticket than they would demand to give up a coffee mug or a lottery ticket that they already own.[7] One question I meant to ask is whether an endowment effect would be observed for use of social media; another question is its magnitude.

For WTP, the median answer was just $1 per month. The average was $7.38. Most strikingly, nearly half of participants (46 percent) said that they would pay $0 for a month of Facebook use. In the context of WTP, valuation of Facebook was extremely low. Many users appear to think that it is worthless!

For WTA, by contrast, the median answer was $59 per month. The average was $74.99.[8] In the context of WTA, Facebook has genuine value, and it is not small. It should be clear that the disparity between WTP and WTA is unusually large. We might describe it as a *superendowment effect*. This is in contrast to the 1:2 ratio often observed in previous studies (and also in contrast of course to the finding of no endowment effect for money tokens, for goods held for resale, and sometimes for goods with well-established economic values).[9]

I followed my first survey with a larger one, involving a nationally representative sample. The survey also divided people into two groups, asking the same two questions. But it focused on a wide assortment of social media platforms, and it included people who do not use those platforms. The results were broadly in line with those in the pilot survey, but with some interesting differences across platforms.

For the entire population, the median WTP for the use of Facebook was $5, with a mean of $16.99. The WTA numbers were much higher: $87.50 and $89.17. The figures were close for Facebook users: a median of $5 and a mean of $17.40 for WTP, and $64.00 and $75.16 for WTA. For people who do not use Facebook, the median WTP number was $4, with a mean of $16.70. The WTA answers were surprisingly high: a median of $98.50 and a mean of $98.90. (The relatively high mean for people who do not use Facebook is a bit of a mystery.)

The patterns were broadly similar for other social media platforms. For simplicity, I will restrict the figures to actual users:

Platform	WTP median	WTP mean	WTA median	WTA mean
Instagram	$5	$21.67	$100	$102.60
LinkedIn	$8	$25.71	$99	$97.80
Pinterest	$5	$20.97	$100	$102.92
Reddit	$10	$27.73	$99	$97.73
Snapchat	$5	$24.92	$100	$106.20
Twitter	$5	$19.94	$100	$104.18
WhatsApp	$10	$34.90	$100	$101.16
YouTube	$5	$17.27	$88	$90.78

For all of the tested media outlets, the patterns are strikingly similar. Most important, WTP is far lower than WTA, sometimes with a ratio (for the medians) of 1:20. I am unaware of any area in which the disparity between WTP and WTA is so high.

The magnitude of the difference raises a puzzle, to which I will turn shortly. By way of comparison, it is useful to consider the environmental setting, in which large disparities have also been observed between WTP and WTA in surveys.[10] One study found that people would demand about five times as much to allow destruction of trees in a park as they would pay to prevent the destruction of those same trees.[11] When hunters were questioned about the potential destruction of a duck habitat, they said that they would be willing to pay an average of $247 to prevent the loss—but would demand no less than $1044 to allow it.[12] In another study, participants required payments to accept degradation of visibility from air pollution ranging from five to more than sixteen times higher than their valuations based on how much they were willing to pay to prevent the same degradation.[13] These disparities are not as high as those observed in the context of social media, but they are also unusually large.

Wasting Time

We will return shortly to the environmental domain. In the social media surveys, the most obvious mystery is the very low median for WTP (with many people saying that they would be willing to pay nothing at all). It is plausible to think that for many digital goods, a similarly low WTP would be observed, at least in surveys. This is a puzzle. From actual behavior, social media seem to have real value for users. Their use, sometimes extending to many hours per week, would seem to be demonstrative of a positive valuation. Is it even plausible to think that for a substantial percentage of them, the value is zero, or close to it?

One possibility is that for such people, social media are a good that they use, but that they also consider, on reflection, to be useless or valueless. Facebook might be a way of spending time, through habit or perhaps even a kind of addiction—but people might nonetheless think that they would be better off, or as well off, doing something else instead. On this account, there are some goods—call them *wasting time goods*—for which there is an interesting but explicable disparity between choices and valuation. People choose to use or consume wasting time goods, but they would not be willing to pay much, if anything, for the right to continue to do so.

In my view, wasting time goods are real, important, and understudied. Social media may well count as such for some users. But I speculate that the low WTP numbers are not adequately or fully explicable in those terms. The reason for the low WTP figures may well be *expressive*. For some people, they are in the nature of protest answers, and to that extent, they are not at all a reliable measure of the welfare benefits of using Facebook, Twitter, or YouTube. In short: having had to pay nothing to use such platforms, people greatly dislike the idea of a monthly fee. When people say that they are willing to pay nothing or only slightly more, they are effectively announcing: "If you are going to start charging me, well, then, forget about it!" The reference point has been zero, and a sudden charge (a price increase, even if it is small) is taken to be unfair, not least because it is a loss from the status quo.[14]

Something similar might be said about those who said that they would pay only a small monthly amount (say, $5). They might well have been registering their displeasure at the idea of suddenly having to buy something that has long been provided gratis. Here, then, is a reason to think that the low median WTP does not offer adequate information about the welfare effects of using social media platforms.

Return to the environmental studies in this light. It would be easy to imagine studies of clean air or clean water that would also generate puzzlingly low willingness-to-pay figures, and for the same reasons: a good once enjoyed for free is now being subject to some kind of charge. Loss aversion undoubtedly plays some kind of role here as well. If people are asked to pay more than the reference point (in this case, zero), they will rebel. They might well think that the change is unfair, and hence the protest answer. If so, there is a fair question whether the response to survey questions would be predictive of actual behavior in real markets. People might say that they would pay nothing or give a very low number in a survey, but once a price actually emerged, they might be willing to pay much more. After a short period, or after the norm changes, they might get over their initial feelings of outrage. Whether and to what extent this is so is of course an empirical question.

But in the environmental studies listed earlier, the real puzzles come from the high WTA numbers. In general, such numbers can be a questionable proxy for welfare effects. One reason is that in the environmental context, a high WTA figure might reflect a kind of *moral outrage* (no less than a zero answer for WTP). For an environmental good (clean air, safe drinking water, an endangered species), the WTA question undoubtedly triggers moral concerns, producing protest answers of their own. Some people might think that it is morally abhorrent to allow members of endangered species to be lost or the air to be made dirtier in return for a specified amount of money. Trading money for some such loss might be seen as a taboo trade-off.

Protest answers can also be found when moral concerns are not present and when people are asked how much they would accept giving up some entitlement that they enjoy, such as a right to vacation time. Some people might well think: "There is no amount of money that can get me to give up my vacation time!"[15] In some settings, people might resent the very idea that "someone" is trying to pay them to stop doing what they are planning to do. Their resentment might well manifest itself in a high WTA figure (including the use of social media).

Here as well, there remains a question whether and to what extent answers in survey questions would map onto actual behavior. It is easy to decline money in a hypothetical survey setting, and much harder to do so when real money is on the line. Nonetheless, it might well be the case that moral concerns, or a sense of entitlement, will be expressed even in market settings.[16]

There is a separate point, and it involves opportunity costs. The WTP question puts opportunity costs on the cognitive table, at least for many people much of the time: when people are asked how much they are willing to pay for some X, they are often going to think about what else they could do with that money. The WTA question is different. When people say that they would demand a very high amount of money to give up some good that they own (coffee mugs, lottery tickets), they might not be focused on the potential uses of that money.[17] For that reason, there is reason to doubt whether a high median, in response to the second question, is sufficiently informative about the welfare effects of using a social media platform.

Welfare

These points suggest severe limitations to both WTP and WTA surveys as measures of the welfare effects of digital goods that have formerly been provided for free. Expressive answers might well be found for WTP questions, and resentment might infect answers to WTA questions.

In real markets, of course, different results might be expected. Some media outlets, such as the *New York Times* and the *Washington Post*, have shifted to require paid subscriptions, rather than providing free content (as they previously did). In surveys, elicited WTP might have been far lower than actual WTP as observed through behavior. For subscribers to formerly free services, initial resentment, resulting in some kind of expressive reaction, might recede in favor of a welfare calculation, in which people decide how much the good is worth to them. As I have noted, it remains to be determined when and by how much WTP or WTA figures, elicited in surveys, would differ from those that are observed in behavior.

In a much more elaborate study, Brynjolfsson et al. tried to value use of Facebook by asking consumers if they would prefer (a) to maintain access to the platform or (b) to give it up for one month in response to a specified payment.[18] With their method—a *discrete choice experiment*—they asked people to choose between two identified options and to specify the one they valued more. It is important to see that a discrete choice experiment ought to avoid some of the distortions of both WTP and WTA.[19] At the same time, it cannot avoid an endowment effect: the relevant questions will be asked to people who either are, or are not, current "owners" of the good at issue.

Brynjolfsson et al. also used a large, nationally representative sample, limited to Facebook users. The median answer was in the vicinity of $40–$50 to give up Facebook for a month (significantly higher than my WTP answers, and significantly lower than my WTA answers). Aware of various technical limitations in their study, Brynjolfsson et al. do not insist on those particular numbers. But they do urge that digital goods, including social media, are producing large, monetizable benefits that are not included in conventional measures of well-being, such as gross domestic product. That conclusion is both important and plausible. Nonetheless, it is important to add two qualifications.

The first, signaled by my own surveys, is that whatever numbers are generated will be an artifact of the particular method that is used. If different methods produce different numbers, then it will be challenging to decide which one is the best measure of economic value. For goods that have been provided for free, WTP numbers might not be reliable because they might well reflect resentment about being asked to pay for such goods. WTA numbers are better, but they have the problems outlined above. If the goal is to capture welfare effects, discrete choice experiments are probably best, but insofar as the relevant questions are posed to current users, they will embody a kind of endowment effect.

The more fundamental point is that we need better measures of the effects of such goods on people's experienced well-being.[20] Brynjolfsson et al. title their impressive paper *Using Massive Online Choice Experiments to Measure Changes in Well-Being*, but well-being is emphatically not what they are measuring. At best, they are measuring *predictions* of well-being.[21]

People might be willing to pay $5 each month for the right to use Facebook, or demand $100 to give up that right. In discrete choice experiments, the median value might turn out to be $50. But what are the effects of Facebook on their actual experience? Are they enjoying life more or less or the same? Those are the more important questions. WTP and WTA numbers and the outcomes of discrete choice experiments are best understood as reflecting people's predictions about effects on well-being, translated into monetary terms. Once more: the actual effects are what matter.[22]

Paying to Be Made Sadder

Another group of economists, led by Hunt Allcott of New York University, tried to explore those actual effects. They found that getting off Facebook appears to increase people's well-being (and significantly decreases political polarization).[23] As we shall see, there is a real puzzle here.

In November 2018, Allcott and his coauthors began by asking 2,884 Facebook users how much money they would demand to deactivate their accounts for a period of four weeks, ending just after the midterm election. To make their experiment manageable, the researchers focused on about 60 percent of users, who said that they would be willing to deactivate their accounts for under $102. The researchers divided those users into two groups. The treatment group was paid to deactivate. The control group was not. Members of both groups were asked a battery of questions, exploring how getting off Facebook affected their lives.

The most striking finding is that even in that short period, those who deactivated their accounts seemed to enjoy their lives more as a result. In response to survey questions, they showed significant decreases in depression and anxiety. They also showed significant improvements in both happiness and life satisfaction. Why is that? One reason may be that deactivating Facebook gave people a nice gift: about 60 minutes per day on average. Those who got off the platform spent that time with friends and family, and also watching television alone. Interestingly, they did not spend more time online (which means that contrary to what you might expect, they did not replace Facebook with other social media platforms, such as Instagram).

Getting off Facebook also led people to pay less attention to politics. Those in the treatment group were less likely to give the right answers to questions about recent news events. They were also less likely to say that they followed political news. Perhaps as a result, deactivating Facebook led to a major decrease in political polarization. On political questions, Democrats and Republicans in the treatment group disagreed less sharply than did those in the control group. (This is not because the groups were different; members of both groups, selected randomly, were equally willing to give up use of Facebook for the right amount of money.) It is reasonable to speculate that while people learn about politics on their Facebook page, what they see is skewed in the direction they prefer—which leads to greater polarization.

At this point, it might be reasonable to think that getting off Facebook really does improve well-being, properly understood. But there is a serious complication. After one month without Facebook, the median amount that users would demand to deactivate their account for another month was still pretty high: $87. The United States has 172 million Facebook users. Assuming that the median user demands $87 to give up use of the platform for a month, a little multiplication suggests that the platform is providing Americans with massive benefits. If each user gets the equivalent of $87 in benefits per month, the total amount is in the hundreds of billions annually.

With that finding in mind, Allcott and his coauthors offer a strong conclusion. Facebook produces "enormous flows of consumer surplus," in the form of those hundreds of billions of dollars in benefits, for which users pay nothing at all (at least not in monetary terms). But that might not be right. Recall that those who deactivated their accounts reported that they were better off along multiple dimensions—happier, more satisfied with their lives, less anxious, less depressed. So here is a real paradox: Facebook users are willing to give up a significant sum of money, each month, to make themselves more miserable!

The Paradox

To resolve the paradox, consider two possibilities. The first is that what matters is people's actual experience. When people say that they would demand $87 to give up use of Facebook for a month, they are making a big mistake. The monetary figure might reflect a simple habit (maybe people are just used to having Facebook in their lives), or a prevailing social norm, or even a kind of addiction. The second possibility is that when people say that they would demand $87, they are not making a mistake at all. They are telling us something important about what they value.

Mistaken Forecasts

Begin with the first possibility. People who use social media platforms might not know that they are being made sad or anxious. They might simply lack that information. They might go online because that is the norm in their social group, or because doing that has become habitual. As with other addictions, the problem might be that the pain of not going online is intense; it is not as if going online is pleasurable. When they break the habit or addiction, they are better off. When they demand $87 to stop using Facebook for another month, they are simply making a mistake.

If that is so, the mystery is why they demand that amount even after they have had a pretty good month without Facebook.

The answer might lie in their failure to solve a prediction problem. Recall that when people buy goods or services, they are usually making forecasts about welfare effects. We have seen that if the good is familiar and if the chooser has experience with it, the prediction problem might not be so serious. But we have also seen that even in such cases, that problem has other dimensions, if it is to be solved properly. *The chooser has to figure out the welfare effects of alternative uses of the money.* That is a complex endeavor.

In a sense, the chooser is in the position of a social(ist) planner, as discussed by Friedrich Hayek: he faces a serious epistemic problem. Suppose that the planner is trying to decide on prices or quantities of goods—shoes, socks, pens, cell phones, cars. As Hayek showed, the problem is that the market, reflecting the judgments and tastes of numerous people, will incorporate an extraordinary amount of dispersed knowledge, inaccessible to the planner who seeks to set prices or to decide quantity. Along one dimension, the case of the individual chooser is analogous. The problem is that at time 1, the chooser may know far too little about the likely experience at times 2, 3, 4, 5, 6, and so forth. The chooser may lack important facts about those items for which he is deciding how much to pay. The chooser may also lack facts about his future self—about exactly what he will be like and will like. The problem is especially acute if people are changed in relevant ways.

As I have emphasized, the epistemic problem is harder for some options than for others. In choosing between vanilla and chocolate ice cream, people know what they like best, and in that sense what will promote their welfare. They also have a rough-and-ready sense of alternative uses of the money; even if they do not, the stakes are not so high. But for many options, people lack experience. What is it like to vacation in Bermuda? To see the

Mona Lisa? To go to the best restaurant in Los Angeles? To live with ringing in the ears or chronic bronchitis? To have heart disease? To lose a child? The prediction problem is formidable. And yet the WTP measure requires people to try to solve it, certainly when they are deciding how much to pay to eliminate risks.

For social media platforms, some of these problems dissipate. Users have relevant experience; the platforms are part of their lives. For that reason, we might trust WTP or WTA measures, if expressive values could be purged, and we might think that discrete choice experiments tell us something important. Even so, welfare is the master value, and monetary amounts, however elicited, are unlikely to tell us everything that we need to know. If people are following a social norm or facing some kind of addiction, there might be a big disconnect between monetary valuations on the one hand and welfare effects on the other. Social media might be making people worse off, even if they are willing to pay for it.

What People Value

The underlying data raise another possibility, and it is equally fundamental. Survey answers about personal well-being—including anxiety and depression—fail to capture everything that people really care about. For example, Allcott and his coauthors show that Facebook users know more about politics. Those who follow politics might become more anxious and depressed—but a lot of people still follow politics. They don't follow politics to be happy. They follow politics because they are curious and because they think that's what good citizens do. Similarly, Facebook users might want to know what their friends are doing and thinking because that's good to know, whether or not that knowledge makes them happier.

There is a large point here. As we have seen, people often want information for reasons that have nothing to do with the hedonic effects. Recall the instrumental value of information—as, for example, when people want health-related information even if it makes them sad, because they might be able to use that information to become healthier. Undoubtedly many people who use social media like doing so for instrumental reasons, even if it makes them anxious or sad. But the motivation is surely broader than that. Many of them think that it is good to know things about family and friends or about the world, even if that information cannot be used in any way. They are undoubtedly thinking about what it means to have a good or full life. Having that kind of information is valuable even if it has no instrumental value and even if its hedonic value is negative.

Answers to hard questions about the welfare effects of social media platforms are starting to emerge.[24] Aside from the Allcott et al. study just described, the results are both complicated and mixed. Use of Facebook and other social media platforms may well have different effects on people with different personality traits and on different demographic groups.[25] It certainly has different effects on qualitatively different *components* of well-being.[26] Moreover, Facebook does not provide a uniform or unitary experience. Different uses of Facebook, and different ways of spending time on the platform, undoubtedly have different effects on users' well-being. We need to know far more about these questions. For current purposes, the most important point is that many users of social media want the relevant information not because of its hedonic effects, but because they can use it and because they like being connected with other people and having a sense of their lives and concerns, for its own sake.

7 Sludge

What information does government want to have? What information does it deserve to get? And what are the limits on its efforts to obtain it? These questions might seem far afield from those raised by mandatory disclosure, but they are close cousins. They too raise the question of how much information is too much information. They too suggest that compulsory disclosure of information can be costly. And in many cases, government is asking for far too much, imposing serious costs in terms of time, frustration, money, humiliation, and sometimes even health.

In the United States, an organizing framework can be found in the Paperwork Reduction Act (PRA), enacted in 1979.[1] The PRA was meant to be a deregulatory statute. It was designed to minimize the paperwork burden imposed on the American people and to maximize the benefit of the information obtained. Its key provision states:

> With respect to the collection of information and the control of paperwork, the Director [of the Office of Management and Budget] shall—
>
> (1) review and approve proposed agency collections of information;
> (2) coordinate the review of the collection of information associated with Federal procurement and acquisition by the Office of

Information and Regulatory Affairs with the Office of Federal
Procurement Policy, with particular emphasis on applying information technology to improve the efficiency and effectiveness
of Federal procurement, acquisition and payment, and to reduce
information collection burdens on the public;

(3) *minimize the Federal information collection burden, with particular
emphasis on those individuals and entities most adversely affected;*

(4) *maximize the practical utility of and public benefit from information
collected by or for the Federal Government;* and

(5) establish and oversee standards and guidelines by which agencies
are to estimate the burden to comply with a proposed collection
of information.[2]

For present purposes, the most important provisions are 3
and 4. The word *minimize* suggests that paperwork burdens
should be no greater than necessary to promote the agency's
goals. The central idea seems to be one of *cost-effectiveness*:
between two approaches to promoting those goals, the least burdensome must be chosen. Taking the word *minimize* together
with the phrase *maximize the practical utility and public benefit*, we can plausibly understand the PRA to suggest a kind of
cost-benefit test as well: *the costs of paperwork burdens must justify
their benefits*. And yet there is no systematic effort, to date, to see
which burdens pass that test. Nor is there an opportunity for
judicial review of arbitrary or capricious collection of information. If an agency is imposing highly burdensome information
collection arbitrarily or without good reason, people cannot get
courts to help them, notwithstanding the general rule in favor of
judicial review for arbitrariness.

All this creates serious problems. Elimination or reduction of
paperwork is not generally understood as an important form of
deregulation. But in view of the toll it takes on human welfare,
paperwork reduction should be considered a priority.

There is an additional point. In recent years, behavioral science has played a significant role in thinking about regulation, leading not merely to academic pleas for behaviorally informed initiatives of various kinds but also to actual initiatives in multiple domains, often producing large benefits at low cost. But if we put a spotlight on paperwork burdens, we will be interested in something different and insufficiently explored: *behaviorally informed deregulation*. To be sure, fully rational people, unaffected by behavioral biases, might be, and are, adversely affected by paperwork burdens. As we shall see, however, behavioral biases of various sorts make such burdens especially harmful and sometimes devastating.

The PRA requires the Office of Management and Budget (OMB) to produce an annual report, called the Information Collection Budget of the United States Government (ICB).[3] The ICB quantifies the annual paperwork burden that the US government imposes on its citizens. The most recent official report finds that in 2015, Americans spent 9.78 billion hours on federal paperwork.[4] In early 2019, an official running count had the number at a whopping 11.3 billion hours.[5] That number is almost certainly more accurate than the 2015 figure, but because it has not been subject to the same level of internal and external scrutiny, I will rely on the 9.78-billion-hour figure here.

It is worth pausing over that figure. Suppose that we assembled every resident of Chicago and insisted that for the entirety of the next year, each one must work forty hours a week engaged in just one task: filling out federal forms. By the end of that year, the 2.7 million citizens of Chicago will not have come within four billion hours of the annual paperwork burden placed on Americans.

The 9.78 billion hours take a significant toll. The Office of Information and Regulatory Affairs (OIRA) has not attempted to monetize those hours, though in 2010 it asked for public comments on whether and how to do so.[6] If we value an hour of work at $20 (a bit lower than the standard government number),[7] then 9.78 billion hours is the equivalent of $195.6 billion—more than double the budget of the Department of State and the Department of Transportation, about triple the budget of the Department of Education, and about eight times the budget of the Department of Energy. The monetary figures greatly understate the problem. Administrative burdens can make it difficult or impossible for people to enjoy fundamental rights (such as the right to vote and the right to free speech), to obtain licenses and permits, to obtain life-changing benefits, and to avoid crushing hardship.[8] With respect to the right to choose abortion, such burdens can be decisive impediments. They can also make it difficult for people to receive the Earned Income Tax Credit, which is one of the nation's most beneficial antipoverty programs. In short, paperwork burdens have massive negative effects on people's lives.

Richard H. Thaler has popularized a helpful term for such burdens: *sludge*.[9] The term should be taken to refer to the kind of friction, large or small, that people face when they want to go in one or another direction.[10] For their own reasons, whether self-interested or altruistic, private and public institutions might impose or increase sludge. In the private sector, companies can use sludge to increase profits. For example, people might want to cancel a subscription to a magazine in which they no longer have the slightest interest, but to do that, they might have to wade through a great deal of sludge.

In the public sector, sludge may be an accident, but it might also be a political choice. People might want to sign their child up for some beneficial program, such as free transportation or free school meals, but the sludge might defeat them. To obtain financial aid for college, students are required to fill out the Free Application for Federal Student Aid (FAFSA).[11] It is long and complicated, and it requires young people to provide information that they might not have (some of it is on their parents' tax returns).[12] Many students give up. The right to vote may be the most fundamental of all, but a sludge-filled registration process disenfranchises many millions of people.[13] A sludge-reduction initiative would be a Voting Rights Act.

A great deal of evidence establishes that reducing administrative burdens can have a large impact on people's lives. Millions of people are now benefiting from the Global Entry program, which reduces time, trouble, and stress in security lines at airports. For free school meals, the US Department of Agriculture has adopted a direct certification program, which means that parents do not have to take the trouble to enroll their children at all.[14] If the school district has enough information to know that they are eligible, they are automatically enrolled. In recent years, more than fifteen million children benefited from the program.

Simplification of FAFSA would dramatically increase the likelihood that low-income people will apply for aid and eventually enroll in college. A number of states have adopted automatic voter registration, which means that if eligible citizens interact with a state agency (say, by receiving a driver's license), they are registered as voters. In less than a year, Oregon's automatic registration program produced more than 250,000 new voters, and almost 100,000 of them actually voted.[15] The private sector can do a great deal more to reduce sludge—to help workers to choose among healthcare plans, to make life easier for consumers and employees with ideas or complaints, and to help people avoid serious risks.

Sludge Hurts

Sludge can make it difficult or impossible for people to enjoy or exercise constitutional rights. For freedom of speech, licensing schemes are the most obvious example; they are a form of sludge and are usually unconstitutional for that reason. In the domain of health care, the sludge imposed on doctors and patients can literally kill.[16] In emergency rooms, for example, sludge has made it unnecessarily difficult for doctors to prescribe medicines that help patients overcome opioid addiction.[17] Efforts to reduce that sludge, through private initiative and through law, can save lives.

To understand why sludge matters, let's begin with the assumption that people are fully rational and that in deciding whether to overcome administrative burdens, they make some calculation about costs and benefits. Even if the benefits are high, the relevant costs might prove overwhelming. These costs can take qualitatively different forms.[18] They might involve acquisition of *information*, which might be difficult and costly. They might involve *time*, which people might not have. They might be *psychological*, in the sense that they involve frustration, stigma, and humiliation. For any of those reasons, it might be very difficult to navigate or overcome the sludge. In some cases, doing the relevant paperwork might be literally impossible; it simply may not be feasible for people to fill out the forms. By themselves, these points help explain low take-up rates for many federal and state programs,[19] as well as the immense difficulty that people often have in obtaining permits or licenses of various sorts. We can even see sludge as an obstacle to freedom, especially insofar as it reduces or impairs navigability.

Everyone Believes in Redemption

An assortment of human biases, emphasized by behavioral economists, amplify the real-world effects of administrative burdens. For many people, inertia is a powerful force,[20] and people tend to procrastinate.[21] If people suffer from inertia and if they procrastinate, they might never do the necessary paperwork. The problem is compounded by present bias.[22] The future often seems like a foreign country—Laterland—and people are not sure that they will ever visit. It is often tempting to put off administrative tasks until another day. That day may never come, even if the consequences of delay are quite serious.

Mail-in forms impose a type of sludge. They provide people with an opportunity to obtain a nontrivial gain, often in the form of a check, but they require people to overcome inertia. As an illustration of the relationship between behavioral biases and sludge, consider a study of people's failure to redeem such forms, with a memorably precise name: *Everyone Believes in Redemption*.[23] Across various markets, redemption rates usually range between 10 percent and 40 percent, which means that a strong majority of customers forget or simply do not bother. Because of the power of inertia, that might not be terribly surprising. What is more striking is the finding that people are unrealistically optimistic about the likelihood that they will ever redeem forms. In the relevant study, people thought that there was about an 80 percent chance that they would do so within the thirty days they were given. The actual redemption rate was 31 percent. It is an overstatement to say that everyone believes in redemption—but most people certainly do.

In the same study, the researchers made three efforts (with different groups of people) to reduce the massive difference between the predicted and actual redemption rates. First, they informed participants, very clearly, that in previous groups with similar people, redemption rates were below one-third. Second, they issued two clear reminders, one soon after purchase and another when the deadline for redemption was near. Third, they made redemption far simpler by eliminating the requirement that people must print out and sign a certification page.

As it turned out, not one of the three interventions reduced people's optimism. In all conditions, people thought there was about an 80 percent chance that they would mail in the forms. Moreover, and somewhat surprisingly, the first two interventions had no effect on what people actually did. When hearing about the behavior of other groups, people apparently thought, "Well, those are *other* groups. What do they have to do with us?" In other contexts, reminders often work because they focus people's attention and reduce the power of inertia. But in this case, reminders turned out to be useless. The only effective intervention was simplification, which had a strong impact on what people actually did. By making it easier to mail in the form and thus reducing sludge, simplification significantly increased people's willingness to act. The redemption rate rose to about 54 percent, which means that the disparity between belief and behavior was cut in half.

Behavioral Biases

The relevant study is of course relatively narrow, but it has large implications. Recall that inertia is a powerful force and that because of inertia, people might not fill out necessary forms or otherwise wade through sludge. That is one reason that participation rates are often much lower with opt-in designs than with opt-out designs.[24] Recall too that inertia is aggravated by present bias, leading people to focus on the short term and neglect the future.

Suppose in this light that under federal regulations, individuals, small businesses, and start-ups must fill out certain forms to be eligible for important benefits or to avoid significant penalties. They might intend to do exactly that, but if the task can be put off, or if it is burdensome or difficult, their behavior might not match their intentions. The actual costs might turn out to be very high; the perceived costs might be far higher. To get slightly ahead of the story: it would make sense for federal regulators to "scrub" existing paperwork burdens to make sure that they are not doing unintended or inadvertent harm. That is the idea of a Sludge Audit.

The right to vote may be the most fundamental of all, and federal law requires states to send mail-in forms ("return cards") before purging voters from electoral rolls on change-of-residence grounds (if a voter has not already confirmed a move).[25] Each state is allowed to choose its own trigger for sending the return card. Some states use change-of-address information provided by the United States Postal Service, but others use methods that can very foreseeably flag voters who have in fact not moved and thus remain eligible.[26] A qualified voter can be struck for failing to mail the return card back and not voting for four years.[27] Voters—along with Congress and the Supreme Court—may be optimistic that they will mail back the return card, but their optimism might be misplaced.

More generally, sludge has a significant impact that many people do not foresee. As the redemption study shows, people are unrealistically optimistic about the likelihood that they will overcome inertia. Even specialists might be surprised at the extent to which apparently promising inertia-reduction strategies fail. In addition, sludge can be used opportunistically by clever marketers who seek to give consumers the impression that they will receive an excellent deal but who know that consumers will not send in a required form. In most cases, government officials do not seek to act opportunistically; they respond to political values and commitments, which is not the same thing. At the same time, sludge might have a damaging effect that they do not anticipate. In particular, officials might not understand the extent to which sludge will adversely affect a population that they are seeking to help.

Cognition and Scarcity

With respect to redemption, the power of simplification puts a spotlight on the large consequences of seemingly modest administrative burdens—on the effects of *choice architecture* in determining outcomes. I have noted that in many domains, participation rates can be dramatically increased with a mere shift from requiring people to apply (opt-in) to automatically enrolling them (opt-out).

An underlying reason for the low take-up rates under opt-in plans is that our cognitive resources are limited.[28] Inevitably, we are able to focus on only a small subset of life's challenges. Each of us has limited mental bandwidth. For those who are busy, poor, disabled, or elderly, the problem of cognitive scarcity is especially serious. If you are busy or poor, you are focused on an assortment of life's challenges. The same is true if you are disabled. If you suffer from a mental disability or if you are elderly, your cognitive limits may be severe. For that reason, it is important to focus on the *distributional* effects of administrative burdens—on whom they are most likely to hurt.[29]

As a practical matter, the answer is often the poorest among us. A central reason is that if you are poor, you have to focus on a wide range of immediately pressing problems. If the government is asking poor people to navigate a complex system or to fill out a lot of forms, they might give up. But the problem is hardly limited to the poor. When programs are designed to benefit the elderly, sludge might be especially damaging, at least if the population suffers from reduced cognitive capacity.

For different reasons, the problem of sex equality deserves particular attention. Because women do a disproportionate amount of administrative work—running the household, arranging meals, taking care of children—a significant reduction in sludge could address a pervasive source of social inequality, with ramifying effects on other areas of life. An important study finds that with a shift from opt-in to opt-out, there is a major increase in the percentage of women who are willing to compete for a promotion. Evidently men are more willing than women to put themselves forward and hence to navigate some sludge. When the sludge is removed, disparities between men and women are essentially eliminated.[30]

Justifying Information Acquisition

Notwithstanding these points, administrative burdens often serve important goals. Sometimes they are indispensable. As the examples suggest, we can readily imagine five possible justifications for sludge: (1) program integrity, (2) acquiring useful data, (3) self-control problems,(4) privacy and security, and (5) targeting.

Program Integrity

When agencies impose paperwork burdens, it is often because of a desire to ensure that programs work in the way that the law requires. One reason involves eligibility restrictions; another involves record-keeping. What is true for the public sector is true for the private sector as well. Those who seek a loan, private or public, face sludge. The central reason is to ensure that they actually qualify. People should not receive Medicare, Medicaid, the EITC, or Social Security unless they are entitled to the relevant benefits, and sludge is often a way of collecting necessary information. Even in the context of voting rights, burdens of various sorts can be and often are justified as a means of ensuring that would-be voters meet existing legal requirements. For spending programs, a usual justification for paperwork burdens points to "fraud, waste, and abuse"; sludge can be an effort to reduce all three.

It is true that with the increasing availability of information and with machine learning, private and public institutions might be able to find the relevant information on their own. In the private sector, some companies use the idea of *prequalification*, which means that they have enough information to know, in advance, that some people are already qualified for goods or services. Sometimes forms can be *prepopulated*; as a result, form-filling might be reduced or unnecessary. In the domain of taxation, one example is the idea of return-free filing, which eliminates the need for taxpayers to fill out forms at all.[31] In the fullness of time, we should see significant movements in this direction.

But those movements remain incipient. For the present and the near future, the most obvious justifications for sludge go by the name of *program integrity*. Suppose that the Internal Revenue

Service decided to send the EITC to apparently eligible taxpayers. If it could do so at low cost and if the apparently eligible taxpayers are in fact eligible, there would be little ground for objection. The problem, of course, is the word *apparently*. It is possible that some of the recipients will not in fact be eligible. Whenever people are automatically enrolled in a program, some of them may not meet the legal criteria.

When this is so, regulators must choose between (1) a design ensuring that some eligible people will not receive a benefit and (2) a design ensuring that some ineligible people will receive a benefit. If the idea of program integrity is meant to refer to the number of errors, the choice between designs 1 and 2 might turn purely on arithmetic. Which group is larger? If automatic enrollment means that 500,000 eligible people receive the benefit who otherwise would not, and if a degree of sludge means that 499,999 ineligible people receive the benefit who otherwise would not, automatic enrollment might seem to be justified.

But it would be possible to see things differently. Suppose that automatic enrollment gives benefits to 200,000 eligible people but also to 200,001 ineligible people. Some people might think that if the 200,001 people are nearly eligible—if they are relatively poor—it is not so terrible if they receive some economic help. But other people might emphasize that taxpayer money is accompanied by clear restrictions and insist that if it is given out in violation of those restrictions, a grave wrong has been committed. On this view, even a modest breach of program integrity, operating to the advantage of those who are not legally eligible, is unacceptable.

The most extreme version of this view would be that a grant of benefits to a very large number of eligibles would not outweigh the grant of benefits to a very small number of ineligibles.

From a welfarist standpoint, the most extreme version is hard or perhaps impossible to defend: a grant of benefits to five people who are almost (but not) eligible would seem to be a price worth paying in exchange for a grant of benefits to a million people who are in fact eligible. But the correct trade-off is not self-evident, and reasonable people might differ.

We can generalize this example. In the direct certification program for school lunches, the level of accuracy appears to be very high; as far as the public record shows, few if any ineligible children are allowed to qualify. When sludge is eliminated through automaticity, any objections are weakened so long as benefits are not conferred on the ineligible. To the extent that they are, trade-offs are inevitable, and different people can make different judgments. Consider the question of voter registration. Sludge has been defended as a way of combating the risk of fraud and thus ensuring the integrity of the voting process. On imaginable assumptions, sludge reduction could ensure that many eligible people are allowed to vote while also allowing some ineligible voters to end up voting. The size of the two categories surely matters.

Acquiring Useful Data

Public officials might impose administrative burdens, including reporting requirements, to acquire data that can be used for multiple purposes, and that might benefit the public a great deal. For example, officials might want to know whether people who receive employment training or funding to help them during a pandemic are actually benefiting from the relevant program. What do they do with that training or that funding? Administrative burdens might be essential to obtain answers to that question. Or suppose that the government is trying to reduce the spread of an infectious disease, to promote highway development, to monitor hazardous waste management, to ensure that pilots are properly certified and that airplanes are properly maintained, or to see how food safety programs are working. Those who receive information-collection requests might complain of sludge. They might be agitated or worse. But the relevant burdens might be justified as a means of ensuring acquisition of important or even indispensable knowledge.

In some of these cases, of course, such burdens might be an effort to ensure program integrity. But I am emphasizing a different point. Even if program integrity were already guaranteed, officials might seek information and require people to provide it in order to provide both short-term and long-term benefits. For example, the government wants to know whether subsidies are being used as intended, and to that end it might ask those who receive subsidies to provide regular reports. The government might ask educational institutions to give detailed accounts of what those institutions have done with money received. Importantly, that information might be made public and used by private and public sectors alike. In the modern era, acquisition of information might promote public and private accountability. It might save money. It might spur innovation. It might even save lives—as, for example, when government requires public reporting on occupational deaths or illnesses and injuries in an effort to incentivize safer workplaces and also to learn where people are getting hurt, with a view toward prevention.

These are important justifications for sludge, and they are easy to overlook. But they should not be taken as a kind of blank check or an open invitation for officials to impose a lot of sludge. For any particular burden, a central question is whether the government is *actually acquiring useful information*. If public officials are asking people to file with paper rather than electronically, refusing to reuse information that they already have, declining to prepopulate forms, or requiring quarterly rather than annual reporting, they should offer a strong justification. In all these cases, they may run into difficulty in meeting that burden.

In the abstract, it is not possible to say whether sludge can be justified as a means of generating useful or important information. Some cases will be easy; any such justification will not be credible. Other cases will also be easy; any such justification is self-evidently convincing. Still other cases will be hard; without investigating the details with care, we cannot know whether such a justification is sufficient. The only point is that the benefit of sludge might be found there.

Self-Control Problems

Administrative burdens of diverse kinds might be designed to promote better decisions—to counteract self-control problems, recklessness, and impulsivity. Sludge can be a way of protecting people against their own errors. For that reason, it can be seen as the right cure for a behavioral problem. For mundane decisions, small administrative burdens are frequently imposed online, with questions asking whether you are "sure you want to" send an email without a subject line, activate a ticket, cancel a recent order, or delete a file. Those burdens can be an excellent idea.

A degree of sludge, imposed by private and public institutions, might make sense for life-altering decisions, such as marriage and divorce.[32] "Cooling-off periods" can be a blessing.[33] If System 1 is leading people to make rash decisions, a mandatory waiting time might be useful as a way of allowing System 2 to have its say.[34] Some sludge might also make sense before the purchase of guns, partly as a way of promoting deliberation.

An important study finds that laws that mandate short waiting periods before the purchase of guns reduce gun homicides by about 17 percent—meaning that in seventeen states, about 750 such homicides were prevented.[35] Impulsive gun purchases can apparently lead to tragedy, and a little sludge, calling for cooler emotions, saves lives.

The abortion right is highly controversial, of course, but for that very reason, it is an especially interesting example. For instance, some people think that counseling requirements and mandatory twenty-four-hour waiting periods are legitimate ways of protecting fetal life, or of protecting women from making decisions that they will regret. Other people think that the burdens are simply an effort to discourage the exercise of a constitutional right. Even if we bracket the deepest issues, it is hardly impossible, in light of the stakes of the decision, to defend some administrative burdens as efforts to promote reflection and to provide valuable information.

Privacy and Security

Administrative burdens are often imposed in order to obtain information about people's backgrounds—their employment history, their income, their criminal history (if any), their credit rating, their family history, their expertise, their interests, their places of residence. Those who seek to work in government, certainly at levels that involve national security, are required to provide a great deal of information of that sort.[36] It is reasonable to think that if private and public institutions are to receive some or all of that information, it must be with people's explicit consent. If so, the question is whether to ask people to face administrative burdens or instead to intrude on their privacy. Perhaps it is not so terrible if the government chooses the former.

At one time, of course, officials had no real option. They could not intrude on privacy because they lacked the means to do so. Increasingly, however, private and public institutions actually have independent access to that information, or they might be able to obtain it with a little effort. As a result, they are in a position to reduce sludge. Return, as a simple example, to the direct certification program of the US Department of Agriculture. In countless other cases, available data can enable private or public institutions to announce, very simply, that certain people are eligible and on what terms. They might be able to prepopulate forms. They might be able to share data.[37] To that extent, sludge can be a thing of the past.

But would that be desirable? Not necessarily. Automatic enrollment might well depend on a great deal of information gathering by institutions that people distrust. In some cases, there is a trade-off between irritating burdens on the one hand and potential invasions of privacy on the other. Consider, for example, the question of how much information credit card companies should acquire before offering cards to customers. We might welcome situations in which such companies can learn what is required and simply send people offers or even cards. Whether we should do so depends in part on what information they have and whether it might be misused—as, for example, when it is transferred to companies that can use it for their own purposes, which may be self-interested or even nefarious. If the government has or acquires the relevant information, the risks of misuse might be thought unacceptable.

The question of security is closely related. To set up an online account, people might be asked to provide, and might be willing to provide, sensitive information—involving, for example, a bank account or a credit card. Sludge might be designed to ensure against security violations. People might have to answer questions about their address, their Social Security number, or their mother's maiden name. These questions are not exactly fun, but they might be justified as a means of ensuring against some kind of breach. Ideally, of course, we would have some clarity about the benefits and costs of obtaining the relevant information. But if costs and benefits are difficult to specify, it might make sense to have a rough-and-ready sense that a little sludge is desirable to prevent the worst-case scenarios.

Targeting

A growing literature on "hassles" and "ordeals" explores how administrative burdens might operate as a good rationing device, ensuring that certain goods go to those who most want or need them.[38] When a movie or a concert is immensely popular, people might have to stay on the telephone or wait in line for a ridiculously long time to buy tickets. If that can be justified, it is because an investment of time, like an expenditure of money, helps measure how intensely people want things. In the same vein, onerous administrative burdens might be a reasonable way of screening applicants for job training or other programs. If people are really willing to run the gauntlet, we might have good reason to think that they will benefit from those programs.

The basic idea here is that it is important to screen those who seek access to scarce resources. In markets, the willingness-to-pay criterion provides the standard screen. We have seen that willingness to pay money is one way to measure need or desire; willingness to pay in terms of time and effort (WTPT, for short) is another. It is possible to argue that the willingness-to-pay criterion discriminates against people without much money, because willingness to pay is dependent on ability to pay. WTPT does not have that defect. There may or may not be a correlation between lacking money and lacking time. Some rich people are wildly busy, while others have plenty of time on their hands. If you are poor, you might be very busy and hence have little time—or you might not be busy at all and hence have plenty of time. It is far too crude to say that WTP discriminates against poor people, whereas WTPT does not. If anything, WTPT discriminates against people without much time.

However that may be, government might choose to use WTPT as a way of *targeting*—as a way of ensuring that goods are allocated to people who really need and want them. Note also that if people are willing to pay others to do a relevant task, such as tax preparation, the difference between WTP and WTPT might be erased.

The problem is that sludge is often a singularly crude method of targeting. A complex, barely comprehensible form for receiving federal aid is not exactly a reliable way to ensure that people who need financial help actually get that help. If the goal is to ensure that people who are eligible for the EITC are able to receive it, a degree of sludge is not the best sorting mechanism. Ordeals have their purposes, and sludge can be an ordeal. But it is an unreliable mechanism for targeting. Actually, it is worse than that. In some cases, ordeals work in concert with the limitations faced by poor people so as specifically to select out those with the very highest need. From the standpoint of targeting, it is actually perverse, which highlights a central point here: *paperwork burdens should be assessed for their distributive effects.* If they have especially adverse consequences for the most disadvantaged members of society, there is a serious problem.

Sludge Reduction

Return to the number with which I began: 9.78 billion. Insofar as we are speaking of federal paperwork programs, that number deserves serious attention. It is also important to see that there are significant disparities across agencies, and these give a fuller picture than the aggregate number, as highlighted in table 7.1.[39]

These numbers provide real help in showing where the problem of sludge is most serious and where the greatest opportunities for sludge reduction can be found. The Department of the Treasury, and the IRS in particular, win Olympic gold for sludge production. The Department of Education is lowest on the list, but ninety million hours of annual paperwork burdens impose serious costs on universities, high schools, and students. From the raw numbers, of course, we cannot know how much of this

Table 7.1

FY 2015 paperwork burden hours by agency (in millions of hours)

Agency	Burden hours
Department of the Treasury/Internal Revenue Service (IRS)	7,357.22
Department of Health and Human Services (HHS)	695.88
Securities and Exchange Commission (SEC)	224.89
Department of Transportation (DOT)	214.21
Department of Homeland Security (DHS)	203.39
Environmental Protection Agency (EPA)	156.89
Department of Labor (DOL)	144.71
Federal Trade Commission (FTC)	135.37
Department of Agriculture (USDA)	127.55
Department of Education	90.84

burden is necessary. Perhaps the Department of Agriculture can and should reduce sludge by 20 percent; perhaps the Department of Health and Human Services can and should reduce sludge by 10 percent. What can be done to know, or to help?

That is an important question, and it can appeal to people who disagree on many political issues. Divisions with respect to climate change, tax rates for the wealthy, and immigration may come up, but they are generally irrelevant to the question of whether to reduce sludge. To be sure, we have seen that on some issues, such as abortion, sludge is introduced for reasons that involve basic values, and in such cases, ideological divisions break out. But a great deal can be done to reduce sludge without getting close to such divisions.

The Office of Information and Regulatory Affairs

The Office of Information and Regulatory Affairs, entrusted with overseeing the PRA, has significant room to maneuver. I served as administrator of that office during the Obama administration, and I learned that it can do a great deal to reduce sludge, if it has the will.

In any particular period, OIRA can work hard to cut paperwork burdens. It can be tough. It can signal to federal agencies that it will give careful scrutiny to their information-collection requests, or not. Because it assesses such requests on an individual basis, it can work in an ad hoc manner to reduce the volume of paperwork burdens added each year, or not.[40] Alternatively, OIRA can work more systematically. Periodically, OIRA can direct agencies to undertake sludge-reduction efforts.[41] It does so through something called a *data call*, by which it asks for information about information gathering and also imposes requirements.

It can issue binding guidance documents, which can include ambitious targets for burden reduction.[42] It can work with other White House offices, and the president personally, to produce presidential memoranda or executive orders. If the president tells agencies to reduce sludge, there will be a lot less sludge.

In fact, OIRA has done all of these things. When I was the administrator of OIRA in 2012, for example, we directed agencies to do a great deal to reduce paperwork burdens.[43] Among other things, we called for "significant quantified reductions" in burdens, with relatively aggressive requirements:

> Agencies that now impose high paperwork burdens [defined to include the Department of Treasury, the Department of Health and Human Services, the Securities and Exchange Commission, the Department of Transportation, the Environmental Protection Agency, the Department of Homeland Security, the Department of Labor, and the Department of Agriculture] should attempt to identify at least one initiative, or combination of initiatives, that would eliminate two million hours or more in annual burden. All agencies should attempt to identify at least one initiative, or combination of initiatives, that would eliminate at least 50,000 hours in annual burden.[44]

For the executive branch, the choice among the various procedural vehicles greatly matters. A presidential directive is the strongest possible statement. If a document comes from the president of the United States, agencies know that it must be taken seriously. In contrast, a data call is the weakest.

To illustrate the point, I will violate my ordinary rule against disclosing conversations with the president of the United States. In a meeting during President Barack Obama's first term, we discussed various options for directing agencies to follow certain principles and requirements, some of them deregulatory. The president decided in favor of a new executive order, which

became Executive Order 13563. I had floated various supplements and alternatives, including a data call that I would issue.
At the end of the meeting, I asked the president what, if anything, to do with the data call. The president responded, with
some combination of pity, mischief, and incredulity, "Cass, the
American people don't really care that much about your darned
data call." (He might have used a word other than *darned*.)

There are also important questions in terms of the *content* of
any sludge-reduction directions. A data call could take the form
of an open-ended standard: "take paperwork burdens seriously"
or "reduce them to the extent feasible." As in the document
quoted previously, it could specify concrete numbers: "eliminate
fifty million burden-hours per year" or "cut the existing burden
by ten percent."[45] A data call could specify, and has in the past
specified,[46] ways to reduce burdens: (1) use short-form options,
(2) allow electronic communication, (3) promote prepopulation,
(4) make less frequent information collections, or (5) reuse information that the government already has.[47] These are standard
formulations, and they can be enforced with different degrees
of energy. It is also worthwhile to consider novel formulations,
which could be far more aggressive.

If we keep the 9.78-billion-hour figure in mind, we might be
able to agree that OIRA should undertake an unprecedently bold
effort to reduce paperwork burdens, with an emphasis on both
the flow of new burdens and the existing stock. For purposes of
illustration: with a presidential directive (preferably) or a directive from OIRA itself (also good), it could announce an initiative
that would require the following in the next six months:

• Identification of at least three steps to cut existing burdens
  through the methods of burden reduction enumerated earlier.

- A reduction of existing burdens by least one hundred thousand hours by all agencies that impose significant burdens (by some standardized definition) and a reduction of at least three million hours by the agencies that currently impose the greatest burdens.
- A focus on reducing burdens imposed on vulnerable subpopulations, including the elderly, the disabled, and the poor.
- A focus on reducing burdens in cases in which those burdens compromise specified policy priorities of special interest to the current administration. (These could of course differ across administrations and within administrations over time.)

An initiative of this kind could be specified in many different ways. Interactions between OIRA and relevant agencies would undoubtedly produce fresh ideas. With respect to policy priorities, different administrations would make different choices. Some administrations might want to reduce information-collection burdens under the Affordable Care Act; others might emphasize sludge imposed on small businesses and start-ups; others might emphasize burdens imposed on the transportation sector or on educational institutions; others might do all of these. Importantly, many administrative burdens are imposed by state and local governments. Although OIRA has no direct authority over them, it might use its convening power to remove sludge, especially where federal, state, and local governments must coordinate.

Courts

There is a lurking question in the background. If the federal government imposes a paperwork burden in violation of the PRA, is there a legal remedy? Suppose, for example, that the Department of Health and Human Services requires hospitals to fill out a host of confusing or difficult forms. Suppose, too, that the burden is plainly inconsistent with the PRA, in the sense that it has not been minimized and has little practical utility. Can hospitals invoke the PRA and seek invalidation of the requirement?

The answer appears to be negative. The general rule is that so long as OIRA has approved an information-collection request, people have to comply with it.[48] As the Court of Claims put it, the PRA creates only "the right of a private citizen not to expend time, effort or financial resources to respond to an information collection request *that has not been approved by OMB*."[49] This holding, followed by many courts,[50] is supported by the relevant provision of the PRA, which says:

(a) Notwithstanding any other provision of law, no person shall be subject to any penalty for failing to comply with a collection of information that is subject to this subchapter if—

    (1) the collection of information *does not display a valid control number assigned by the Director in accordance with this subchapter*; or

    (2) the agency fails to inform the person who is to respond to the collection of information that such person is not required to respond to the collection of information *unless it displays a valid control number*.

(b) The protection provided by this section may be raised in the form of a complete defense, bar, or otherwise at any time during the agency administrative process or judicial action applicable thereto.[51]

The clear language suggests that the PRA requires only that an information collection have and display a control number, which shows that it has been approved by OIRA. There is a good argument that the PRA should be amended to allow private persons to object more broadly, perhaps on the ground that OIRA approval was arbitrary or capricious, given the text of the PRA, at least in cases in which the information collection is mandatory and in which it exceeds a certain threshold. The Administrative Procedure Act generally allows judicial review of arbitrary or capricious decisions by public officials.[52] That standard should be applied to information collections as well, given their serious cost and intrusiveness.

Congress

Should the PRA be amended in other ways? Absolutely. In particular, three reforms would do a great deal to improve the current situation.

First, Congress should require a periodic "look back" at existing paperwork burdens to see if the current stock of requirements can be justified and to eliminate those that seem outmoded, pointless, or too costly. This reform would build on existing look-back requirements for regulation in general.[53] With respect to paperwork burdens, the look back could occur every two years, alongside a requirement of a publicly available report to Congress. Second, Congress should explicitly require agencies to choose the least burdensome method for achieving their goals. This is essentially a requirement of cost-effectiveness. If, for example, annual reporting would be as effective as quarterly reporting, then agencies should choose annual reporting. As we have seen, current law can be understood to require cost-effectiveness, but an explicit legislative signal would do considerable good. Third, Congress should explicitly require the benefits of paperwork to justify the costs. As we have seen, cost-benefit balancing can also be seen as required by the PRA in its current form. But the statute is hardly clear on that point and, again, Congress should give an explicit signal to this effect.

With respect to paperwork, as with regulation in general, it is important to appreciate the difference between cost-effectiveness and cost-benefit analysis. The former requires the least costly way of achieving a specified goal. For that reason, cost-effectiveness is a modest idea, and it should not be contentious. A burden might be cost-effective but nonetheless fail cost-benefit analysis—and therefore be a bad idea. Even if a burden is cost-effective, it should also be assessed in cost-benefit terms to ensure that it is worthwhile on balance.

It is true and important that cost-benefit balancing is not always simple for paperwork burdens. When agencies engage in such balancing, the general goal is to compare the social benefits and the social costs, understood in economic terms. A paperwork burden may or may not generate *social* benefits, understood in those terms. When the IRS imposes paperwork burdens on taxpayers, it might be trying to ensure that they do what the law requires. We can speak of economic costs (in terms, perhaps, of monetized hours) and of economic benefits (in terms, perhaps, of dollars gained by the Treasury). But that is not standard cost-benefit analysis. Or paperwork might be designed to ensure that people applying for benefits actually deserve those benefits, as, for example, when the effort is to avoid giving transfers to people who are not entitled to them.

In such cases, a crude approach would be to understand the cost-benefit justification not as an effort to compare social costs and social benefits, understood in economic terms, but instead as entailing an assessment of *proportionality*. Are significant costs likely to serve significant purposes? What is the magnitude of the costs, and what is the magnitude of the gains? Real numbers would help inform decisions and combat sludge.

It is worth emphasizing the fact that even a crude form of cost-benefit analysis would be *information forcing*. It would create a stronger incentive for agencies to offer accurate accounts of the number of burden hours and also to turn them into monetary equivalents. It would simultaneously create an incentive for agencies to be more specific, and more quantitative, about the expected benefits of information collections. What does the government actually want to know? What does it need to know? Why?

We need far more information on the question whether collection of information really is beneficial and worth the trouble; in that regard, a requirement of cost-benefit balancing should help. It should also help spur improved and perhaps creative ways to test whether the benefits of information collections justify the costs.

Sludge Audits

Many institutions should be conducting regular Sludge Audits. Governments should certainly be doing so. The same is true of a wide assortment of private institutions. Banks, insurance companies, hospitals, universities, and publishers could save a great deal of money by reducing sludge, and they could greatly improve the experience of people who interact with them. They might even be able to change people's lives. It is worth underscoring the case of hospitals, where sludge can not only create immense frustration but also impair health and even cost lives.

I have noted that Sludge Audits can take both formal and informal forms. They might involve a great deal of quantification, or they might be more qualitative. In the easiest cases, Sludge Audits would immediately show institutions, both public and private, that the existing level of sludge is not in their interest. With respect to the public sector: If it turns out to be difficult for children to have access to free school meals because the sludge is excessive, officials might take steps to reduce it. If it turns out to be hard for students to obtain financial aid because the forms have more than one hundred questions, an understanding of that fact might produce serious sludge-reduction efforts. If it turns out that needy families have a hard time receiving food to which they have a legal right, sludge reduction, perhaps through the use of online services, might seem quite appealing.

With respect to the private sector: If it turns out to be difficult for consumers to do what must be done to buy a product—say, an automobile—a company might simplify the experience. Doing so might attract more customers and produce a wide range of reputational benefits. It is not exactly news that consumers will have a far worse experience with a company if it is difficult to obtain a response to their complaints. Many companies have innovated creatively in an effort to reduce such problems. We could easily imagine a kind of competition to be a sludge-free government or company with respect to everything that matters to citizens or consumers. The same could be true for employees, investors, and students.

At the opposite pole, public or private institutions might know, or learn, that sludge is in their interest, and a Sludge Audit would not create an incentive to reduce it. If sludge discourages immigration, some officials would be pleased to impose sludge, and perhaps to increase it. If sludge reduces entry into certain professions, officials, attuned to the interests of existing entrants, might not be displeased. It might well be good business to make it very easy to start a subscription—and sludgy to stop. Careful testing might show that such a strategy is optimal. A complaint process that involves a degree of sludge might not merely filter out unjustified complaints; it might also save money when complaints are justified. Under imaginable circumstances, sludge is in the competitive interest of firms. If so, the question remains: Is this a kind of behavioral market failure for which a regulatory response is appropriate? The answer will often be "yes."

The largest point is that for public institutions, a Sludge Audit will often reveal that there are significant opportunities for improving performance. It should not be difficult for governments all over the world to produce an information collection budget, cataloging paperwork burdens. To be sure, some of those burdens are undoubtedly justified. In addition, the worst forms of sludge might not be paperwork at all (consider time waiting in line). But for governments, an information collection budget is an important start, not least because it is likely to spur sludge-reduction efforts. Private institutions should be producing similar documents, if only for internal use—and public transparency might well be a good idea.

Less Is More

The idea of deregulation is usually understood as the removal of formal regulations—those governing the environment, food safety, and motor vehicles, for example. But administrative burdens are regulatory in their own way, and they impose a kind of tax. If they require nearly ten billion hours of paperwork annually, they are imposing, at a minimum, a cost equivalent to about $200 billion. For both rational actors and those who display behavioral biases (such as inertia and present bias), administrative burdens can impose excessive costs, frustrate enjoyment of rights, and prevent access to important benefits of multiple sorts. The $200 billion figure greatly understates the actual impact, economic and psychological. Sludge infringes on the most fundamental rights; it can also cost lives.

In these circumstances, there is a strong argument for a behaviorally informed deregulatory effort, aimed at paperwork burdens. Such an effort would call for reductions at the level of program design, including radical simplification of existing requirements and (even better) use of default options to cut learning and compliance costs. Automatic enrollment can drive administrative burdens down to zero and have very large effects for that reason. Where automatic enrollment is not possible, officials might use an assortment of tools: frequent reminders; simplification and plain language; online, telephone, or in-person help; and welcoming messages to reduce psychological costs.

What is necessary is a heavily empirical approach to administrative burdens, including an effort to weigh their benefits against their costs and a careful assessment of their distributional effects. Are they really helping to reduce fraud? By how much? What are the take-up rates, and how do they vary across populations, including the most vulnerable? What are the compliance costs, in terms of time and money?

To be sure, the answers to these questions will not always be self-evident. If sludge discourages exercise of the abortion right, people will disagree about whether that is a benefit or a cost. To know whether sludge causes losses or gains, we will sometimes run into intense disagreements about values. But in many cases, such disagreements are uninteresting and irrelevant, and acquisition of the relevant information will demonstrate that sludge is not worth the candle. In the future, it should be a high priority for deregulation and deregulators.

Time is the most precious commodity that human beings have. Public officials should find ways to give them more of it.

Epilogue

Here is one of humanity's best-known tales about the value of information:

> Now the serpent was more subtil than any beast of the field which the Lord God had made. And he said unto the woman, Yea, hath God said, Ye shall not eat of every tree of the garden?
>
> And the woman said unto the serpent, We may eat of the fruit of the trees of the garden:
>
> But of the fruit of the tree which is in the midst of the garden, God hath said, Ye shall not eat of it, neither shall ye touch it, lest ye die.
>
> And the serpent said unto the woman, Ye shall not surely die:
>
> For God doth know that in the day ye eat thereof, then your eyes shall be opened, and ye shall be as gods, knowing good and evil.
>
> And when the woman saw that the tree was good for food, and that it was pleasant to the eyes, and a tree to be desired to make *one* wise, she took of the fruit thereof, and did eat, and gave also unto her husband with her; and he did eat.
>
> And the eyes of them both were opened, and they knew that they were naked; and they sewed fig leaves together, and made themselves aprons.[1]

After Adam and Eve ate the apple, their eyes were indeed opened. The serpent told the truth on that point. And once their eyes were opened, they felt shame ("they knew that they were naked"). They knew good and evil, and so the serpent told the truth on that point as well. Also from Genesis: "And the LORD God said, Behold, the man is become as one of us, to know good and evil." When they were expelled from the Garden of Eden, Adam and Eve lost everything. But they did gain something whose importance Genesis clearly signifies: knowledge.

Was the serpent God's agent? Was he an instrument of God's will? Did God wish human beings to know? The standard reading answers "no" to all three questions. On the evidence of the text, the standard reading is right. But it's not self-evidently right. The power of the tale of Adam and Eve lies in the inevitable question that the text tempts every reader to ask: Mightn't Adam and Eve have been better off—freer and more truly human—after they ate the apple?

My topic here has been knowledge of facts, not of morality. But in some cases, those who obtain information are cursed. In the most obvious cases, information gives rise to agitation, terror, shame, and even despair. The decision whether to obtain information is a gamble: Should you turn over that particular card? Many gambles are lost. In other cases, information is useless or affirmatively harmful. You might not be able to perform well if you know, in advance, whether other people think that you will perform well or whether you are as well-prepared as you think. (Would you really like to know what all of your friends think about you? In my own surveys, most people say no.)

I have emphasized the instrumental value of information, which can lengthen and even save lives, and also its hedonic value. Much of life's news is good; receiving it is fun or joyful, or a big relief. Even when it is not exactly fun, people like getting it. And if they aren't glad that they got it today, they might be glad tomorrow, and exceedingly glad the day after. I have tried to place a bright spotlight on the immense importance of people's emotional reactions to information and to the prospect of having their questions answered. If we want to know whether and when people want to know, we have to focus on how people think that they will *feel* if they end up knowing. And if we want to know whether people *should* want to know, we will give a lot of attention to those feelings. Ignoring them can be obtuse, or even a kind of cruelty.

Of course, there is a great deal more to say and to learn about when people want to seek or avoid information and whether they are mistaken to seek or avoid it. But the essentials of the story are, I think, captured in these remarks. In any case, they provide a foundation for thinking about some insistent questions of public policy, which are likely to help define the coming decades. In countless areas, disclosure is the recommended approach whenever people are running risks. And whenever behavior raises serious moral questions, it is tempting to insist: consumers have a right to know.

If the argument here is correct, the language of *right to know* is usually unhelpful; the real question is whether information will make people better off, all things considered. To answer that question, we need to get traction on how information will benefit people and how it will hurt them. We also need to know something about distributive effects—about who is being helped and who is being hurt. In some cases, information can help people at the bottom of the social ladder. In some cases, information can save lives. In other cases, there is a serious risk of false inferences. Current evidence suggests, for example, that calorie labels are probably a good idea and that GMO labels are almost certainly a bad idea. The particular conclusions are less important than the insistence on exploring the actual consequences of mandatory disclosure.

An intriguing lesson emerges from the Facebook data: people would demand a significant amount of money to give up use of a platform that seems to make them a bit less happy. We don't know exactly why that is so, but it is plausible to speculate that the information they receive—about friends, about family, about politics—is important to them, whether or not it makes them happy. There is a large clue here to the complexity of the idea of human welfare and the inadequacy of understanding it simply in terms of happiness. John Stuart Mill's objection to Bentham's version of utilitarianism is relevant here. In Mill's words, Bentham

> but faintly recognizes, as a fact in human nature, the pursuit of any other ideal end for its own sake. The sense of honour, and personal dignity,—that feeling of personal exaltation and degradation which acts independently of other people's opinion, or even in defiance of it; the love of beauty, the passion of the artist; the love of order, of congruity, of consistency in all things, and conformity to their end; the love of power, not in the limited form of power over other human beings, but abstract power, the power of making our volitions effectual; the love of action, the thirst for movement and activity, a principle scarcely of less influence in human life than its opposite, the love of ease. . . . Man, that most complex being, is a very simple one in his eyes.[2]

These words help explain the multiple reasons that people might seek information, and the difficulty of speaking of those reasons in narrowly hedonic terms.

The government is not a person, but it does want information—a lot of it. As for people, so for government: the question is the consequences of obtaining information. Sometimes the benefits are high and the costs are low. The government can use information to improve people's lives and to ensure that programs operate as they should. But sometimes information acquisition involves a lot of sludge. One thing is clear: 9.78 billion hours of paperwork, every year, is far too many. All over the world, governments (and private institutions as well) should be doing Sludge Audits.

Possession, A. S. Byatt's masterpiece, can be seen as an extended variation on the tale of the Garden of Eden. It is intensely focused on the acquisition of knowledge. It is subtle and ambivalent on the subject, seeing knowledge as both blessing and curse. In a defining passage, Randolph Ash writes these words to Christabel LaMotte, his lover and soulmate: "We must come to grief and regret anyway—and I for one would rather regret the reality than its phantasm, knowledge than hope, the deed than the hesitation, true life and not mere sickly potentialities."[3] There is joy and life, not fatalism or despair, in these words. Ash is making a decisive argument in favor of seeking knowledge, even when the consequence is a kind of fall.

In ordinary life, Ash's argument is generally convincing (certainly with respect to matters of the heart). For governments and regulators, things are much more complicated. The coming decades will provide unprecedented opportunities for them to require disclosure of information, with the salutary goal of helping consumers, employees, investors, and ordinary citizens going about their lives. Often that will be a terrific idea. But in some contexts, less is more, and more is less. The challenge is to increase the likelihood that information will actually make people's days and years go better—and contribute to both the enjoyment and the length of "true life."

Acknowledgments

I am grateful to many friends and collaborators for help with this book. Special thanks to George Loewenstein, Oren Bar-Gill, David Schkade, Russell Golman, and Eric Posner for collaborations that were fun and fabulous and that have made their way into these pages. It is an understatement to say that my understanding of the topics here has been enriched by the opportunity to work with them. (More, please.) Thanks too to Tali Sharot for many discussions and for collaborative work on information seeking and information avoidance, from which this book has greatly benefited.

My interest in the subject of wanting to know was initially triggered, and continues to be framed, by a brilliant, crisp essay by the late Edna Ullmann-Margalit, *On Not Wanting to Know*, which can be found in her book Normal Rationality (2017). I am grateful to Ullmann-Margalit for many valuable discussions. Richard Thaler is a wonderful, creative, lovable, fun, and occasionally truculent discussant, and our joint work on nudges, nudging, and sludge has been a sine qua non. Thanks as well to Jon Elster, a long-time colleague at the University of Chicago. Once upon a time, we planned to collaborate on a paper asking whether ignorance is bliss. We never did that, but I learned a ton from him, and I continue to do that, just about every day.

Many thanks to Emily Taber, an amazing editor and friend, who made this book better in ways large and small. (Okay, okay: she fundamentally reoriented it.) Kathleen Caruso did sensational, careful work in transforming the manuscript into an actual book. Three anonymous reviewers provided terrific help. Superb research assistance came from Andrew Heinrich, Ethan Lowens, Zach Manley, and Cody Westphal. The Behavioral Economics and Public Policy Program at Harvard Law School provided essential support. Sarah Chalfant, my agent, made the book possible. Samantha Power makes all things possible, and if she is skillful at ruining popcorn, well, it's usually for the best.

I have borrowed here from previous work, though in all cases, it has been substantially revised. Chapter 2 draws on Cass R. Sunstein, *Ruining Popcorn? The Welfare Effects of Information*, 58 J. Risk and Uncertainty 121 (2019); chapter 3 draws on George Loewenstein, Cass R. Sunstein, and Russell Golman, *Disclosure: Psychology Changes Everything*, 6 Annual Review of Economics 391 (2014); chapter 4 draws on Oren Bar-Gill, David Schkade, and Cass R. Sunstein, *Drawing False Inferences from Mandated Disclosures*, 3 Behavioural Public Policy 209 (2019); chapter 5 draws (a fair bit) from Eric Posner and Cass R. Sunstein, *Moral Commitments in Cost-Benefit Analysis*, 103 Virginia Law Review 1809 (2017); chapter 6 draws on Cass R. Sunstein, *Valuing Facebook*, Behavioural Public Policy (2019); and chapter 7 draws on Cass R. Sunstein, *Sludge and Ordeals*, 68 Duke L. J. 1843 (2019). Special thanks again to my coauthors—Loewenstein, Golman, Bar-Gill, Schkade, and Posner—for permission to use joint work and for allowing various revisions, deletions, and edits. None of them is responsible for my revisions and mistakes. Readers who are interested in fuller treatments, often dealing with issues not explored here, are strongly encouraged to consult the original publications.

Notes

1 Knowledge Is Power, but Ignorance Is Bliss

1. See Edna Ullmann-Margalit, *On Not Wanting to Know*, in Normal Rationality 80 (Avishai Margalit & Cass R. Sunstein eds., 2017).

2. Russell Golman et al., *Information Avoidance*, 55 J. Econ. Literature 96 (2017); Ralph Hertwig & Christopher Engel, *Homo Ignorans: Deliberately Choosing Not to Know*, 11 Persp. Psychol. Sci. 359 (2016), https://doi.org/10.1177/1745691616635594.

3. See Ullmann-Margalit, supra note 1.

4. For valuable discussions from which I have learned a great deal, see Linda Thunstrom et al., *Strategic Self-Ignorance*, 52 J. Risk and Uncertainty 117 (2016); Jonas Nordstrom et al., Strategic Self-Ignorance Negates the Effect of Risk Information, https://editorialexpress.com/cgi-bin/conference/download.cgi?db_name=EEAESEM2016&paper_id=1949; Golman et al., supra note 2; Hertwig & Engel, supra note 2; Caroline J. Charpentier et al., *Valuation of Knowledge and Ignorance in Mesolimbic Reward Circuitry*, 115 PNAS E7255 (2018).

5. See Tali Sharot & Cass R. Sunstein, *How People Decide What They Want to Know*, 4 Nat. Hum. Behav. 14 (2020).

6. See Daniel Kahneman, Thinking, Fast and Slow (2011).

7. See Linda Thunstrom & Chian Jones Ritten, *Endogenous Attention to Costs*, 59 J. Risk and Uncertainty 1 (2019).

8. Chip Heath & Dan Heath, *The Curse of Knowledge*, Harv. Bus. Rev. (Dec. 2006), https://hbr.org/2006/12/the-curse-of-knowledge.

9. For relevant discussion, see Sharot & Sunstein, supra note 5.

10. See Jon Elster, Sour Grapes (1983).

11. See Thunstrom et al., supra note 4.

12. Id.

13. Id.; see also Nordstrom et al., supra note 4.

14. Daniel Kahneman et al., *Experimental Tests of the Endowment Effect and the Coase Theorem*, 98 J. Pol. Econ. 1325 (1990).

15. Jada Hamilton et al., *Emotional Distress Following Genetic Testing for Hereditary Breast and Ovarian Cancer: A Meta-Analytic Review*, 28 Health Psych. 510 (2009).

16. See Marta Broadstreet et al., *Psychological Consequences of Predictive Genetic Testing: A Systematic Review*, 8 European Journal of Genetics 731 (2000).

17. Id. Valuable in this regard is research on "emotional self-regulation." See, e.g., Charles S. Carver & Michael F. Scheier, *Cybernetic Control Processes and the Self-Regulation of Behavior*, in Oxford Handbook on Motivation 28 (Richard Ryan ed., 2012).

18. See Cass R. Sunstein, *Illusory Losses*, 37 J. Legal Stud. S157 (2008).

19. David Schkade and Daniel Kahneman, *Does Living in California Make People Happy? A Focusing Illusion in Judgments of Life Satisfaction*, 9 Psych. Science 340, 346 (1996).

20. Tali Sharot, The Optimism Bias (2012).

21. Amos Tversky & Daniel Kahneman, *Judgment under Uncertainty: Heuristics and Biases*, *in* Judgment under Uncertainty: Heuristics and Biases 3, 11 (Daniel Kahneman et al. eds., 1982).

22. Niklas Karlsson et al., *The Ostrich Effect: Selective Attention to Information*, 38 J. Risk and Uncertainty 95 (2009), https://www.cmu.edu/dietrich/sds/docs/loewenstein/OstrichEffect.pdf.

23. See Charles Dorison et al., *Selective Exposure Partly Relies on Faulty Affective Forecasts*, 188 Cognition 98 (2019).

24. Linda Thunstrom, *Welfare Effects of Nudges: The Emotional Tax of Calorie Menu Labeling*, 14 Judgment and Decision Making 11 (2019), http://journal.sjdm.org/18/18829/jdm18829.html.

25. Id. See also Nordstrom et al., supra note 4.

26. See Thunstrom, supra note 24.

27. Id.

28. Gerd Gigerenzer & Rocio Garcia-Retamero, *Cassandra's Regret: The Psychology of Not Wanting to Know*, 124 Psych. Rev. 179 (2017), https://www.apa.org/pubs/journals/releases/rev-rev0000055.pdf.

29. Charpentier et al., supra note 4.

30. For relevant data, see Yumi Iwamitsu et al., *Anxiety, Emotional Suppression, and Psychological Distress before and after Breast Cancer Diagnosis*, 46 Psychosomatics 19 (2005); Theresa Marteau & John Weinman, *Self-Regulation and the Behavioural Response to DNA Risk Information: A Theoretical Analysis and Framework for Future Research*, 62 Soc. Sci. & Med. 1360 (2006); Jada Hamilton et al., *Emotional Distress Following Genetic Testing for Hereditary Breast and Ovarian Cancer: A Meta-Analytic Review*, 28 Health Psychol. 510 (2009).

31. See Cass R. Sunstein, The Ethics of Influence (2015).

32. Thunstrom et al., supra note 4.

2 Measuring Welfare

1. For defenses of deontological approaches, see John Rawls, A Theory of Justice (1972); Joseph Raz, The Morality of Freedom (1985). A form of

welfarism is defended in Matthew Adler, Well-Being and Fair Distribution: Beyond Cost-Benefit Analysis (2011).

2. The proposal can be found at https://www.federalregister.gov/documents/2019/08/16/2019-17481/tobacco-products-required-warnings-for-cigarette-packages-and-advertisements.

3. See Adler, supra note 1; Matthew D. Adler, Measuring Social Welfare: An Introduction (2019).

4. Id.

5. In this section, and in other parts of this chapter, I borrow from a much briefer, earlier account in Cass R. Sunstein, The Cost-Benefit Revolution (2018), and a fuller account in Cass R. Sunstein, *Ruining Popcorn? The Welfare Effects of Information*, 58 J. Risk and Uncertainty 121 (2019). Those accounts, especially the former, are significantly revised and, I hope, improved here. (If a degree of repetition is not exactly ideal, perhaps it is better than self-contradiction? Compare André Gide's remark: "Everything that needs to be said has already been said. But since no one was listening, everything must be said again.")

6. For a defense of this claim, see Cass R. Sunstein, The Cost-Benefit Revolution (2018).

7. W. Kip Viscusi, Pricing Lives (2018).

8. Kenneth Arrow, *Economic Welfare and the Allocation of Resources for Invention*, in The Rate and Direction of Inventive Activity: Economic and Social Factors 6–5 (1962).

9. Richard H. Thaler & Cass R. Sunstein, Nudge: Improving Decisions about Health, Wealth, and Happiness (2008).

10. Shlomo Benartzi et al., *Should Governments Invest More in Nudging?*, 28 Psychol. Sci. 1041 (2017).

11. On reminder warnings, see W. Kip Viscusi, Reforming Products Liability (1991). On ineffective nudges in general, see Cass R. Sunstein, *Nudges That Fail*, 1 Behav. Pub. Pol'y 4 (2017).

12. H. Gilbert Welch, Should I Be Tested for Cancer? (2004). See also H. Gilbert Welch et al., Overdiagnosed (2012).

13. Wesley A. Magat & W. Kip Viscusi, Informational Approaches to Regulation (1992). See also Cass R. Sunstein, Simpler: The Future of Government (2013).

14. Omri Ben-Shahar & Carl Schneider, More Than You Wanted to Know: The Failure of Mandated Disclosure (2016).

15. See Natalina Zlatevska et al., *Mandatory Calorie Disclosure: A Comprehensive Analysis of Its Effect on Consumers and Retailers*, 94 J. Retailing 89 (2018).

16. See Zlatevska et al., supra note 15, at 93 (Table 1).

17. See Joel Monárrez-Espino et al., *Systematic Review of the Effect of Pictorial Warnings on Cigarette Packages in Smoking Behavior*, 104 Am. J. Pub. Health e11 (2014); Sven Schneider et al., *Does the Effect Go Up in Smoke? A Randomized Controlled Trial of Pictorial Warnings on Cigarette Packaging*, 86 Patient Educ. and Counseling 77 (2012).

18. See, e.g., Monárrez-Espino et al., supra note 17. Of the 2,456 papers published on the effect of pictorial warnings on smokers between 1989 and 2014, only five included original randomized control trials. Note that when the peer reviewers scored a paper's study design, they gave the highest score to randomized control trials.

19. See, e.g., Abigail Evans et al., *Graphic Warning Labels Elicit Affective and Thoughtful Responses from Smokers: Results of a Randomized Clinical Trial*, 10 PLOS One 1 (2015). Researchers had long debated whether smokers actually reflect on the content of the warning labels or whether their message was tuned out. This study suggests that such labels have a strong effect on smokers, and because the study involved randomized controlled trials, it was able to isolate the effects of pictorial warnings. It yielded some results in line with findings from other studies: the less information on the label, the more thoughtfully smokers responded to it.

20. For a helpful overview, see Kent D. Messer et al., Labeling Food Processes: The Good, the Bad and the Ugly, 39 Applied Econ. Persp. & Pol'y 407 (2017), https://academic.oup.com/aepp/article/39/3/407/4085217.

21. Erica Myers et al., *Effects of Mandatory Energy Efficiency Disclosure in Housing Markets* (Nat'l Bureau of Econ. Research, Working Paper No. 26436, 2019), https://www.nber.org/papers/w26436.

22. Jens Hainmueller et al., *Consumer Demand for Fair Trade*, 97 Rev. Econ. and Stat. 242 (2015), https://www.mitpressjournals.org/doi/abs/10.1162/REST_a_00467.

23. Nat'l Res. Council, Dolphins and the Tuna Industry, Nat'l Acad. Press, PL 42 (1992).

24. Mary J. Christoph & Ruopeng An, *Effect of Nutrition Labels on Dietary Quality among College Students*, 76 Nutrition Rev. 187 (2018), https://www.ncbi.nlm.nih.gov/pubmed/29373747.

25. Ctrs. for Disease Control and Prevention, *CDC Study Finds Levels of Trans-Fatty Acids in Blood of U.S. White Adults Has Decreased* (Feb. 8, 2012), https://www.cdc.gov/media/releases/2012/p0208_trans-fatty_acids.html.

26. Anne N. Thorndike et al., *Traffic-Light Labels and Choice Architecture Promoting Healthy Food Choices*, 46 Am. J. Preventive Med. 143 (2014), https://www.ncbi.nlm.nih.gov/pmc/articles/PMC3911887/. But see M. W. Seward et al., *A Traffic-Light Label Intervention and Dietary Choices in College Cafeterias*, 106 Am. J. Pub. Health 1808 (2016), https://www.ncbi.nlm.nih.gov/pubmed/27552277.

27. Gicheol Jeong & Yeunjoong Kim, *The Effects of Energy Efficiency and Environmental Labels on Appliance Choice in South Korea*, 8 Energy Efficiency 559 (2015), https://link.springer.com/article/10.1007/s12053-014-9307-1.

28. Kamila M. Kiszko et al., *The Influence of Calorie Labeling on Food Orders and Consumption*, 39 J. Community Health, 1248 (2014), https://www.ncbi.nlm.nih.gov/pmc/articles/PMC4209007/; Brian Elbel et al., *Calorie Labeling and Food Choices*, 28 Health Aff. 1110 (2009), https://

www.ncbi.nlm.nih.gov/pubmed/19808705; Sara N. Bleich et al., *A Systematic Review of Calorie Labeling and Modified Calorie Labeling Interventions*, 25 Obesity 2018 (2017), https://www.ncbi.nlm.nih.gov/pmc/articles/PMC5752125/.

29. Julie S. Downs et al., *Supplementing Menu Labeling with Calorie Recommendations to Test for Facilitation Effects*, 103 Am. J. Pub. Health 1604 (2013), https://ajph.aphapublications.org/doi/full/10.2105/AJPH.2013.301218.

30. Partha Deb & Carmen Vargas, *Who Benefits from Calorie Labeling?* 1–29 (Nat'l Bureau of Econ. Research, Working Paper No. 21992, 2016), https://www.nber.org/papers/w21992; see also Bryan Bollinger et al., *Calorie Posting in Chain Restaurants* (Nat'l Bureau of Econ. Research, Working Paper No. 15648, 2010), https://www.nber.org/papers/w15648.

31. Steven K. Dallas et al., *Don't Count Calorie Labeling Out*, 29 J. Consumer Psychol. 60 (2018).

32. For an important decision upholding a refusal to quantify benefits, on the ground that quantification was not feasible, see Inv. Co. Inst. v. Commodity Futures Trading Comm'n, 720 F.3d 370 (D.C. Cir. 2013). In the context of disclosure, the leading decision is Nat'l Ass'n of Mfr. v. SEC (D.C. Cir. 2014), which upheld against arbitrariness review a regulation that would require disclosure of the use of "conflict minerals":

> An agency is not required "to measure the immeasurable," and need not conduct a "rigorous, quantitative economic analysis" unless the statute explicitly directs it to do so. Here, the rule's benefits would occur half-a-world away in the midst of an opaque conflict about which little reliable information exists, and concern a subject about which the Commission has no particular expertise. Even if one could estimate how many lives are saved or rapes prevented as a direct result of the final rule, doing so would be pointless because the costs of the rule—measured in dollars—would create an apples-to-bricks comparison. Despite the lack of data, the Commission *had* to promulgate a disclosure rule.

Quoting Inv. Co. Inst., v. Commodity Futures Trading Comm'n 720 F.3d 370 (D.C. Cir. 2013).

33. Ben-Shahar & Schneider, supra note 14.

34. Daniel Kahneman & Richard H. Thaler, *Anomalies: Utility Maximization and Experienced Utility*, 20 J. Econ. Persp. 221 (2006).

35. The final rule can be found at https://www.federalregister.gov/documents/2018/12/21/2018-27283/national-bioengineered-food-disclosure-standard.

36. Hunt Allcott & Judd B. Kessler, *The Welfare Effects of Nudges: A Case Study of Energy Use Social Comparisons*, 11 American Economic Review: Applied Economics 236 (2019).

37. Preference Change: Approaches from Philosophy, Economics and Psychology 4 (Till Grune-Yanoff & Sven Ove Hansson eds., 2009).

38. For example, according to the Environmental Protection Agency and the Department of Transportation (2011), speaking of new fuel economy labels, "any assessment of quantitative effects of label design on vehicle sales involves a great deal of speculation." In a nutshell: "The primary benefits associated with this rule are associated with improved consumer decision-making resulting from improved presentation of information. At this time, EPA and NHTSA do not have data to quantify these impacts." Revisions and Additions to Motor Vehicle Fuel Economy Label, 76 Fed. Reg. 39,517 (July 6, 2011).

39. W. Kip Viscusi & Wesley A. Magat, Learning about Risk (1987).

40. Wesley A. Magat & W. Kip Viscusi, Informational Approaches to Regulation (1992).

41. Allcott & Kessler, supra note 35.

42. The defining work here comes from W. Kip Viscusi, Pricing Lives (2018); many people draw on his research. See, e.g., Thomson and Monje, who explain: "On the basis of the best available evidence, this guidance identifies $9.4 million as the value of a statistical life." Kathryn Thomason & Carlos Monje, Guidance on Treatment of the Economic Value of a Statistical Life in U.S. Department of Transportation Analyses, Memorandum, US Department of Transportation (2015), https://perma.cc/C6RQ-4ZXR. See also Sunstein, who provides the underlying theory and a discussion of how "agencies . . . assign monetary values to

the human lives that would be saved by a proposed regulation." Cass R. Sunstein, Valuing Life: Humanizing the Regulatory State (2014).

43. See Loureiro et al., who find that "on average, consumers are willing to pay close to 11 per cent above the initial price to obtain cookies with nutritional labelling." Maria L. Loureiro et al., *Do Consumers Value Nutritional Labels?*, 33 Eur. Rev. Agric. Econ. 249, 263 (2006). Further, "Consistent with prior expectations, our results also indicate a difference between the [willingness-to-pay] of individuals suffering from diet-related health problems (estimated mean 13 per cent) and those who do not suffer any diet-related health problems (estimated mean 9 per cent)." Id. at 249.

44. See US Food and Drug Administration, Food Labeling: Nutrition Labeling of Standard Menu Items in Restaurants and Similar Retail Food Establishments, Report FDA-2011-F-0172, 11, 64 (2014), https://www.fda.gov/media/90450/download. As before, however, the willingness-to-pay criterion may run into normative objections, even from the standpoint of welfare. See generally Bronsteen et al., who raise questions about willingness to pay in view of people's occasional failure to know what will promote their welfare. John Bronsteen et al., Happiness and the Law (2015).

45. Jonathan Gruber & Sendhil Mullainathan, *Do Cigarette Taxes Make Smokers Happier?* (Nat'l Bureau of Econ. Research, Working Paper No. 8872, 2002), http://www.nber.org/papers/w8872.

46. See the US Food and Drug Administration, which notes the longer lifespans, fewer cancers and diseases, and increased property and monetary values of nonsmokers. US Food and Drug Administration, Required Warnings for Cigarette Packages and Advertisements, 76 Fed. Reg. 36719 (June 22, 2011). See also the US Department of Labor requiring that employees have access to OSHA logs. US Department of Labor, Improve Tracking of Workplace Injuries and Illnesses, 81 Fed. Reg. 29628 (May 12, 2016). And see the US Environmental Protection Agency and US Department of Transportation, which explains, "The agencies believe that informed choice is an end in itself, even if it is hard to quantify; the agencies also believe that the new labels will provide significant benefits

for consumers, including economic benefits, though these benefits cannot be quantified at this time." US Environmental Protection Agency & US Department of Transportation, Revisions and Additions to Motor Vehicle Fuel Economy Label, 76 Fed. Reg. 39517 (July 6, 2011). Finally, see the US Food and Drug Administration, which explains, "The final rule may also assist consumers by making the long-term health consequences of consumer food choices more salient and by providing contextual cues of food consumption." US Food and Drug Administration, Food Labeling: Nutrition Labeling of Standard Menu Items in Restaurants and Similar Retail Food Establishments, Report FDA-2011-F-0172, 11 (2014), https://www.fda.gov/media/90450/download.

47. The proposal can be found at https://www.federalregister.gov/documents/2019/08/16/2019-17481/tobacco-products-required-warnings-for-cigarette-packages-and-advertisements.

3 Psychology

1. Omri Ben-Shahar & Carl E. Schneider, *The Failure of Mandated Disclosure*, 159 U. Pa. L. Rev. 647 (2010). The paper was the foundation for an excellent book: Omri Ben-Shahar & Carl E. Schneider, More than You Want to Know (2014).

2. Even when information cannot be verified, some honest communication can occur. Vincent P. Crawford & Joel Sobel, *Strategic Information Transmission*, 50 Econometrica 1431 (1982); Joseph Farrell & Matthew Rabin, *Cheap Talk*, 10 J. Econ. Persp. 103 (1996).

3. For example, Ulrike Malmendier & Devin Shanthikumar, *Are Small Investors Naïve about Incentives?*, 85 J. Fin. Econ. 457 (2007).

4. Vijay Krishna & John Morgan, *A Model of Expertise*, 116 Q. J. Econ. 747 (2001).

5. Carlos Jensen et al., *Privacy Practices of Internet Users: Self-Reports versus Observed Behavior*, 63 Intl. J. Man-Machine Stud. 203 (2005).

6. Joseph Turrow et al., *The Federal Trade Commission and Consumer Privacy in the Coming Decade*, 3 I/S: J. L. Pol. Info. Soc'y 723 (2008).

7. This lack of attention, and resultant misconceptions, should come as no surprise. It has been estimated that 54 percent of privacy policies are beyond the grasp of 57 percent of the internet population—see Carlos Jensen & Colin Potts, *Privacy Policies as Decision-Making Tools: An Evaluation of Online Privacy Notices* in Proceedings of the SIGCHI Conference on Human Factors in Computing Systems 471 (2004)—and, somewhat amusingly, that the aggregate dollar value of the time it would take for US consumers *actually* to read privacy policies would be $652 billion/ year. Aleeccia M. McDonald & Lorrie Faith Cranor, *Cost of Reading Privacy Policies*, 4 I/S: J. L. Pol. Info. Soc'y 543 (2008).

8. Roger McCarthy et al., *Product Information Presentation, User Behavior, and Safety*, 28 Proc. Hum. Factors Ergonomics Soc'y Ann. Meeting 81 (1984).

9. The research is summarized in Richard E. Nisbett & Lee Ross, Human Inference: Strategies and Shortcomings of Social Judgment (1980).

10. Alexander L. Brown et al., *To Review or Not to Review? Limited Strategic Thinking at the Movie Box Office*, 4 Am. Econ. J. Microecon. 1 (2012); Alexander L. Brown et al., *Estimating Structural Models of Equilibrium and Cognitive Hierarchy Thinking in the Field: The Case of Withheld Movie Critic Reviews*, 59 Mgmt. Sci. 733 (2013).

11. Sunita Sah & George Loewenstein, *Nothing to Declare: Mandatory and Voluntary Disclosure Leads Advisors to Avoid Conflicts of Interest*, 25 Psychol. Sci. 575 (2014).

12. Alan D. Mathios, *The Impact of Mandatory Disclosure Laws on Product Choices: An Analysis of the Salad Dressing Market*, 43 J. L. Econ. 651 (2000).

13. Botond Kőszegi, *Utility from Anticipation and Personal Equilibrium*, 44 Econ. Theory 415 (2010), https://doi.org/10.1007/s00199-009-0465-x. For example, see Markus K. Brunnermeier & Jonathan A. Parker, *Optimal Expectations*, 95 Am. Econ. Rev. 1092 (2005); Andrew Caplin & John Leahy, *Psychological Expected Utility Theory and Anticipatory Feelings*, 116 Q. J. Econ. 55 (2001); George Loewenstein, *Anticipation and the Valuation of Delayed Consumption*, 97 Econ. J. 666 (1987); Thomas C. Schelling, *The Mind as a Consuming Organ*, in The Multiple Self (ed. J. Elster 1987).

14. Niklas Karlson et al., *The Ostrich Effect: Selective Avoidance of Information*, 38 J. Risk Uncertainty 95 (2009); Nachum Sicherman et al., *Financial Attention*, 29 Rev. Fin. Stud. 863 (2016), http://dx.doi.org/10.2139/ssrn.2120955.

15. Rebecca L. Thornton, *The Demand for, and Impact of, Learning HIV Status*, 98 Am. Econ. Rev. 1829 (2008).

16. Emily Oster et al., *Optimal Expectations and Limited Medical Testing: Evidence from Huntington Disease*, 103 Am. Econ. Rev. 804 (2013).

17. See, e.g., Yumi Iwamitsu et al., *Anxiety, Emotional Suppression, and Psychological Distress before and after Breast Cancer Diagnosis*, 46 Psychosomatics 19 (2005).

18. See Eun Kyoung Choi et al., *Associated with Emotional Response of Parents at the Time of Diagnosis of Down Syndrome*, 16 J. for Specialists in Pediatric Nursing 113 (2011).

19. See Theresa Marteau and John Weinman, *Self-Regulation and the Behavioural Response to DNA Risk Information: A Theoretical Analysis and Framework for Future Research*, 62 Soc. Sci. & Med. 1360 (2006).

20. Howard Leventhal, *Fear Appeals and Persuasion: The Differentiation of a Motivational Construct*, 61 Am. J. Pub. Health 1208 (1971); Ronald W. Rogers, *A Protection Motivation Theory of Fear Appeals and Attitude Change*, 91 J. Psych. 93 (1975); Sabine Loeber et al., *The Effect of Pictorial Warnings on Cigarette Packages on Attentional Bias of Smokers*, 98 Pharmacology Biochemistry Behav. 292 (2011).

21. Tali Sharot, The Optimism Bias (2012).

22. For example, Amos Tversky & Daniel Kahneman, *Judgment under Uncertainty: Heuristics and Biases*, *in* Judgment under Uncertainty: Heuristics and Biases 3, 11 (Daniel Kahneman et al. eds., 1982).

23. Bryan Bollinger et al., *Calorie Posting in Chain Restaurants* (Nat'l Bureau of Econ. Research, Working Paper No. 15648, 2010), https://www.nber.org/papers/w15648.

24. Robert Jensen, *The (Perceived) Returns to Education and the Demand for Schooling*, 125 Q. J. Econ. 515 (2010).

25. Hunt Allcott, *Social Norms and Energy Conservation*, 95 J. Pub. Econ. 1082 (2011).

26. W. Kip Viscusi, *Do Smokers Underestimate Risks?*, 98 J. Pol. Econ. 1253 (1990).

27. Paul Slovic, *Rejoinder: The Perils of Viscusi's Analyses of Smoking Risk Perceptions*, 13 J. Behav. Decision Making 273 (2000).

28. Uri Gneezy, *Deception: The Role of Consequences*, 95 Am. Econ. Rev. 384 (2005).

29. For example, see Kathleen Valley, *How Communication Improves Efficiency in Bargaining Games*, 38 Games Econ. Behav. 127 (2002).

30. Cognitive biases can, in some situations, have a similar effect. The "curse of knowledge" refers to the fact that people with private information often overestimate the extent to which it is shared. Colin F. Camerer, *The Curse of Knowledge in Economic Settings: An Experimental Analysis*, 97 J. Pol. Econ. 1232, 1245 (1989). According to the author's note, "By making better-informed agents think that their knowledge is shared by others, the curse helps alleviate the inefficiencies that result from information asymmetries, bringing outcomes closer to complete information (first-best) outcomes. In such settings, the curse on individuals may actually improve social welfare." Id.

31. Daylian M. Cain et al., *The Dirt on Coming Clean: Perverse Effects of Disclosing Conflicts of Interest*, 34 J. Legal Stud. 1 (2005).

32. Daylian M. Cain et al., *When Sunlight Fails to Disinfect: Understanding the Perverse Effects of Disclosing Conflicts of Interest*, 37 J. Consumer Res. 836 (2010).

33. Id.

34. Id.

35. Sunita Sah et al., *The Burden of Disclosure: Increased Compliance with Distrusted Advice*, 104 J. Personality Soc. Psychol. 289 (2013); Sunita Sah et al., *Insinuation Anxiety: Concern that Advice Rejection Will Signal Distrust after Conflict of Interest Disclosures*, 45 Pers. Soc. Psychol. B. 1099 (2019).

36. For example, Archon Fung et al., Full Disclosure: The Perils and Promise of Transparency (2007).

37. Ginger Zhe Jin & Phillip Leslie, *The Effect of Information on Product Quality: Evidence from Restaurant Hygiene Grade Cards*, 118 Q. J. Econ. 409 (2003). The same authors also obtained evidence that mandatory disclosure was more effective than voluntary disclosure and that although the grade cards did lead to real improvements in hygiene, they also led inspectors to distort their ratings.

38. Thomas Gilovich et al., *The Spotlight Effect in Social Judgement: An Egocentric Bias in Estimates of the Salience of One's Own Actions and Appearance*, 78 J. Personality Soc. Psychol. 211 (2000).

39. Edgar Allen Poe, *The Tell-Tale Heart* (1843).

40. For example, see Maureen O'Dougherty et al., *Nutrition Labeling and Value Size Pricing at Fast Food Restaurants: A Consumer Perspective*, 20 Am. J. Health Promotion 247 (2006). See, however, Bollinger et al., supra note 23, who find a nontrivial effect on consumer choices.

41. Alexa Namba et al., *Exploratory Analysis of Fast-Food Chain Restaurant Menus before and after Implementation of Local Calorie-Labeling Policies, 2005–2011*, 10 Preventing Chronic Disease 1 (2013).

42. The average calorie content for entrée items showed no similar type of change across the two groups of restaurants (presumably because with calorie labeling, unhealthier options got even worse).

43. Pierre Chandon & Brian Wansink, *The Biasing Health Halos of Fast-Food Restaurant Health Claims: Lower Calorie Estimates and Higher Side-Dish Consumption Intentions*, 34 J. Consumer Res. 301 (2007).

44. Jessica Wisdom, *Promoting Healthy Choices: Information vs. Convenience*, 99 Am. Econ. J.: Applied 159 (2010).

45. Richard G. Newell et al., *The Induced Innovation Hypothesis and Energy-Saving Technological Change*, 114 Q. J. Econ. 941 (1999).

46. Paul Waide, Energy Labeling around the Globe, paper presented at Energy Labels—A Tool for Energy Agencies (Oct. 19, 2004).

47. Cynthia L. Estlund, *Just the Facts: The Case for Workplace Transparency*, 63 Stan. L. Rev. 351 (2011).

48. Susanna Kim Ripken, *The Dangers and Drawbacks of the Disclosure Antidote: Toward a More Substantive Approach to Securities Regulation*, 58 Baylor L. Rev. 139 (2006).

49. Saurabh Bhargava & Dayanand Manoli, Psychological Frictions and the Incomplete Take-Up of Social Benefits: Evidence from an IRS Field Experiment, 105 Am. Econ. Rev. 3489 (2015).

50. Jennifer Thorne & Christine Egan, *An Evaluation of the Federal Trade Commission's EnergyGuide Appliance Label: Final Report and Recommendations*, American Council for an Energy-Efficient Economy (2002), http://aceee.org/research-report/a021; Stephen Wiel & James E. McMahon, *Governments Should Implement Energy-Efficiency Standards and Labels-Cautiously*, 31 Energy Pol'y 1403 (2003).

51. Richard G. Newell & Juha V. Siikamäki, *Nudging Energy Efficiency Behavior: The Role of Information Labels* 1–41 (Nat'l Bureau of Econ. Research, Working Paper No. 19224, 2013), https://www.nber.org/papers/w19224.

52. Id.; Appliance Labeling Rule, 72 Fed. Reg. 6,836 (Feb. 13, 2007) (16 C.F.R. pt. 305). However, for 15 percent of the consumers in this study, the presence of CO_2 information *decreased* willingness to pay for a lower operating cost. This surprising result may be a product of political reactions to "environmental issues" and may reflect how those reactions can negatively affect energy efficiency adoption. Dena M. Gromet et al., *Political Ideology Affects Energy-Efficiency Attitudes and Choices*, 110 Proc. Nat'l Acad. Sci. 9314 (2013).

53. See Steven K. Dallas et al., *Don't Count Calorie Labeling Out*, 29 J. Consumer Psychology 260 (2018).

54. For example, see Christopher K. Hsee et al., *Preference Reversals between Joint and Separate Evaluations of Options: A Review and Theoretical Analysis*, 125 Psychol. Bulletin 576 (1999).

55. Jeffrey Kling et al., *Comparison Friction: Experimental Evidence from Medicare Drug Plans*, 127 Q. J. Econ. 199 (2012).

56. Marianne Bertrand & Adair Morse, *Information Disclosure, Cognitive Biases, and Payday Borrowing*, 66 J. Fin. 1865 (2011).

57. Justine S. Hastings & Lydia Tejeda-Ashton, *Financial Literacy, Information, and Demand Elasticity: Survey and Experimental Evidence from Mexico*, 1–34 (Nat'l Bureau of Econ. Research, Working Paper No. 14538, 2008).

58. Michael Luca & Jonathan Smith, *Salience in Quality Disclosure: Evidence from the U.S. News College Rankings*, 22 J. Econ. Mgmt. Strategy 58 (2013).

59. Similarly, Pope finds that changes in the ranking of hospitals (and specialties within hospitals) have a major impact on patient volume, even though the continuous score on which the rankings are based (which is arguably a finer-grained measure of the same thing) has no significant additional impact. Devin G. Pope, *Reacting to Rankings: Evidence from "America's Best Hospitals"*, 28 J. Health Econ. 1154 (2009).

60. Justine S. Hastings & Jeffrey M. Weinstein, *Information, School Choice, and Academic Achievement: Evidence from Two Experiments*, 123 Q. J. Econ. 1373 (2008).

61. The natural experiment did, however, provide support for the idea that mailing parents information (albeit somewhat complicated information) about school performance did improve their school choice decisions.

62. In a clever experiment, Duffy and Kornienko found that subjects who played a sequential "dictator game" gave more when placed in a generosity tournament (in which subjects were publically ranked from most to least generous) as compared with an "earnings" tournament in which subjects were ranked according to how much they kept, even

though there was no award associated with winning the tournament. John Duffy & Tatiana Kornienko, *Does Competition Affect Giving?*, 74 J. Econ. Behav. Org. 82 (2010).

63. P. Wesley Schultz et al., *The Constructive, Destructive, and Reconstructive Power of Social Norms*, 18 Psych. Sci. 429 (2007).

64. Hunt Allcott & Todd Rogers, *The Short-Run and Long-Run Effects of Behavioral Interventions: Experimental Evidence from Energy Conservation*, 104 Am. Econ. Rev. 3003 (2014); Hunt Allcott, Social Norms and Energy Conservation, 95 J. Public Econ. 1082 (2011).

65. Bhargava & Manoli, supra note 49.

66. Aaron K. Chatterji & Michael W. Toffel, *How Firms Respond to Being Rated*, 31 Strategic Mgmt. 917 (2010).

67. Archon Fung & Dara O'Rourke, *Reinventing Environmental Regulation from the Grassroots Up*, 25 Env. Mgmt. 115 (2000); James T. Hamilton, Regulation through Revelation (2005); Shameek Konar & Mark Cohen, *Information as Regulation: The Effect of Community Right to Know Laws on Toxic Emissions*, 32 J. Env. Econ. Mgmt. 109 (1997).

68. See Sah & Loewenstein, supra note 11.

69. The George Washington University School of Public Health and Health Services, Pharmaceutical Marketing Expenditures in the District of Columbia, 2010 (2012), http://doh.dc.gov/sites/default/files/dc/sites/doh/publication/attachments/pharmaceutical_marketing_expenditures_in_the_district_of_columbia_2010.pdf.

70. Mary Graham, *Regulation by Shaming*, Atlantic Monthly, Apr. 2000.

71. Wendy Nelson Espeland & Michael Sauder, *Rankings and Reactivity: How Public Measures Recreate Social Worlds*, 113 Am. J. Soc. 1 (2007).

72. Schultz et al., supra note 63; see also Dora L. Costa & Matthew E. Kahn, *Energy Conservation "Nudges" and Environmentalist Ideology: Evidence from a Randomized Residential Electricity Field Experiment*, 11 J. Eur. Econ. Ass'n 680 (2010), who find that Republicans increased their energy usage.

73. See, for example, Nisbett & Ross, supra note 9.

74. Ron Borland et al., *Impact of Graphic and Text Warnings on Cigarette Packs: Findings from Four Countries Over Five Years*, 18 Tobacco Control 358 (2009); David Hammond et al., *Effectiveness of Cigarette Warning Labels in Informing Smokers about the Risks of Smoking: Findings from the International Tobacco Control (ITC) Four Country Survey*, 15 Tobacco Control iii19 (2006); Michelle M. O'Hegarty et al., *Reactions of Young Adult Smokers to Warning Labels on Cigarette Packages*, 30 Am. J. Preventive Med. 467 (2006); James F. Thrasher et al., *Estimating the Impact of Pictorial Health Warnings and "Plain" Cigarette Packaging: Evidence from Experimental Auctions among Adult Smokers in the United States*, 102 Health Pol'y 41 (2011).

75. Zain Ul Abedeen Sobani et al., *Graphic Tobacco Health Warnings: Which Genre to Choose?*, 14 Int'l J. Tuberculosis Lung Disease 356 (2010).

76. See, for example, Sabine Loeber et al., *The Effect of Pictorial Warnings on Cigarette Packages on Attentional Bias of Smokers*, 98 Pharmacology Biochemistry Behav. 292 (2011).

77. Cass R. Sunstein, Simpler: The Future of Government (2013).

4 Learning the Wrong Thing

1. A similar inference problem is studied in Juanjuan Zhang, Policy and Inference: The Case of Product Labeling (Sept. 23, 2014) (unpublished manuscript), http://jjzhang.scripts.mit.edu/docs/Zhang_2014_GMO.pdf. Zhang reports an interesting initial empirical study showing that people perceive higher risk following a GMO disclosure mandate (compared to no action).

2. See id.

3. Oren Bar-Gill et al., *Drawing False Inferences from Mandated Disclosures*, 3 Behavioural Public Policy 209 (2019).

4. US Food and Drug Administration, Guidance for Industry: Voluntary Labeling Indicating Whether Foods Have or Have Not Been Derived from Genetically Engineered Plants 7 (2015).

5. See Cass R. Sunstein, *The Limits of Quantification*, 102 Cal. L. Rev. 1369 (2014).

5   Moral Wrongs

1. Conflict Minerals, 77 Fed. Reg. 56,274, 56,277–78 (Sept. 12, 2012) (codified at 17 C.F.R. pts. 240 and 249b).

2. 16 U.S.C. § 1385 (2012).

3. Id.

4. Sydney E. Scott et al., *Evidence for Absolute Moral Opposition to Genetically Modified Food in the United States*, 11 Persp. Psychol. Sci. 315, 316 (2016).

5. National Bioengineered Food Disclosure Standard, Pub. L. No. 114-216 (2016) (codified at 7 U.S.C. § 1621 et seq. (2016)).

6. See Denis Swords, *Ohio v. United States Department of the Interior: A Contingent Step Forward for Environmentalists*, 51 La. L. Rev. 1347 (1991). On the theoretical issues, see Robert Goodin, Green Political Theory (1992).

7. These issues are engaged in detail in Eric Posner & Cass R. Sunstein, *Moral Commitments in Cost-Benefit Analysis*, 103 Va. L. Rev. 1809 (2017), and somewhat more briefly in Cass R. Sunstein, The Cost-Benefit Revolution (2017). I borrow from those discussions here.

8. See Deven Carlson et al., Monetizing Bowser: A Contingent Valuation of the Statistical Value of Dog Life (2019), https://www.cambridge .org/core/journals/journal-of-benefit-cost-analysis/article/monetizing -bowser-a-contingent-valuation-of-the-statistical-value-of-dog-life/86EB 120F86F7376DC366F6578C8CFEF1.

9. See Conflict Minerals, 77 Fed. Reg. 56,274, 56,333–36 (Sept. 12, 2012) (codified at 17 C.F.R. pts. 240, 249b).

10. 21 U.S.C. § 343(w) (2012).

11. See Peter Singer, Animal Liberation 5–7 (1975).

12. Jeremy Bentham, An Introduction to the Principles of Morals and Legislation 282–83 (J. H. Burns & H. L. A. Hart eds., 1996).

13. See 15 U.S.C. §§ 78m(p) (2012).

14. Nat'l Ass'n of Mfrs. v. SEC, 748 F.3d 359, 369–70 (D.C. Cir. 2014).

15. Conflict Minerals, 77 Fed. Reg. 56,274, 56,334 (Sept. 12, 2012) (codified at 17 C.F.R. pts. 240 and 249b).

16. Id. at 56,350.

17. National Ass'n of Mfrs., 748 F.3d at 370.

18. Id. at 369.

6 Valuing Facebook

1. There are also controversies, of course, centered on whether people's privacy is being invaded and whether they know how their information is being used. For relevant discussion, overlapping with the analysis here, see Angela G. Winegar & Cass R. Sunstein, *How Much Is Data Privacy Worth? A Preliminary Investigation*, 42 J. Consumer Pol'y 440 (2019).

2. See Richard H. Thaler, Misbehaving (2016).

3. Charles Plott & Kathryn Zeiler, *The Willingness to Pay–Willingness to Accept Gap, the "Endowment Effect," Subject Misconceptions, and Experimental Procedures for Eliciting Valuations*, 95 Am. Econ. Rev. 530 (2005).

4. The sample was not nationally representative, but it did have a significant level of demographic diversity. I am now engaged in a nationally representative survey; this is not the place to report the results, but they are broadly consistent with those in the pilot survey.

5. See Daniel Kahneman et al., *Experimental Tests of the Endowment Effect and the Coase Theorem*, 98 J. Pol. Econ. 1325 (1998).

6. See id.; Keith M. Marzilli Ericson & Andreas Fuster, *The Endowment Effect* 1–34 (Nat'l Bureau of Econ. Research, Working Paper No. 19384, 2013), http://www.nber.org/papers/w19384; Carey K. Morewedge &

Colleen E. Giblin, *Explanations of the Endowment Effect: An Integrative Review*, 18 Trends Cognitive Sci. 339 (2015).

7. See, e.g., Christoph Kogler et al., *Real and Hypothetical Endowment Effects when Exchanging Lottery Tickets: Is Regret a Better Explanation than Loss Aversion?*, 37 J. Econ. Psychol. 42 (2013). The endowment effect is often attributed to loss aversion, but that explanation does not appear to be complete. See Morewedge & Giblin, supra note 6.

8. None of the demographic differences (sex, race, education, income, region) was significant, but in light of the small sample, it would be a mistake to make much of this. I might note, however, that for both men and women, the median response to the first question was $1 and that the male average was $7.98 and the female $6.92; that the Republican median was $2, with an average of $11; that the Democratic median was $1, with an average of $8.74; and that the independent median was zero, with an average of $3.36. For the second question, the male median was $57, and the average was $75.44; the female median was $59, and the average was $74.63. The Republican median was $59, with an average of $78.25; the Democratic median was $53, with an average of $71.34; the independent median was $60, with an average of $77.14.

9. Some questions about the underpinnings and domain of the endowment effect are raised in Plott & Zeiler, supra note 3. Clarifying discussions can be found in Ericson & Fuster, supra note 6, and Andrea Isoni et al., *The Willingness to Pay–Willingness to Accept Gap, the "Endowment Effect," Subject Misconceptions, and Experimental Procedures for Eliciting Valuations: Comment*, 101 Am. Econ. Rev. 991 (2011).

10. See Cass R. Sunstein, *Endogenous Preferences, Environmental Law*, 22 J. Legal Stud. 217 (1993); Simon Dietz and Frank Venmans, *The Endowment Effect and Environmental Discounting* (Ctr. Climate Change Econ. Pol'y Working Paper No. 264, 2017), http://www.lse.ac.uk/GranthamInstitute/wp-content/uploads/2016/08/Working-paper-233-Dietz-Venmans-updateMarch17.pdf.

11. Dan Brookshire & Don Coursey, *Measuring the Value of a Public Good: An Empirical Comparison of Elictation Procedures*, 77 Am. Econ. Rev. 554 (1987).

12. Judd Hammock & G. M. Brown, Waterfowl and Wetlands: Toward Bioeconomic Analysis (1974).

13. Robert Rowe et al., *An Experiment on the Economic Value of Visibility*, 7 J. Env't Econ. Mgmt. 1 (1980).

14. Daniel Kahneman et al., *Fairness and the Assumptions of Economics*, 59 J. Bus. S285 (1986).

15. Id.

16. See Truman Bewley, Why Wages Don't Fall During A Recession (1995).

17. Shane Frederick et al., *Opportunity Cost Neglect*, 36 J. Consumer Res. 551 (2009). In the environmental context, another factor is at work: conscience. If people are being asked how much they would demand to allow destruction of (say) polar bears, they might say that no amount is high enough, or they might give an amount that signals not the welfare effects (for them) of destruction of polar bears, but their feeling of responsibility for a terrible loss. On some of the issues here, see Eric Posner & Cass R. Sunstein, *Moral Commitments in Cost-Benefit Analysis*, 103 Va. L. Rev. 1809 (2017).

18. Erik Brynjolfsson et al., *Using Massive Online Choice Experiments to Measure Changes in Well-Being* (Nat'l Bureau of Econ. Res. Working Paper No. 24514, 2018), http://www.nber.org/papers/w24514. I am focusing only on a portion of their studies here; it has a number of illuminating findings.

19. See Edward McCaffery et al., *Framing the Jury: Cognitive Perspectives on Pain and Suffering Awards*, 81 Va. L. Rev. 1341 (1995).

20. For relevant discussion, see Paul Dolan, Happiness by Design (2014).

21. I am bracketing here the possibility that the answers may reflect reactions, cognitive or emotional, to being asked the questions, as in the case of protest answers.

22. See John Bronsteen et al., *Well-Being Analysis vs. Cost-Benefit Analysis*, 62 Duke L. J. 1603 (2013); Cass R. Sunstein, The Cost-Benefit

Revolution (2018). On two of the different components of well-being—pleasure and purpose—see Dolan, supra note 20. It is possible that for many users of social media, pleasure is increased, but not purpose. It is possible that for many users, neither pleasure nor purpose is increased, and use is in the nature of an addiction, reducing rather than increasing welfare. It is also true that an analysis of welfare effects will ultimately lead to serious philosophical issues. See Matthew Adler, Well-Being and Fair Distribution (2011).

23. Hunt Allcott et al., The Welfare Effects of Social Media (unpublished draft 2019).

24. Xiaomeng Hu et al., *The Facebook Paradox: Effects of Facebooking on Individuals' Social Relationships and Psychological Well-Being*, 8 Frontiers Psychol. 87 (2017); Sebastian Valenzuela et al., *Is There Social Capital in a Social Network Site? Facebook Use and College Students' Life Satisfaction, Trust, and Participation*, 14 J. Computer-Mediated Comm. 875 (2009); E. C. Tandoc et al., *Facebook Use, Envy, and Depression among College Students*, 43 Computer Hum. Behav. 139 (2015); Ethan Kloss et al., *Facebook Use Predicts Declines in Subjective Well-Being in Young Adults*, PLOS One (2013), http://journals.plos.org/plosone/article?id=10.1371/journal.pone .0069841.

25. Kloss et al., supra note 24.

26. See, e.g., Sebastian Valenzuela et al., supra note 24.

7 Sludge

1. Paperwork Reduction Act of 1995, Pub. L. 104-13, 109 Stat. 163 (codified as amended at 44 U.S.C. §§ 3501–3521 (2012)).

2. 44 U.S.C. § 3504(c) (2012) (emphasis added).

3. 44 U.S.C. § 3514(a) (2012).

4. Off. of Mgmt. & Budget, Information Collection Budget of the United States Government 2 (2016), https://www.whitehouse.gov/sites/ whitehouse.gov/files/omb/inforeg/inforeg/icb/icb_2016.pdf (https://perma

.cc/3FYG-M93W) (hereinafter Information Collection Budget 2016). Puzzlingly, the Trump administration has failed to produce the annual report, though it is required by law. See Office of Management and Budget Reports, WhiteHouse.gov, https://www.whitehouse.gov/omb/information-regulatory-affairs/reports (https://perma.cc/B75H-FAL3), which lists the 2016 Information Collection Budget as the most recent.

5. Government-Wide Totals for Active Information Collections, OIRA, https://www.reginfo.gov/public/do/PRAReport?operation=11 (https://perma.cc/H9K2-J424).

6. See Request for Comments on Implementation of the Paperwork Reduction Act, 74 Fed. Reg. 55,269 (Oct. 27, 2009). I served as administrator of OIRA at the time. OMB and OIRA asked similar questions in 1999. See Notice of Reevaluation of OMB Guidance on Estimating Paperwork Burden, 64 Fed. Reg. 55,788 (Oct. 14, 1999). For a valuable relevant discussion, see generally Adam M. Samaha, *Death and Paperwork Reduction*, 65 Duke L. J. 279 (2015).

7. The figure of $27 is used to simplify the illustration. The federal government does not have a standard number, but in regulatory impact analysis it has used numbers from the Bureau of Labor Statistics, which reports an average in the vicinity of $27. See, e.g., Dep't of Health and Hum. Serv. & Food and Drug Admin., Docket No. FDA-2016-N-2527, Tobacco Product Standard for N-Nitrosonornicotine Level in Finished Smokeless Tobacco Products 78 (Jan. 2017), https://www.fda.gov/downloads/aboutfda/reportsmanualsforms/reports/economicanalyses/ucm537872.pdf (https://perma.cc/46HT-25RZ): "Labor hours are valued at the current market wage as reported by the May 2015 Occupational Employment Statistics published by the Bureau of Labor Statistics (US Bureau of Labor Statistics, 2015)"; *Average Hourly and Weekly Earnings of All Employees on Private Nonfarm Payrolls by Industry Sector, Seasonally Adjusted*, Bureau of Lab. Stat., https://www.bls.gov/news.release/empsit.t19.htm (https://perma.cc/42WN-8CDG), listing the average hourly wage across private industries in January 2019 as $27.56; see also Samaha, supra note 6, at 298: "Not knowing who would be randomly selected for the survey, the [Institute of Museum and Library Services]

used the national average per capita income of about $20 per hour to convert respondent time into dollar cost."

8. Cf. Pamela Herd & Donald Moynihan, Administrative Burden: Policymaking by Other Means 22–30 (2019), discussing the concept of administrative burden and outlining its components; see generally Elizabeth F. Emens, *Admin*, 103 Geo. L. J. 1409 (2015), explaining how administrative tasks, like paperwork, hinder the leisure, sleep, relationships, and work of individuals, especially women; Elizabeth F. Emens, Life Admin: How I Learned to Do Less, Do Better, and Live More (2019), illustrating the impact of administrative burdens in life and offering advice to mitigate it.

9. Richard H. Thaler, *Nudge, Not Sludge*, 361 Sci. 431 (2018).

10. I am bracketing here the precise relationship between nudge and sludge. It should be clear that nudges can be for good or for bad; on the bad, see George Akerlof & Robert Shiller, Phishing for Phools (2015), describing, among other examples, the strategies that Cinnabon founder Rich and Greg Komen developed to push people to make the "unhealthy" decision to eat a Cinnabon. I am offering an understanding of sludge that includes "sludge for good," but it might be useful to restrict sludge to bad kinds of frictions. More work remains to be done on definitional issues. My hope is that the examples will be sufficient for purposes of the current discussion.

11. See Eric Bettinger et al., *The Role of Simplification and Information in College Decisions: Results from the H&R Block FAFSA Experiment* 1 (Nat'l Bureau of Econ. Research, Working Paper No. 15361, 2009), https://www.nber.org/papers/w15361 (https://perma.cc/66EG-VQXD): "To determine eligibility, students and their families must fill out an eight-page, detailed application called the Free Application for Federal Student Aid (FAFSA), which has over 100 questions."

12. See Susan Dynarski & Mark Wiederspan, *Student Aid Simplification: Looking Back and Looking Ahead* 8–11 (Nat'l Bureau of Econ. Research, Working Paper No. 17834, 2012), https://www.nber.org/papers/w17834 (https://perma.cc/5VTH-682V).

13. See, e.g., Herd & Moynihan, supra note 8, at 47–60; La. Advisory Committee for the US Commission on Civil Rights, Barriers to Voting in Louisiana 25–26 (2018), https://www.usccr.gov/pubs/2018/08-20-LA -Voting-Barriers.pdf (https://perma.cc/VCV4-BVQB), recommending reduction in paperwork associated with voter registration to increase access to the polls; Jonathan Brater et al., Brennan Ctr. for Justice, Purges: A Growing Threat to the Right to Vote (2018), http://www.brennancenter.org/ publication/purges-growing-threat-right-vote (https://perma.cc/74YE-P6ZP); The Leadership Conf. Educ. Fund, The Great Poll Closure (2016), http://civilrightsdocs.info/pdf/reports/2016/poll-closure-report-web.pdf (https://perma.cc/GRS7-953K).

14. See Dept. of Agriculture, Direct Certification in the National School Lunch Program: State Implementation Progress, School Year 2014–2015 (2015), https://www.fns.usda.gov/direct-certification-national-school-lunch-program-report-congress-state-implementation-progress-0 (https://perma.cc/D6PP-X4GL), at 2: "Direct certification typically involves matching SNAP, TANF, and FDPIR records against student enrollment lists, at either the State or the LEA level."

15. Rob Griffin et al., Who Votes with Automatic Voter Registration? Impact Analysis of Oregon's First-in-the-Nation Program (2017), https:// www.americanprogress.org/issues/democracy/reports/2017/06/07/ 433677/votes-automatic-voter-registration/#fn-433677-2 (https://perma .cc/9L7K-YPWX).

16. See Felice J. Freyer, *Emergency Rooms Once Offered Little for Drug Users: That's Starting to Change*, Boston Globe (Dec. 10, 2018), https:// www.bostonglobe.com/metro/2018/12/09/emergency-rooms-once -had-little-offer-addicted-people-that-starting-change/guX2LGPqG1 Af9xUV9rXI/story.html [https://perma.cc/FH6P-C2UF].

17. See id.

18. See Herd & Moynihan, supra note 8, at 23; Donald Moynihan et al., *Administrative Burden: Learning, Psychological, and Compliance Costs in Citizen-State Interactions*, 25 J. Pub. Admin. Res. Theory 43, 45–46 (2014).

19. See Janet Currie, *The Take up of Social Benefits* 11–12 (Inst. for the Study of Labor in Bonn, Discussion Paper No. 1103, 2004), examining rates of enrollment in social benefits within the United States and United Kingdom; see generally Katherine Baicker et al., *Health Insurance Coverage and Take-Up: Lessons from Behavioral Economics*, 90 Milbank Q. 107 (2012), examining low health-insurance take-up rates from a behavioral-economic perspective; Carole Roan Gresenz et al., *Take-Up of Public Insurance and Crowd-Out of Private Insurance under Recent CHIP Expansions to Higher Income Children*, 47 Health Servs. Res. 1999 (2012), analyzing the effect of expanding CHIP eligibility on health insurance take-up rates; Saurabh Bhargava & Dayanand Manoli, *Improving Take-Up of Tax Benefits in the United States*, Abdul Latif Jameel Poverty Action Lab (2015), https://www.povertyactionlab.org/evaluation/improving-take-tax-benefits-united-states (https://perma.cc/TPW8-XDHU), noting that "many people who are eligible for social and economic benefits do not claim those benefits" in the United States.

20. Brigitte C. Madrian & Dennis F. Shea, *The Power of Suggestion: Inertia in 401(k) Participation and Savings Behavior*, 116 Q. J. Econ. 1149, 1185 (2001), identifying inertia as a force working against participation in 401(k) plans; see also John Pottow & Omri Ben-Shahar, *On the Stickiness of Default Rules*, 33 Fla. St. U. L. Rev. 651, 651 (2006): "It is by now recognized that factors beyond drafting costs might also cause parties to stick with an undesirable default rule."

21. George Akerlof, *Procrastination and Obedience*, 81 Am. Econ. Rev. 1, 1–17 (1991), which examines several "behavioral pathologies," including procrastination.

22. See Ted O'Donoghue & Matthew Rabin, *Present Bias: Lessons Learned and to be Learned*, 105 Am. Econ. Rev. 273, 273–78 (2015).

23. Joshua Tasoff & Robert Letzler, *Everyone Believes in Redemption: Nudges and Overoptimism in Costly Task Completion*, 107 J. Econ. Behav. & Org. 107, 115 (2014).

24. For an especially dramatic illustration, see Peter Bergman, Jessica Laskey-Fink, & Todd Rogers, *Simplification and Defaults Affect Adoption*

and Impact of Technology, but Decision Makers Do Not Realize This (Harvard Kennedy School Faculty Research Working Paper Series, Working Paper No. RWP17-021, 2018), https://ssrn.com/abstract=3233874 (https://perma.cc/YWN6-BBCJ).

25. National Voter Registration Act of 1993, 52 U.S.C. § 20507(d) (2012). This provision of the National Voter Registration Act, among other purposes, is aimed to "ensure that accurate and current voter registration rolls are maintained." 52 U.S.C. § 20501(b)(4).

26. See, e.g., Iowa Code § 48A.28.3 (2018), permitting the sending of a notice each year; Ga. Code Ann. § 21-2-234(a)(1)–(2) (2018), notice sent to registrants with whom there has been "no contact" for three years; Pa. Stat. Ann., tit. 25, § 1901(b)(3) (2018), notice sent to voters who have not voted in five years; Ohio Rev. Code Ann. § 3503.21(B)(2) (2018), notice sent to those who fail to vote in two consecutive federal elections. Note also that some states trigger notices based on dubious interstate databases. See, e.g., Okla. Admin. Code § 230:15-11-19(a) (3) (2018), notice sent to those who have not voted since the "second previous General Election" and those who fail references to interstate databases; Wis. Stat. Ann. § 6.50(1) (2018), notice sent to voters who have not voted in four years. See also Brater et al., supra note 13, at 7–8, which explains how the system used by Oklahoma, "Crosscheck," is unreliable and inaccurate.

27. See 52 U.S.C. § 20507(d)(1)(ii).

28. See Xavier Gabaix, *Behavioral Inattention* (Nat'l Bureau of Econ. Research, Working Paper No. 24096, 2018), https://www.nber.org/papers/w24096 (https://perma.cc/FQ2L-M3VN).

29. See Herd & Moynihan, supra note 8. For helpful related discussion, see Jessica Roberts, *Nudge-Proof: Distributive Justice and the Ethics of Nudging*, 116 Mich. L. Rev. 1045 (2018). The idea has support in the PRA, which requires "particular emphasis on those individuals and entities most adversely affected." 44 U.S.C. § 3504(c)(3) (2012).

30. See Joyce He et al., Leaning In or Not Leaning Out? Opt-Out Choice Framing Attenuates Gender Differences in the Decision to Compete

(Nat'l Bureau of Econ. Research, Working Paper No. 24096, 2019), https://www.nber.org/papers/w26484.

31. See Austan Goolsbee, The "Simple Return": Reducing America's Tax Burden through Return-Free Filing 2 (2006), https://www.brookings.edu/wp-content/uploads/2016/06/200607goolsbee.pdf (https://perma.cc/C695-5YQL): "For the millions of taxpayers who could use the Simple Return, however, filing a tax return would entail nothing more than checking the numbers, signing the return, and then either sending a check or getting a refund."

32. See, e.g., Fla. Stat. Ann. § 741.04 (2018), making the effective date of marriage licenses three days after application unless both partners take a premarital education course; Mass. Ann. Laws ch. 208, § 21 (2018), allowing divorce to become absolute ninety days after the initial judgment.

33. See Pamaria Rekaiti & Roger Van den Bergh, *Cooling-Off Periods in the Consumer Laws of the EC Member States: A Comparative Law and Economics Approach*, 23 J. Consumer Pol'y 371, 397 (2000): "Cooling-off periods are potential remedies for the problems of irrational behaviour, situational monopoly, and informational asymmetry"; Dainn Wie & Hyoungjong Kim, *Between Calm and Passion: The Cooling-Off Period and Divorce Decisions in Korea*, 21 Feminist Econ. 187, 209 (2015): "The cooling-off period has no significant impact on divorce rates when the cause of divorce is . . . dishonesty, abuse, or discord with other family members. . . . Couples reporting the cause of divorce as personality difference or financial distress responded to the cooling-off periods."

34. See Cass R. Sunstein & Richard H. Thaler, *Libertarian Paternalism Is Not an Oxymoron*, 70 U. Chi. L. Rev. 1159, 1187–1188 (2003); see generally Wie & Kim, supra note 32, finding that the mandatory cooling-off period for divorce reduced the final divorce rate in Korea.

35. See Michael Luca et al., Handgun Waiting Periods Reduce Gun Deaths, 114 PNAS 12162 (2017).

36. For an example, see US Office of Pers. Mgmt., Standard Form 86: Questionnaire for National Security Positions (2010), https://www.opm.gov/forms/pdf_fill/sf86-non508.pdf (https://perma.cc/KB9P-JJ8D).

37. On some of the relevant trade-offs, see generally Memorandum from Jeffrey D. Zients, Dep. Dir. for Mgmt., & Cass R. Sunstein, Admin., OIRA, to Heads of Executive Departments and Agencies (Nov. 3, 2010), https://obamawhitehouse.archives.gov/sites/default/files/omb/memoranda/2011/m11-02.pdf (https://perma.cc/56QK-7HCR), encouraging federal agencies to share data to improve program implementation while complying with privacy laws.

38. Examples include Albert Nichols & Richard Zeckhauser, *Targeting Transfers through Restrictions on Recipients*, 72 Am. Econ. Rev. 372 (1982); Vivi Alatas et al., *Ordeal Mechanisms in Targeting: Theory and Evidence from a Field Experiment in Indonesia* (Nat'l Bureau of Econ. Research, Working Paper No. 19127, 2013), https://www.nber.org/papers/w19127 (https://perma.cc/6XFF-QP8E); Amedeo Fossati & Rosella Levaggi, Public Expenditure Determination in a Mixed Market for Health Care (May 4, 2004) (unpublished manuscript), https://papers.ssrn.com/sol3/papers.cfm?abstract_id=539382 (https://perma.cc/GF5A-YRY5); Sarika Gupta, Perils of the Paperwork: The Impact of Information and Application Assistance on Welfare Program Take-Up in India (Nov. 15, 2017) (unpublished PhD job market paper, Harvard University Kennedy School of Government), https://scholar.harvard.edu/files/sarikagupta/files/gupta_jmp_11_1.pdf (https://perma.cc/K4HY-3YK4).

39. See Information Collection Budget 2016, supra note 4, at 7.

40. OIRA provides a public account of information-collection requests under review. The account deserves far more attention, academic and otherwise, than it has received to date. See Information Collection Review Dashboard, OIRA, https://www.reginfo.gov/public/jsp/PRA/praDashboard.myjsp?agency_cd=0000&agency_nm=All&reviewType=RV&from_page=index.jsp&sub_index=1 (https://perma.cc/PD5L-9BNJ).

41. See, e.g., Memorandum from Neomi Rao, Admin., OIRA, to Chief Information Officers 8 (Aug. 6, 2018), https://www.whitehouse.gov/wpcontent/uploads/2018/08/Minimizing-Paperwork-and-Reporting-Burdens-Data-Call-for-the2018-ICB.pdf (https://perma.cc/KF9L-N6NZ); Memorandum from Cass R. Sunstein, Admin., OIRA, to the Heads of Exec. Dep'ts & Agencies (June 22, 2012), https://www.dol.gov/sites/default/

files/oira-reducing-rep-paperwork-burdens-2012.pdf (https://perma.cc/FRA5-M5P2).

42. Memorandum from Cass R. Sunstein, Admin., OIRA, to the Heads of Exec. Dep'ts & Agencies & Indep. Reg. Agencies (Apr. 7, 2010), https://www.whitehouse.gov/sites/whitehouse.gov/files/omb/assets/inforeg/PRAPrimer_04072010.pdf (https://perma.cc/D3VW-ZD8T).

43. See Memorandum from Cass R. Sunstein, Admin., OIRA, to the Heads of Exec. Dep'ts & Agencies (June 22, 2012), https://www.dol.gov/sites/default/files/oira-reducing-rep-paperwork-burdens-2012.pdf (https://perma.cc/FRA5-M5P2).

44. Id.

45. For a mixture of approaches, see id.

46. See, e.g., Memorandum from Neomi Rao, Admin., OIRA, to Chief Info. Offs. (July 21, 2017), https://www.whitehouse.gov/wp-content/uploads/2017/12/MEMORANDUM-FOR-CHIEF-INFORMATION-OFFICERS.pdf (https://perma.cc/6PD4-25N7), same subject.

47. Memorandum from Neomi Rao, Admin., OIRA, to Chief Info. Offs. 8 (Aug. 6, 2018), https://www.whitehouse.gov/wpcontent/uploads/2018/08/Minimizing-Paperwork-and-Reporting-Burdens-Data-Call-for-the2018-ICB.pdf [https://perma.cc/KF9L-N6NZ]; see also Memorandum from Howard Shelanski, Admin., OIRA, and John P. Holdren, Dir., Off. of Sci. & Tech. Pol'y, to the Heads of Exec. Dep'ts & Agencies and of the Indep. Reg. Agencies (Sept. 15, 2015) https://obamawhitehouse.archives.gov/sites/default/files/omb/inforeg/memos/2015/behavioral-science-insights-and-federal-forms.pdf (https://perma.cc/M8MX-9K6C), which recommends the use of behavioral sciences when crafting initiatives to reduce paperwork-burden hours.

48. See Pac. Nat. Cellular v. United States, 41 Fed. Cl. 20, 29 (1998).

49. Id. (emphasis added).

50. Id.; see also Util. Air Regulatory Grp. v. EPA, 744 F.3d 741, 750 n.6 (D.C. Cir. 2014), explaining that the PRA merely provides a defense, not

a private cause of action, to those of whom information is improperly requested; Smith v. United States, 2008 WL 5069783 at *1 (5th Cir. 2008), same subject; Springer v. IRS, 2007 WL 1252475 at *4 (10th Cir. 2007), same subject; Sutton v. Providence St. Joseph Med. Ctr., 192 F.3d 826, 844 (9th Cir. 1999), same subject; Alegent Health-Immanuel Med. Ctr. v. Sebelius, 34 F.Supp.3d 160, 170 (D.D.C. 2014), same subject.

51. 44 U.S.C. § 3512(b) (2012) (emphasis added).

52. 42 U.S.C. § 706.

53. See Cass R. Sunstein, *The Regulatory Lookback*, 94 B. U. L. Rev. 579, 592–596 (2014).

Epilogue

1. King James Bible Online, Gen. 3.1–3.7, https://www.kingjamesbible-online.org/Genesis-3-kjv/.

2. John Stuart Mill, Utilitarianism (Oskar Priest ed., 1957).

3. A. S. Byatt, Possession 212 (1990).

Index

Page numbers followed by t refer to tables; page numbers followed by f refer to figures.

Addiction
  cigarettes and, 73, 111
  opioids and, 158
  social media and, 8, 142, 149, 151, 216n22
Administrative burden
  choice architecture and, 162
  cost-benefit analysis of, 158
  fundamental rights and, 156
  procrastination and, 159
  program integrity and, 163–167
  sludge and, 8, 156–159, 162–171, 177, 183–184, 219n8
  targeting and, 163, 171–172
Advertising, 75–76, 96, 116, 136
Affective value, 15–16, 25
Affordable Care Act, 84, 177
Allcott, Hunt, 68–71, 103, 147–148, 151–152
Alzheimer's disease, 12, 30, 32, 33t

Amazon Mechanical Turk, 26, 32, 138
American Medical Student Association, 104
Anchoring, 71–72
Anger, 129
Animal welfare
  canine influenza and, 125
  dogs and, 125, 129
  dolphins and, 44, 54, 120, 122f, 125–130
  false inferences and, 110
  morals and, 16, 26, 43–44, 90, 110, 119–122, 128
  psychology and, 90
Anxiety
  information avoidance and, 23
  insinuation, 92–93
  panhandler effects and, 92–93, 108
  psychology and, 88, 92–93, 108

Anxiety (cont.)
  social media and, 135, 147,
    149–152
  welfare and, 48–49
Appliances, 29–31, 34t, 44, 55, 79,
  95, 100, 209n52
Arrow, Kenneth, 46
Ash, Randolph, 191
Attention
  bounded, 85
  emotions and, 189
  inattention and, 18, 86–87, 94
  information avoidance and, 18
  limited, 84–86, 107
  mandatory disclosure and, 16
  missing information and, 86–87
  motivated, 87–89, 106
  psychology and, 82–89, 94,
    96–100, 106–107, 205n7
  simplification and, 96–100
  sludge and, 160, 163, 173
  social media and, 136, 148
  welfare and, 50, 56, 75–76
Auerbach, Red, 109
Automobiles, 150
  fuel economy and, 2, 15, 26,
    39, 44, 57, 59, 63, 65–68, 71,
    79, 82–83, 89, 100, 120–123,
    202n38
  information avoidance and,
    11–12, 15, 24
  morals and, 121, 124
  psychology and, 79–83, 89,
    100–101
  safety and, 2, 35, 36t, 79–80
  sludge and, 182
  welfare and, 65, 68, 71, 74

Autonomy, 1–2, 40–42, 79
Availability heuristic, 24–25
Awareness, 75, 83–86, 104, 106

Bad news, 4, 7, 22–25, 30, 48–49,
  87–88
Bar-Gill, Oren, 109–117
Behavior
  addictive, 8, 73, 111, 142, 149,
    151, 158, 216n22
  altering, 15
  cancer and, 15, 21
  cognition and, 14 (see also
    Cognition)
  conflict of interest and, 44, 84,
    87, 91–93, 104–106
  conscience and, 16, 216n17
  decision-making and, 21 (see
    also Decision-making)
  discrete choice experiments and,
    145–146, 151
  disease and, 15, 21–22, 48, 61,
    81
  distributional effects and, 43,
    162–163, 184
  focusing illusion and, 24
  information avoidance and,
    14–15, 21–22, 28, 35–36
  information seeking and, 21, 28,
    42, 189
  irrationality and, 223n33
  loss aversion and, 22–25, 37, 61,
    143, 215n7
  morals and, 90–92, 144, 189 (see
    also Morals)
  nudges and, 28, 47–49, 95,
    198n11, 219n10

optimism and, 4, 24–25, 37,
    71–72, 77–78, 88–89, 159–161
procrastination and, 159, 221n21
psychology and, 14, 21–22, 81,
    85, 90, 95–96, 104, 106–108,
    155, 225n47
rational, 13, 21, 25, 61, 85, 100,
    116, 155, 158, 184
sludge and, 155, 159–161, 168,
    183–184, 221n21, 225n47
social media and, 137–145
welfare and, 42, 44, 47–53,
    61–63, 66–67, 72, 78
Behavioral economics, 81, 137,
    139, 159, 221n19
Behaviorally informed
    deregulation, 155, 184
Behavioral market failures, 81
Ben-Shahar, Omri, 79–80
Bentham, Jeremy, 40, 128, 190
Bhargava, Saurabh, 97, 104
Bias
    availability, 13
    behavioral, 160–162
    cognitive, 13, 25, 207n30
    false inferences and, 109–117
    focusing illusion and, 24
    information avoidance and, 13,
        21–25, 35–36
    information seeking and, 21–23,
        25, 42
    present, 13, 21–25, 48, 61, 72,
        78, 159, 161, 184
    psychology and, 84, 89–91, 93,
        108
    sludge and, 155, 159–162, 184
    social media and, 155, 159–161

welfare and, 42, 48, 61–63,
    71–73, 78
Bisphenol A (BPA), 111
Bisphenol S (BPS), 111
Boomerang effects, 105
Breakeven analysis, 56–57, 75–78,
    123
Brynjolfsson, Erik, 145–146
Byatt, A. S., 191

Cain, Daylian M., 91, 93
Calories
    disclosure and, 2–3, 5, 7, 17,
        31, 39, 70, 79, 82, 84, 94, 119,
        124, 194
    halo effect and, 95
    information avoidance and,
        26–28, 31–32, 34, 36
    labels and, 3, 26–28, 31–32, 34,
        36, 39, 44–45, 49, 53, 55, 58,
        61, 64, 66, 70, 72–73, 94–95,
        98, 189, 208n42
    psychology and, 79, 82, 89,
        94–95, 98–99, 208n42
    welfare and, 39, 44–45, 49, 53,
        55, 58, 61–64, 66, 70, 72–73

Cancer, 2
    behavior and, 15, 21–22, 48,
        61, 81
    breast, 23
    false inferences and, 109
    information avoidance and, 15,
        21–23, 30, 32, 33t
    lung, 81
    ovarian, 23
    prostate, 48

Cancer (cont.)
  psychology and, 81, 88, 90
  skin, 57
  susceptibility to, 12
  welfare and, 48, 57, 203n46
Canine influenza, 125
Carbon, 122
Centers for Disease Control and
    Prevention, 55, 200n25
Chandon, Pierre, 95
Channel factors, 103–104
Charities, 127–129
Charlotte-Mecklenburg Schools
    study, 102
Choice architecture, 162
Choosemyplate.gov, 52–53
Cigarettes
  addiction to, 73, 111
  cancer and, 81
  labels and, 3, 9, 39–40, 44,
      54, 61, 67, 73, 75, 106, 109,
      198n2, 199n19, 203n46
  psychology and, 81, 90, 106
  US Food and Drug
      Administration (FDA) and, 40,
      203n46, 218n7
  warnings on, 9, 39–40, 44,
      67, 75, 106, 109, 198n2,
      199nn18,19, 203n46, 212n74
  welfare and, 54, 60–61, 73,
      199nn18,19, 203n46
Cinnabon, 219n10
Climate change, 2, 16, 120, 174
Cognition
  awareness and, 75, 83–86, 104,
      106

bias and, 13, 25, 207n30
distributional effects and, 43,
    162–163, 184
information avoidance and,
    13–14, 25
information seeking and, 25, 60
limitations of, 162–163
morals and, 123
psychology and, 87, 100, 102,
    207n30
scarcity and, 162–163
sludge and, 162–163
social media and, 144, 216n21
System 1 operations and, 14–15,
    168
System 2 operations and, 14–15,
    168
tax of, 60
welfare and, 60, 67, 73
Cold release, 86
Comparative information,
    100–105
Complexity
  disclosure and, 49–50, 60, 88,
      91, 97, 106–108, 111, 131,
      150, 163, 172, 190
  psychology and, 49–50, 108
Conflict of interest, 44, 84, 87,
    91–93, 104–106
Conflict minerals, 35, 36t, 44,
    120, 126, 130–133, 201n32
Conscience, 16, 216n17
Consumer Financial Protection
    Bureau, 2
Consumers' Checkbook, 107
Consumer welfare loss, 64–65

Corporate social responsibility
(CSR), 96
Cost-benefit analysis
  cognitive tax and, 60
  conscience and, 216n17
  disclosure and, 6, 43–44, 49, 56,
    60, 75, 77, 81–82, 100, 105,
    114–117, 123, 126, 130, 153,
    201n32
  efficiency and, 15 (*see also*
    Efficiency)
  emotions and, 28, 70
  endogenous preferences and,
    65–66
  end points and, 57–58, 66–68,
    72–75
  Facebook and, 144
  false inferences and, 113–117
  fuel economy and, 2, 15, 26,
    39, 44, 57, 59, 63, 65–68, 71,
    82–83, 89, 120–123, 202n38
  government and, 190–191
  hedonic tax and, 60–64
  information avoidance and, 12,
    17–18, 22, 28–31, 34
  Information Collection Budget
    (ICB) and, 155
  information forcing and, 181
  internalities and, 81–82
  measurement of, 43
  morals and, 122–123, 126–133
  operating costs and, 29–31,
    34t, 44, 55, 79, 95, 100,
    209n52
  personalization and, 62–63
  proportionality and, 180–181

psychology and, 8, 81–82,
    97–101, 104–105, 129, 158,
    184, 209n52
  regulations and, 60–65
  sludge and, 153–155, 158, 161,
    165, 171, 173, 179–181, 184
  social costs and, 122, 180
  spendthrifts and, 17–18
  useless information and, 6
  welfare and, 43–46, 49, 56,
    59–68, 75–77, 113–117,
    123, 126, 129, 144, 197n1,
    198nn5,6, 201n32, 216n17
  WTP and, 12–13 (*see also*
    Willingness to pay [WTP])
Courts, 80, 130–131, 154, 161,
  177–179
Credit cards, 2, 34, 36, 44, 80,
  101, 170

Dallas, Steven K., 99
Data calls, 174–176
Death
  information seeking/avoidance
    and, 12, 17, 28–29, 31–32,
    34t
  morals and, 125–126
  psychology and, 90
  sludge and, 167
  welfare and, 47–48, 54, 67,
    72–73, 76
Decision-making
  autonomy and, 1–2, 40–42, 79
  bias and, 42 (*see also* Bias)
  comparative information and,
    100–102

Decision-making (cont.)
consumer loss and, 64–65
delegation of, 41
discrete choice experiments and,
145–146, 151
false inferences and, 110–115
freedom of choice and, 79
information avoidance and, 21,
28, 36, 188
informed choice and, 83, 107,
203n46
judgments and, 5, 18, 21, 25,
28, 74, 89–90, 107, 150, 166,
223n32
loss aversion and, 22–24, 61,
143, 215n7
psychology and, 79–82, 85–89,
97–98, 100, 210n61
rational, 13, 21, 25, 61, 85, 100,
116, 155, 158, 184
"right to know" and, 1, 110,
112, 189
sludge and, 168–169, 179, 181,
219n10
social media and, 137
standardized information and,
100–102
useful information and, 49–56
welfare and, 39–42, 49, 55–58,
64, 66, 201n32, 202n38
Decision utility, 58–59
Deliberation, 14, 168
Democratic Republic of Congo
(DRC), 131–132
Deontological approaches,
40–41, 197n1

Depression, 23, 135, 147, 149,
151
Deprivation, 13, 21, 25, 63, 119,
132
Deregulation, 153–155, 175,
183–185
Diabetes, 15, 30, 33t, 61, 74
Dictator game, 210n62
Disclosure
bad news and, 4, 7, 22–25, 30,
48–49, 87–88
breakeven analysis and, 56–57,
75–78, 123
calories and, 2–3, 5, 7, 17, 31,
36, 39, 44–45, 62, 70, 72, 79,
82, 89, 119, 124, 194
complexity and, 49–50, 60, 88,
91, 97, 106–107, 111, 131,
150, 163, 172, 190
consumer choice and, 32–37
cost-benefit analysis and, 6,
43–44, 49, 56, 60, 75, 77,
81–82, 100, 105, 114–117, 123,
126, 130, 153, 201n32
credit cards and, 2, 34, 36, 44,
80, 101, 170
end points and, 57–58, 66–68,
72–75
free market and, 79
intermediaries and, 106–107
labels and, 6 (see also Labels)
mandatory, 2–3 (see also
Mandatory disclosure)
McCarthy on, 85
morals and, 119–123, 126–127,
130–133

personalized information and,
35–36, 49, 62–63, 77, 101, 103,
135

privacy and, 50, 85, 106, 163,
169–171, 205n7, 214n1,
224n37

regulations and, 2–3, 42–43,
56, 75, 77–82, 89, 96, 99, 115,
120–121, 126, 130, 132, 175,
191, 201n32

restaurants and, 3, 31, 79, 82,
84, 94

simplification and, 96–100, 102,
108, 157, 160, 162, 182, 184

smart, 106–107

social media and, 7–8, 136–140

voluntary, 86–87, 116, 208n37

well-being and, 6

Discrete choice experiment,
145–146, 151

Disease

Alzheimer's, 12, 30, 32, 33t

ataxia, 23

behavior and, 15, 21–22, 48,
61, 81

cancer, 2 (*see also* Cancer)

Centers for Disease Control and
Prevention and, 55, 200n25

diabetes, 15, 30, 33t, 61, 74

Down syndrome, 88

false inferences and, 109

familial adenomatous polyposis,
23

heart, 12, 30, 33t, 48, 61, 74,
151

Huntington's, 23, 87

information avoidance and, 12,
15, 21–23, 30, 32, 33t, 61, 74

lifespan and, 203n46

psychology and, 15, 21–22, 48,
61, 81, 87–88, 90, 106

sludge and, 167

spinocerebellar ataxia, 23

welfare and, 48, 55, 57, 61–62,
74, 203n46

Distress, 13–14, 17, 22–23, 48, 88,
129, 157, 223n33

Distributional effects, 43,
162–163, 184

Dodd-Frank Act, 130

Dogs, 125, 129

Dolphin Protection Consumer
Information Act, 120, 127

Dolphins, 44, 54, 55, 120, 122f,
125–130

Down syndrome, 88

Duffy, John, 210n62

Earned Income Tax Credit (EITC),
97, 104, 156, 164–165, 172

Efficiency

comparative information and,
100–102

energy, 26, 39, 44, 47, 54–55,
63, 68–72, 75, 79, 89, 95–100,
103–104, 107, 176, 209n52

false inferences and, 114–115

fuel, 2, 15, 26, 39, 44, 57, 59, 63,
65–68, 71, 82–83, 89, 120–123,
202n38

information avoidance and,
15, 26

Efficiency (cont.)
  morals and, 121
  Paperwork Reduction Act (PRA)
    and, 153–155, 174, 177–179,
    222n29, 225n50
  psychology and, 79, 95–100,
    207n30, 209n52
  sludge and, 154
  welfare and, 39, 44, 47, 54–55,
    65, 68, 71, 75
Emotions
  anger, 129
  anxiety, 23, 48–49, 88, 92–93,
    108, 135, 147, 149–152
  attention and, 189
  cost of, 28, 70
  depression, 23, 135, 147, 149,
    151
  distress, 13–14, 17, 22–23, 48,
    88, 129, 157, 223n33
  effects of information on, 1,
    5–9, 189
  fear, 12, 18, 30, 48, 88, 93, 104,
    110, 129, 133
  frustration, 5–8, 14–15, 17, 125,
    153, 158, 181, 184
  happiness, 1, 6–9, 14, 16, 19, 26,
    58, 62, 73, 82, 123, 125, 127–
    131, 135–136, 147–151, 190
  information avoidance and,
    14–15, 28, 30
  information seeking and, 14–20,
    28–29, 37
  negative, 30
  optimistic, 4, 24–25, 37, 71–72,
    77–78, 88–89, 159–161

  pleasure, 12, 15, 89, 142,
    216n22
  positive, 5, 14–15, 17, 19–20,
    28–29
  psychology and, 82, 88, 106
  sadness, 7, 14, 17, 22, 26–27, 31,
    149, 152
  self-regulation and, 196n17
  sludge and, 169
  social media and, 147–149,
    216n21
  tax of, 70
Endogenous preferences, 65–66
Endowment effect, 137–141,
    145–146, 215nn7,9
End points, 57–58, 66–68, 72–75
Energy
  conservation and, 63, 104,
    211n72
  efficiency and, 26, 39, 44, 47,
    54–55, 63, 68–72, 75, 79, 89,
    95–100, 103–104, 107, 176,
    209n52
  home energy reports and, 69f,
    71–72, 103
  labels and, 26, 39, 44, 55, 71,
    95, 97–98, 100
  welfare and, 39, 44, 47, 54–55,
    63, 68–72, 75
Environmental issues
  carbon and, 122
  conscience and, 216n17
  greenhouse gases and, 2,
    120–124
  green products and, 7, 14, 81
  packaging and, 15

political reactions and, 209n52
psychology and, 81, 104,
    216n17
recycling, 5
social media and, 143
Toxics Release Inventory and,
    104
welfare and, 43, 47, 66–67
Estlund, Cynthia L., 96
Ethics, 84, 91, 95–96, 123
European Union (EU), 95
Executive orders, 43, 77, 175–176
Experienced utility, 58–59

Facebook
addiction to, 142, 149, 151,
    216n22
anxiety and, 135
attention and, 136, 148
cost-benefit analysis and, 144
depression and, 135, 147, 149,
    151
discrete choice experiments and,
    145–146, 151
endowment effect and,
    137–141, 145–146, 215nn7,9
happiness and, 8, 135–136,
    147–151, 190
hedonic value and, 152
information seeking and, 138,
    150
mistaken forecasts and, 149–151
money and, 8, 136, 138–139,
    143–144, 147–150, 190
morals and, 143
privacy and, 214n1

revenue and, 136
sadness and, 147–149
stopping use of, 137–151, 215n8
useful information and, 135,
    141
useless information and, 142
value of, 135–152
wasting time and, 141–144
welfare and, 144–147
well-being and, 8, 137–138, 142,
    144, 146–147, 151–152, 190
willingness to accept (WTA)
    and, 137–146, 151
willingness to pay (WTP) and,
    136–146
"Failure of Mandated Disclosure,
    The" (Ben-Shahar and
    Schneider), 79–80
Fair Trade labels, 54, 124
False inferences, 189
bias and, 109–117
cost-benefit analysis and,
    113–117
counteracting, 115–117
decision-making and, 110–115
disease and, 109
efficiency and, 114–115
food and, 109–116
genetically modified organisms
    (GMOs) and, 109–113,
    116–117, 212n1
government and, 109–114, 117
labels and, 113, 116
mandatory disclosure and, 111
predisclosure and, 110–111, 114
regulations and, 115

False inferences (cont.)
  safety and, 113, 116
  useful information and, 115
  US Food and Drug
    Administration (FDA) and,
    113, 212n4
  voluntary disclosure and, 116
  warnings and, 109–110
  welfare costs of, 113–115
  Zhang on, 212n1
Familial adenomatous polyposis,
  23
Fear, 12, 18, 30, 48, 88, 93, 104,
  110, 129, 133
Fitbit, 62
Focusing illusion, 24
Food
  BPA and, 111
  calories and, 2 (*see also* Calories)
  choosemyplate.gov and, 52–53
  dolphins and, 44, 54, 120, 122f,
    125–130
  false inferences and, 109–116
  genetically modified
    organisms (GMOs) and, 2,
    34–35, 36t, 44–45, 59, 109,
    111–113, 116–117, 120, 122f,
    123, 189, 212n1
  halo effect and, 95
  healthier, 3
  information avoidance and, 12,
    34, 36
  menus and, 82, 84, 94–95,
    98–99, 203nn44,46
  morals and, 120–121, 123,
    127

  nutrition and, 2, 39, 44, 52, 55,
    62, 81, 84, 87, 203nn43,44,46
  psychology and, 81–82, 89,
    94–95, 98
  restaurants and, 3, 12, 31–32,
    34, 60, 62, 79–82, 84, 94–95,
    151, 208n42
  safety of, 113, 116, 167, 183
  sludge and, 167, 182–183,
    219n10
  trans fats and, 55, 111
  tuna, 44, 54, 120, 127
  USDA and, 51–52, 59, 121,
    123, 157, 170, 173t, 174–175,
    220n14
  warnings and, 44, 50
  welfare and, 40, 44, 47, 50–55,
    59–62, 72, 75, 78, 203n46
Food Allergen Labeling and
  Consumer Protection Act, 127
Food Pyramid, 51–53
Forbes magazine, 103
Fraud, 164, 166, 184
Free Application for Federal
  Student Aid (FAFSA), 157
Free market, 79
Frustration, 5–8, 14–15, 17, 125,
  153, 158, 181, 184
Fuel
  efficiency and, 2, 15, 26, 39,
    44, 57, 59, 63, 65–68, 71,
    79, 82–83, 89, 100, 120–123,
    202n38
  labels and, 26, 39, 44, 57,
    59, 65–68, 71, 83, 120–123,
    202n38, 203n46

Genetically modified organisms
(GMOs)
    false inferences and, 109–113,
        116–117, 212n1
    food and, 2, 34–35, 36t, 44–45,
        59, 109, 111–113, 116,
        120–123
    information avoidance and,
        34–35, 36t
    labels and, 44–45, 59, 113, 116,
        121–123, 189
    morals and, 120–123
    US Food and Drug
        Administration (FDA) and, 113
    warnings and, 44
    welfare and, 44–45, 59
    willingness to pay (WTP) and,
        35
Gide, André, 198n5
Global Entry program, 157
Golman, Russell, 79–108
Good news, 4, 19, 24–25, 28, 30,
    36, 41, 70
Google Maps, 135
Government. *See also specific
    agencies*
    choosemyplate.gov and, 52–53
    cost-benefit analysis and,
        190–191
    executive orders and, 43, 77,
        175–176
    false inferences and, 109–114,
        117
    information avoidance and, 32
    Information Collection Budget
        (ICB) and, 155

    mandatory disclosure and, 2,
        6–7, 9, 25, 32, 39–41, 44–49,
        54, 78, 80, 82–83, 87–88, 94,
        96, 99, 105, 111, 153, 190,
        208n37
    morals and, 117, 119, 121,
        124
    perceiving motives of, 112–
        113
    regulations and, 2 (*see also*
        Regulations)
    sludge and, 8, 153–155, 162–
        163, 167–172, 177, 181–183,
        191, 218n7
    welfare and, 39–42, 44, 50–51,
        62, 66
GPS, 9, 49, 107
Greenhouse gases, 2, 120–124
Green products, 7, 14, 81

Halo effect, 95
Happiness
    effects of information on, 1,
        6–9
    information avoidance and, 14,
        16, 19, 26
    morals and, 123, 125, 127,
        129–131
    social media and, 8, 135–136,
        147–151, 190
    welfare and, 58, 62, 73
    willingness to pay (WTP) and,
        26, 58, 73, 149
Hayek, Friedrich, 150
Heart disease, 12, 30, 33t, 48, 61,
    74, 151

Hedonic value
  information seeking/avoidance
    and, 15–16, 21, 27–29, 188–
    190
  morals and, 123–124, 133
  psychology and, 87
  social media and, 152
  welfare and, 48–49, 60–64, 67,
    70, 73, 77
Heterogeneity, 7, 14, 25–27, 30,
    34, 64, 70, 79
Home energy reports, 69f, 71–72,
    103
Huntington's disease, 23, 87
Hygiene, 94, 208n37

Inattention, 18, 86–87, 94
Inequality, 25, 163
Inertia, 159–162, 184, 221n20
Inference
  false, 109–117, 189, 212n1
  inattention and, 86
  problem of, 110–111, 212n1
  psychology and, 86
Information avoidance
  active steps in, 11–12
  attention and, 18
  automobiles and, 11–12, 15, 24
  availability heuristic and, 24–25
  bad news and, 4, 7, 22–25, 30,
    48–49, 87–88
  behavior and, 14–15, 21–22, 28,
    35–36
  bias and, 13, 21–25, 35–36
  calories and, 26–28, 31–32, 34,
    36

cognition and, 13–14, 25
complexity and, 49–50, 60, 88,
    91, 97, 106–108, 111, 131,
    150, 163, 172, 190
cost-benefit analysis and, 12,
    17–18, 22, 28–31, 34
dark side of information and,
    17–20
death and, 12, 17, 28–29,
    31–32, 34t
decision-making and, 21, 28,
    36, 188
disease and, 12, 15, 21–23, 30,
    32, 33t
efficiency and, 15, 26
emotions and, 14–15, 17, 19–20,
    28–30
food and, 12, 34, 36
genetically modified organisms
    (GMOs) and, 34–35, 36t
government and, 32
happiness and, 14, 16, 19, 26
hedonic value and, 15–16, 21,
    27–29, 63–64, 188–190
heterogeneity and, 7, 14, 25–27,
    30, 34
injustice and, 13, 21, 25, 35
instrumental value and, 14–21,
    28–29, 152
judgments and, 18, 21, 25,
    28
labels and, 16, 26–28, 31–32,
    34, 36
loss aversion and, 22–24, 61,
    143, 215n7
mandatory disclosure and, 25

money and, 13–15, 20–21, 26, 29, 31–32
motivations for, 14–20, 29, 189–191
regulations and, 34
safety and, 35
strategic self-ignorance and, 22
useful information and, 15, 20, 24, 26, 29–30, 34, 36
useless information and, 17
well-being and, 12, 16
willingness to pay (WTP) and, 3, 12–14, 26–28, 31–35, 36t
Information Collection Budget (ICB), 155
Information forcing, 181
Information overload, 49, 60. *See also* Sludge
Information seeking
affective value and, 15–16, 25
behavior and, 21, 28, 42, 189
bias and, 21–23, 25, 42
cognition and, 25, 60
emotions and, 14–20, 28–29, 37
hedonic value and, 15–16, 21, 27–29, 188–190
heterogeneity and, 7, 14, 25–27, 30, 34
judgments and, 18, 21, 25, 28
knowledge is power idea and, 15
money and, 13–15, 20–21, 26, 29, 31–32
morals and, 119, 125, 132
motivation for, 6, 8, 14–20, 26–29, 37, 189
optimism and, 24–25, 37

personalized information and, 35–36, 49, 62–63, 77, 101, 103, 135
psychology and, 83
salience and, 96–100
simplification and, 96–100, 102, 108, 157, 160, 162, 182, 184
sludge and, 162–172, 178
social media and, 135–152
useful information and, 15, 20, 24, 26, 29–30, 34–36
verification and, 82–83, 86, 123, 204n2
welfare and, 42, 58, 60
willingness to pay (WTP) and, 12–14, 26–28, 31–35, 36t
Informed choice, 83, 107, 203n46
Injustice, 13, 21, 25, 35, 41
Insinuation anxiety, 92–93
Instagram, 138, 140, 148
Instrumental value
hedonic value of, 188
information avoidance and, 14–21, 28–29, 152
knowledge is power idea and, 15
negative, 18–20, 152
online information and, 135
well-being and, 16
Insurance, 80, 181, 221n19
Intermediaries, 106–107
Internalities, 81–82
Internal Revenue Service (IRS), 164, 173, 180, 209n49
Investment, 6, 15, 26, 41, 54, 80, 93, 102, 106, 171
Irrationality, 223n33

Judgments
  biased probability, 89–90
  decision-making and, 5, 18, 21,
    25, 28, 74, 89–90, 107, 150,
    166, 223n32
  Hayek on, 150
  information seeking/avoidance
    and, 18, 21, 25, 28
  optimistic bias and, 24–25, 72,
    78, 159
  psychology and, 89–90, 107
  sludge and, 166, 223n32
  welfare and, 74

Kahneman, Daniel, 24
Kessler, Judd B., 68–71, 103
Know Before You Owe, 2
Komen, Greg, 219n10
Komen, Rich, 219n10
Kornienko, Tatiana, 210n62

Labels
  accentuating positive and,
    119–120
  breakeven analysis and, 56–57,
    75–78, 123
  calories and, 3, 26–28, 31–32,
    34, 36, 39, 44–45, 49, 53, 55,
    58, 61, 64, 66, 70, 72–73,
    94–95, 98, 189, 208n42
  choosemyplate.gov and, 52–53
  cigarettes and, 3, 9, 39–40,
    44, 54, 61, 67, 73, 75,
    106, 109, 198n2, 199n19,
    203n46, 218n7
  effectiveness of, 7, 49

energy, 26, 39, 44, 55, 71, 95,
    97–98, 100
Fair Trade, 54, 124
false inferences and, 113, 116
Food Allergen Labeling and
    Consumer Protection Act and,
    127
Food Pyramid and, 51–53
fuel economy, 26, 39, 44, 57,
    59, 65–68, 71, 83, 120–123,
    202n38, 203n46
genetically modified organisms
    (GMOs) and, 2, 35, 44–45, 59,
    112–113, 116–117, 121–123,
    189, 212n1
information avoidance and, 16,
    26–28, 31–32, 34, 36
mandatory, 6, 16, 44, 53–54,
    56, 64
McCarthy on, 85
menus and, 84, 94–95, 98–99,
    203nn44,46
morals and, 119–124, 127
nutrition and, 39, 44, 55, 87,
    203nn43,44,46
psychology and, 83, 85, 87,
    94–100
safety and, 54, 85, 113, 116,
    120, 122, 122f, 127
salience and, 94, 96–100, 102
trans fats and, 55, 111
vividness and, 106
warnings and, 9, 39–40, 44 (see
    also Warnings)
welfare and, 39, 44–50, 53–76,
    199n19, 202n38, 203n46

LaMotte, Christabel, 191
Lifespan, 203n46
Loans, 2, 80, 100–102, 164
Loewenstein, George, 79–108
Loss aversion, 22–25, 37, 61,
    143, 215n7
Loureiro, Maria L., 203n43
Luca, Michael, 102

Mandatory disclosure
  attention and, 16
  Ben-Shahar and Schneider essay
    on, 79–80
  calories and, 2–3, 31, 36, 39,
    44–45, 62, 72, 79, 82, 89
  circumstances for, 42–44
  dolphin-safe tuna and, 44,
    54–55, 120, 127
  effectiveness of, 40, 54–56,
    208n37
  executive orders and, 43, 77,
    175–176
  false inferences and, 111
  FDA and, 40–41
  government and, 2, 6–7, 9, 25,
    32, 41–49, 54, 78, 80, 82–83,
    87–88, 94, 96, 99, 105, 111,
    153, 190, 208n37
  information avoidance and, 25
  labels and, 6, 16, 44, 53–54, 56,
    64
  nudges and, 47–49
  psychology and, 80–83, 87–88,
    94, 96, 99, 105, 208n37
  restaurants and, 62–63
  sludge and, 153

unknown responses to, 44–49
unverifiable information and,
    83
warnings and, 6, 54, 88, 99
welfare and, 39–49, 54, 78
willingness to pay (WTP) and,
    46–47, 78
Manoli, Dayanand, 97, 104
Mass atrocities, 130–133
McCarthy, Roger, 85
McDonald's, 95
Mill, John Stuart, 40, 190
Misinformation, 49, 82
Missing information, 86–87
Money
  information seeking/avoidance
    and, 13–15, 20–21, 26, 29,
    31–32
  investment and, 6, 15, 26, 41,
    54, 80, 93, 102, 106, 171
  lack of, 13
  morals and, 125, 127, 129, 143
  psychology and, 81, 91
  saving, 13, 15, 29, 47, 56, 67,
    127, 167, 181, 183
  sludge and, 153, 165, 167,
    171–172, 181–184
  social media and, 8, 136,
    138–139, 143–144, 147–150,
    190
  welfare and, 44, 47, 56, 67, 72,
    77
  WTP and, 3 (*see also* Willingness
    to pay [WTP])
Moore, 91
Moral effect, 129–130

Moral outrage, 143
Morals
  animal welfare and, 16, 26,
    43–44, 90, 110, 119–122, 128
  automobiles and, 121, 124
  behavior and, 144, 189
  breakeven analysis and, 56–57,
    75–78
  cognition and, 123
  conflict minerals and, 35, 36t,
    44, 120, 126, 130–133, 201n32
  conflict of interest and, 44, 84,
    87, 91–93, 104–106
  conscience and, 16, 216n17
  consumer choices and,
    130–133
  cost-benefit analysis and,
    122–123, 126–133
  death and, 125–126
  disclosure and, 119–123,
    126–127, 130–133
  effect of, 129–130
  efficiency and, 121
  ethics and, 84, 91, 95–96, 123
  food and, 120–121, 123, 127
  genetically modified organisms
    (GMOs) and, 120–123
  government and, 117, 119, 121,
    124
  happiness and, 123, 125, 127,
    129–131
  hedonic value and, 123–124,
    133
  information seeking and, 119,
    125, 132
  labels and, 119–124, 127
  licensing and, 90–92
  mass atrocities and, 130–133
  money and, 125, 127, 129, 143
  psychology and, 129
  regulations and, 121, 124,
    126–133, 201n32
  righting wrongs and, 120–121
  safety and, 120, 122f
  social media and, 143
  useful information and, 120
  useless information and, 188
  vindicating commitments and,
    124–130
  welfare and, 121–124
  well-being and, 127–129
  willingness to pay (WTP) and,
    124–129, 132–133
Mortgages, 2, 44, 50, 101, 127
Movie theaters, 3, 86, 171

National Association of
    Manufacturers (NAM), 130,
    201n32
Newell, Richard G., 95, 97
Nudges
  choosemyplate.gov and, 52–53
  Food Pyramid and, 51–53
  reminders and, 9, 57–58, 160,
    184, 198n11
  sludge and, 219n10
  welfare and, 28, 47–49, 95,
    198n11
Nutrition, 2
  labels and, 39, 44, 55, 87,
    203nn43,44,46
  psychology and, 81, 84, 87

welfare and, 39, 44, 52, 55, 62, 203nn43,44,46

Obama administration, 2, 107, 122, 174–176
Office of Federal Procurement Policy, 153–154
Office of Information and Regulatory Affairs (OIRA)
data calls and, 174–176
Obama administration and, 174–176
Paperwork Reduction Act (PRA) and, 153–155, 174, 177–179
sludge reduction and, 153–155, 174–179, 218n6, 224n40
Office of Management and Budget (OMB), 155, 178, 218n6
Operating costs, 29–31, 34t, 44, 55, 79, 95, 100, 209n52
Opower, 103, 105
Optimism
behavior and, 4, 24–25, 37, 71–72, 77–78, 88–89, 159–161
bias and, 24–25, 72, 78, 159
information seeking and, 24–25, 37
judgment and, 24–25, 72, 78, 159
psychology and, 88–89
sludge and, 159–161
unrealistic, 88
welfare and, 71–72, 77–78
willingness to pay and, 71–72

Packaging, 5–8, 14–15
Pain relievers, 35, 36t, 50

Panhandler effects, 92–93, 108
Paperwork Reduction Act (PRA), 153–155, 174, 177–179, 222n29, 225n50
Personalized information, 35–36, 49, 62–63, 77, 101, 103, 135
Pharmaceutical industry, 83, 105
PharmFree Scorecards, 104
Pleasure, 12, 15, 89, 142, 216n22
Poe, Edgar Allen, 94
Pope, David G., 210n59
Positive feelings, 14–15, 17, 19–20, 29
Posner, Eric, 119–133
Possession (Byatt), 191
Postdisclosure beliefs, 110–111, 114–115
Poverty, 2, 21, 156
Predisclosure beliefs, 110–111, 114
Prequalification, 164
Prescription drugs, 9, 83, 104–105, 158
Privacy, 50, 85, 106, 163, 169–171, 205n7, 214n1, 224n37
Probability, 18, 20–21, 24–25, 89–90
Procrastination, 159, 221n21
Profit, 94, 156
Program integrity, 163–167
Proportionality, 180–181
Prostate-specific antigen (PSA) testing, 48

Psychology
  addiction and, 8, 73, 111, 142,
    149, 151, 158, 216n22
  attention and, 82–89, 94,
    96–100, 106–107, 205n7
  automobiles and, 79–83, 89,
    100–101
  behavior and, 14, 21–22, 81, 85,
    90, 95–96, 104, 106–108, 155,
    225n47
  Ben-Shahar and Schneider essay
    and, 79–80
  bias and, 84, 89–91, 93, 108
  bounded attention and, 85
  calories and, 79, 82, 89, 94–95,
    98–99
  cancer and, 81, 88, 90
  channel factors and, 103–104
  cognition and, 87, 100, 102,
    207n30
  comparative information and,
    100–102
  complexity and, 49–50, 108
  conflict of interest and, 44, 84,
    87, 91–93, 104–106
  conscience and, 16, 216n17
  cost-benefit analysis and, 8,
    81–82, 97–101, 104–105, 129,
    158, 184, 209n52
  decision-making and, 79–
    82, 85–89, 97–98, 100,
    210n61
  disease and, 15, 21–22, 48, 61,
    81, 87–88, 90, 106
  distributional effects and, 43,
    162–163, 184

  efficiency and, 79, 95–100,
    207n30, 209n52
  emotions and, 82, 88, 106
  environmental issues and, 81,
    104, 216n17
  focusing illusion and, 24
  food and, 81–82, 89, 94–95, 98
  genetic testing and, 23
  hedonic value and, 87
  inattention and, 18, 86, 94
  inference and, 86
  information seeking and, 83
  intermediaries and, 106–107
  internalities and, 81–82
  irrationality and, 223n33
  judgments and, 89–90, 107
  labels and, 83, 85, 87, 94–100
  limited awareness and, 83–86
  loss aversion and, 22–25, 37, 61,
    143, 215n7
  mandatory disclosure and,
    80–83, 87–88, 94, 96, 99, 105,
    208n37
  money and, 81, 91
  morals and, 90–92, 129
  nudges and, 28, 47–49, 95,
    198n11, 219n10
  optimism and, 88–89
  panhandler effects and, 92–93,
    108
  procrastination and, 159,
    221n21
  rationality and, 13, 21, 25, 61,
    85, 100, 116, 155, 158, 184
  regulations and, 79–82, 86, 89,
    95–96, 99, 105

safety and, 79–80, 85
salience and, 94, 96–100, 102
simplification and, 96–100, 102,
    108, 157, 160, 162, 182, 184
sludge and, 158, 184
smokers and, 81, 90, 106
social comparison information
    and, 103–105
spotlight effect and, 94
standardized information and,
    100–102
telltale heart effect and, 93–96,
    108
useful information and, 107
useless information and, 83, 85
verifiable information and,
    82–83, 86
vividness and, 106
voluntary disclosure and, 86–87,
    208n37
warnings and, 83, 85, 88, 99,
    106
willingness to pay (WTP) and,
    209n52

Randomized control trials and,
    53–54, 66–67, 98, 101–102,
    148, 199nn18,19, 218n7
Rationality, 13, 21, 25, 61, 85,
    100, 116, 155, 158, 184
Reagan, Ronald, 43
Recycling, 5
Regulations. *See also specific agency*
    Ben-Shahar/Schneider essay on,
    79–80
    boomerang effects and, 105

cost-benefit analysis and, 60–65
deregulation and, 153–155, 175,
    183–185
disclosure and, 2–3, 42–43, 56,
    75, 77–82, 89, 96, 99, 115,
    120–121, 126, 130, 132, 175,
    191, 201n32
end points and, 72–75
European Union (EU) and, 95
false inferences and, 115
free market and, 79
hedonic tax and, 60–62
information avoidance and, 34
internalities and, 81–82
morals and, 121, 124, 126–133,
    201n32
psychology and, 79–82, 86, 89,
    95–96, 99, 105
self-regulation and, 206n19
shaming and, 105
sludge and, 153–155, 161, 165,
    174–175, 179–180, 183–185
social media and, 137
US Securities and Exchange
    Commission (SEC) and, 120,
    126, 130–133, 173t, 175,
    201n32, 214n14
welfare and, 40, 42–43, 56,
    58–61, 64, 66, 68, 71–78,
    201n32, 202n43
Regulatory impact analysis,
    56, 218n7
Reminders, 9, 57–58, 160, 184,
    198n11
Repopulated forms, 164, 168, 170,
    176

Restaurants
  disclosure and, 3, 31, 79, 82,
    84, 94
  food and, 3, 12, 31–32, 34, 60,
    62, 79–84, 94–95, 151, 208n42
  halo effect and, 95
  hedonic tax and, 60–62
  hygiene and, 94, 208n37
  mandatory disclosure and,
    62–63
  menus and, 82, 84, 94–95,
    98–99, 203nn44,46
Revenue, 131–132, 136
"Right to know," 1, 110, 112, 189
Ripken, Susanna Kim, 96
Risk aversion, 93
Ritten, Chian Jones, 17–18

Sadness, 7, 14, 17, 22, 26–27, 31,
    149, 152
Safety
  automobiles and, 2, 35, 36t,
    79–80
  false inferences and, 113, 116
  food, 2, 35, 112–113, 116–117,
    122f, 167, 183, 189, 212n1
  genetically modified organisms
    (GMOs), 2, 35, 112–113, 117,
    122f, 189, 212n1
  information avoidance and, 35
  labels and, 54, 85, 113, 116,
    120, 122f, 127
  morals and, 120, 122f
  optimistic bias and, 24
  psychology and, 79–80, 85
  sludge and, 167

  warnings and, 9 (see also
    Warnings)
  water and, 143
  welfare and, 39, 50
  workplace, 2, 167
Sah, Sunita, 93
Salience, 94, 96–100, 102
Scarcity, 162–163
Schkade, David, 24, 109–117
Schneider, Carl, 79–80
Security, 157, 163, 169–171, 173t,
    175
Self-control, 27–28, 163, 168–169
Self-regulation, 196n17, 206n19
Shaming, 105
Siikamaki, Juha V., 97
Simplification, 96–100, 102, 108,
    157, 160, 162, 182, 184
Slate magazine, 103
Sludge
  administrative burden of,
    8, 156–159, 162–171, 177,
    183–184, 219n8
  attention and, 160, 163, 173
  audits of, 181–183, 191
  automobiles and, 182
  behavior and, 155, 159–161,
    168, 183–184, 221n21, 225n47
  bias and, 155, 159–162, 184
  clutter from, 11
  cognition and, 162–163
  collection burden and, 154, 177
  cost-benefit analysis and,
    153–155, 158, 161, 165, 171,
    173, 179–181, 184
  courts and, 177–179

data calls and, 174–176
death and, 167
decision-making and, 168–169, 179, 181, 219n10
deregulation and, 153–155, 175, 183–185
detrimental effects of, 158
disease and, 167
distributional effects and, 162–163, 184
efficiency and, 154
emotions and, 169
Everyone Believes in Redemption study and, 159–160
food and, 167, 182–183, 219n10
government and, 8, 153–155, 162–163, 167–172, 177, 181–183, 191, 218n7
inertia and, 159–162, 184, 221n20
Information Collection Budget (ICB) and, 155
information forcing and, 181
information seeking and, 162–172, 178
judgments and, 166, 223n32
justifying information acquisition and, 163–172
mandatory disclosure and, 153
money and, 153, 165, 167, 171–172, 181–184
nudges and, 219n10
OIRA and, 153–155, 174–179, 218n6, 224n40
OMB and, 155, 178, 218n6
optimism and, 159–161

Paperwork Reduction Act (PRA) and, 153–155, 174, 177–179, 222n29, 225n50
prequalification and, 164
privacy and, 163, 169–171, 224n37
procrastination and, 159, 221n21
program integrity and, 163–167
proportionality and, 180–181
psychology and, 158, 184
reduction of paperwork and, 153–161, 164, 172–180, 183–184, 220n13
regulations and, 153–155, 161, 165, 174–175, 179–180, 183–185
repopulating forms and, 164, 168, 170, 176
safety and, 167
scarcity and, 162–163
security and, 157, 163, 169–171, 173t, 175
self-control problems and, 163, 168–169
simplification and, 157, 160, 162, 182, 184
targeting and, 163, 171–172
tax returns and, 157, 223n31
US Congress and, 161, 179–181
useful information and, 163–171, 185, 219n10
useless information and, 160
willingness to pay (WTP) and, 171–172
Smith, Jonathan, 102

Smokers
  hedonic tax and, 60–62
  labels and, 54, 61, 73, 199n19,
    203n46
  lung cancer and, 81
  psychology and, 81, 90, 106
  welfare and, 54, 60–61, 73,
    199nn18,19, 203n46
Social comparison information,
  103–105
Social costs, 122, 180
Social media
  addiction to, 8, 142, 149, 151,
    216n22
  advertising and, 136
  anxiety and, 135
  attention and, 136, 148
  behavior and, 137–145
  bias and, 155, 159–161
  cognition and, 144, 216n21
  decision-making and, 137
  depression and, 135, 147, 149,
    151
  disclosure and, 7–8, 136–140
  discrete choice experiments and,
    145–146, 151
  emotions and, 147–149, 216n21
  endowment effect and,
    137–141, 145–146, 215nn7,9
  environmental issues and, 143
  Facebook, 8, 135–152, 190
  happiness and, 8, 135–136,
    147–151, 190
  hedonic value and, 152
  information seeking and, 138,
    150

Instagram, 138, 140, 148
loss aversion and, 143, 215n7
mistaken forecasts and, 149–151
money and, 8, 136, 138–139,
  143–144, 147–150, 190
morals and, 143
pleasure and, 142, 216n22
privacy and, 214n1
regulations and, 137
revenue and, 136
sadness and, 147–149
stopping use of, 137–151, 215n8
Twitter, 136, 138, 140, 142
useful information and,
  135–136, 141, 152
useless information and, 142
value of, 135–152
wasting time and, 141–144
welfare and, 144–147
well-being and, 8, 137–138,
  142–147, 151–152, 190
willingness to pay (WTP) and,
  136–146
YouTube, 140, 142
Spendthrifts, 17–18
Spinocerebellar ataxia, 23
Spotlight effect, 94
Standardized information, 100–
  102
St. Augustine, 22
Strategic self-ignorance, 22
Stroke, 75
Subway, 95
Superendowment effect, 138–141
System 1 operations, 14–15, 168
System 2 operations, 14–15, 168

Targeting, 163, 171–172
Tax returns, 157, 223n31
"Tell-Tale Heart, The" (Poe), 94
Telltale heart effect, 93–96, 108
Thaler, Richard H., 156, 193
Thunstrom, Linda, 17–18
Toxics Release Inventory, 104
Trans fats, 55, 111
Trump, Donald, 122, 217n4
Tuna, 44, 54, 120, 127
Turner, Ted, 103
Twitter, 136, 138, 140, 142

US Congress, 77, 120–121,
    126–127, 130–131, 161,
    179–181
US Department of Agriculture
    (USDA), 51–52, 59, 121, 123,
    157, 170, 173t, 174–175,
    220n14
US Department of Education, 156,
    173
US Department of Energy, 156
US Department of Health and
    Human Services, 174, 178
US Department of Homeland
    Security, 173t, 175
US Department of Labor, 173t,
    175, 203n46
US Department of State, 156
US Department of the Treasury,
    173
US Department of Transportation,
    43, 120, 156, 202n38, 203n46
Useful information, 7
    false inferences and, 115

information seeking/avoidance
    and, 15, 20, 24, 26, 29–30,
    34–36
    morals and, 120
    psychology and, 107
    salience and, 94, 96–100, 102
    sludge and, 163–171, 185,
    219n10
    social media and, 135–136, 141,
    152
    welfare and, 49–56, 67–68, 74,
    77
Useless information, 1
    cost of, 6
    information avoidance and, 17
    morals and, 188
    preferences and, 7
    psychology and, 83, 85
    sludge and, 160
    social media and, 142
    welfare and, 50
US Environmental Protection
    Agency (EPA), 43, 104, 110,
    120, 173t, 175, 202n38,
    203n46
US Food and Drug Administration
    (FDA)
    calories and, 3
    cigarettes and, 40,
    203n46, 218n7
    false inferences and, 113,
    212n4
    genetically modified organisms
    (GMOs) and, 113
    mandatory disclosure and,
    40–41

US Food and Drug Administration (FDA) (cont.)
  nutrition information and, 203n44
  trans fats and, 55
  welfare and, 40, 55, 75–76, 203nn44,46
Using Massive Online Choice Experiments to Measure Changes in Well-Being (Brynjolfsson et al.), 146
US News & World Report magazine, 102
US Securities and Exchange Commission (SEC), 120, 126, 130–133, 173t, 175, 201n32, 214n14
Utilitarianism, 40, 128, 190

Verification, 82–83, 86, 123, 204n2
Vividness, 106
Voluntary disclosure, 86–87, 116, 208n37
Voters, 157, 161, 164, 166, 220n13
Voting Rights Act, 157

Waide, Paul, 95
Warnings
  choosemyplate.gov and, 52–53
  cigarettes and, 9, 39–40, 44, 67, 75, 106, 109, 198n2, 199nn18,19, 203n46, 212n74
  effectivenss of, 7
  false inferences and, 109–110
  food and, 44, 50–53
  increasing understanding of, 75–76
  mandatory disclosure and, 6, 54, 88, 99
  McCarthy on, 85
  psychology and, 83, 85, 88, 99, 106
  reminders and, 9, 47–48, 198n11
  welfare and, 39–40, 44–50, 54, 57, 60, 67, 70, 75–76
Waste, 5, 50, 53, 164, 167
Wasting time goods, 141–144
Welfare
  animal, 16, 26, 43–44, 90, 110, 119–122, 128
  attention and, 50, 56, 75–76
  automobiles and, 65, 68, 71, 74
  bad news and, 24
  behavior and, 42, 44, 47–53, 61–63, 66–67, 72, 78
  bias and, 42, 48, 61–63, 71–73, 78
  breakeven analysis and, 56–57, 75–78
  calories and, 39, 44–45, 49, 53, 55, 58, 61–64, 66, 70, 72–73
  choosemyplate.gov and, 52–53
  cigarettes and, 3 (*see also* Cigarettes)
  cognition and, 60, 67, 73
  consumer loss and, 64–65
  cost-benefit analysis and, 43–46, 49, 56, 59–68, 75–77, 113–117, 123, 126, 129, 144, 197n1, 198nn5,6, 201n32, 216n17

death and, 47–48, 54, 67, 72–73, 76

decision-making and, 39–42, 49, 55–59, 64, 66, 201n32, 202n38

disease and, 48, 55, 57, 61–62, 74, 203n46

effect of, 24, 45–49, 58–59, 68, 71–72, 74, 121–125, 129–130, 137–138, 142–144, 146, 150–152, 216nn17,22

efficiency and, 39, 44, 47, 54–55, 65, 68, 71, 75

endogenous preferences and, 65–66

end points and, 57–58, 66–68, 72–75

energy and, 39, 44, 47, 54–55, 63, 68–72, 75

environmental issues and, 43, 47, 66–67

experienced utility and, 58–59

false inferences and, 113–115

food and, 2, 40, 44, 47, 50–55, 59–62, 72, 75, 78, 203n46

genetically modified organisms (GMOs) and, 44–45, 59

government and, 39–42, 44, 50–51, 62, 66

happiness and, 58, 62, 73

hedonic value and, 48–49, 60–64, 67, 70, 73, 77

information seeking and, 42, 58, 60

judgments and, 74

labels and, 39, 44–50, 53–76, 199n19, 202n38, 203n46

loss of, 46, 48, 64–65, 70, 109, 117, 123, 126, 130

mandatory disclosure and, 39–49, 54, 78

menus and, 82, 84, 94–95, 98–99, 203nn44,46

money and, 44, 47, 56, 67, 72, 77

morals and, 121–124

nudges and, 28, 47–49, 95, 198n11, 219n10

optimism and, 71–72, 77–78

personalized information and, 35–36, 49, 62–63, 77, 101, 103, 135

predicting, 74–76

regulations and, 40, 42–43, 56, 58–61, 64, 66, 68, 71–78, 201n32, 202n43

safety and, 39, 50

smokers and, 54, 60–61, 73, 199nn18,19, 203n46

social media and, 8, 137–138, 142, 144–147, 151–152

useful information and, 49–56, 67, 68, 74, 77

useless information and, 50

US Food and Drug Administration (FDA) and, 40, 55, 75–76, 203nn44,46

utilitarianism and, 40, 128, 190

warnings and, 39–40, 44–50, 54, 57, 60, 67, 70, 75–76

well-being and, 42 (*see also* Well-being)

Welfare (cont.)
  willingness to pay (WTP) and,
    45–47, 55, 58–59, 68–74,
    77–78, 203nn43,44
Welfarism, 40–42, 61, 197n1
Well-being
  Brynjolfsson on, 145–146
  disclosure and, 6
  information avoidance and,
    12, 16
  instrumental value and, 16
  measuring welfare and, 42
  morals and, 127–129
  predictions of, 146
  social media and, 8, 137–138,
    142, 144, 146–147, 151–152,
    190
  welfare and, 42
Willingness to accept (WTA),
  137–146, 151
Willingness to pay in time
  (WTPT), 171–172
Willingness to pay (WTP)
  Allcott-Kessler study and, 68–71
  canine influenza and, 125
  changing preferences and, 78
  decision utility and, 58–59
  dogs and, 125, 129
  experienced utility and, 58–59
  Facebook and, 137–138
  genetically modified organisms
    (GMOs) and, 35
  happiness and, 26, 58, 73, 149
  information seeking/
    avoidance and, 3, 12–14,
    26–28, 31–35, 36t

  mandatory disclosure and,
    46–47, 78
  morals and, 124–129, 132–133
  optimism and, 71–72
  psychology and, 209n52
  sludge and, 171–172
  social media and, 136–146
  wasting time and, 141–144
  welfare and, 45–47, 55, 58–59,
    68–74, 77–78, 144–147,
    203nn43,44
Workplace risk, 2, 167

YouTube, 140, 142

Zhang, Juanjuan, 212n1